THE YOMPERS

With 45 Commando in the Falklands War

Ian Gardiner

Pen & Sword
MILITARY

First Published in Great Britain in 2012
and reprinted in 2012 (twice), 2013 and 2016 by
Pen & Sword Military
an imprint of
Pen & Sword Books Ltd
47 Church Street
Barnsley
South Yorkshire
S70 2AS

Copyright © Ian Gardiner, 2012, 2013, 2016

ISBN 978-1-47385-342-3

A CIP catalogue record for this book is
available from the British Library

Typeset in 10/12pt Palatino
by Concept, Huddersfield

Printed and bound in England by
CPI Group (UK) Ltd, Croydon, CR0 4YY

For a complete list of Pen & Sword titles please contact

PEN & SWORD BOOKS LIMITED
47 Church Street, Barnsley, South Yorkshire, S70 2AS, England
e-mail: enquiries@pen-and-sword.co.uk
Website: www.pen-and-sword.co.uk

Dedicated to all ranks of
45 Commando Group Royal Marines 1982
and to
the families of the soldiers, sailors, airmen, marines and civilians
of the United Kingdom and Argentina
who bore the real burden of the Falklands War.

Contents

List of Maps

Foreword

This book tells the story of 45 Commando Royal Marines in the Falklands War from the perspective of the point of the spear; a rifle company: Ian Gardiner's X Ray Company. When all the manoeuvring has been done and the time has come to take a piece of ground held by the opposition, a rifle company is the sharp end of the spear thrust into the antagonist's flesh, sometimes literally. I have used this analogy because, in any battle, surprisingly few men actually close with and kill the enemy; the spearhead is small compared with the haft. Take 3 Commando Brigade in the Falklands War of 1982 consisting of some 5,500 'braves' mostly wearing green or red berets, a handful with hats of a different hue. Together the infantry element: three Royal Marine Commandos and two parachute battalions produced fifteen rifle companies, each of around 100 men, say 1,500 total. Add recce troops, patrol companies, and special forces, and the total rises to around 1,700. So the other two thirds are the haft of the spear. At any point in time, a good proportion of these 1,700 will not be fighting, because the whole brigade will not be engaged. So in a typical brigade attack the number of rifle companies engaged might be nine, say 900 soldiers and marines, sometimes far fewer. Everybody else will be in reserve, or form part of the haft of the spear.

Of course without the haft, the point lacks striking power and direction, and soon becomes useless. For the haft contains all the supporting elements, in terms of additional fire-power (artillery, armoured vehicles, naval guns, ground attack aircraft), ammunition, food (logistics), and means of delivery (helicopters, landing craft, and vehicles). Some of these belong to the brigade, but much is owned by others – Royal Navy, Air Force, Merchant Navy and so on. So the proportion of point to haft is actually tiny. Consider that some 29,000 people are entitled to wear the South Atlantic medal, indicating that the wearer took part in the

Falklands War in some capacity or other, in a 'pipeline' stretching all the way from Ascension Island 4,000 miles to the South Atlantic. All that so that Marines Dave O'Connor, Howie Watson, and Alex Gibb, and others like them mentioned in this book, and many, many more not mentioned, could engage the Queen's enemies at close quarters; and take their bayonets to them.

Those in the 'haft' also encountered death and destruction. Ship's companies were trapped in flooded compartments or burnt alive, gunners shelled, crews of light tanks and other vehicles blown up on mines, and logistic units bombed. Ian Gardiner pays tribute to the 'haft', acknowledging the vital part it played. But only the infantryman – and those from supporting arms, gunners and sappers, actually moving with him – had to expose his body to enemy fire again and again, and again; to get up and advance when his instincts were telling him to stay behind cover or take advantage of darkness to 'opt out'; not by running away, but by lying doggo. Sometimes he had to get so close to his enemy that he could smell him; before sticking a bayonet in him. He has, as Ian Gardiner has written, 'the most difficult job in the world'. He is not, as some civilians might imagine, a mindless automaton. Even the most junior member of a rifle section has to master numerous skills and put them into practice in rain, snow, darkness, cold, numbed by exhaustion and half starved, while under fire: field craft; fire and movement; map reading; using the radio, controlling gun and mortar fire; and firing all his section weapons, rifle, machine gun, and two types of shoulder-launched anti-tank weapon. Without warning he may be called upon to take over command of his mates from his section commander, if the latter has been killed or wounded. Very different from the crew of a gun, a tank, or a ship, many of whose tasks can be carried out by rote within prescribed limits; often under close supervision.

I maintain that an infantry company commander from the Second World War would have felt almost at home in the Falklands. He might have found the helicopters a bit strange. He would certainly have enquired why we lacked the array of swimming armoured vehicles and other assorted hardware with which he had assaulted beaches, or crossed the Rhine. But he would *not* have been baffled by the total absence of mobile phones, iPods, computers, the internet, and television sets to while away off-duty hours. He would not have asked why he could not e-mail or telephone his wife or girlfriend on a regular basis, indeed ever; and why the mail only arrived about every four weeks, if he was lucky. He would have taken comfort from the fact that we still used the same cumbersome low-level code: Slidex. He would have found it perfectly normal that nobody could tell him how long this 'do' was going to last, or when his R&R was due. He would have found living for an indeterminate time without benefit of a roof, or even a tent, unexceptional. That was the land campaign in the Falklands in 1982. It was not as bloody as, say Normandy or Italy, but bloody enough. In just under four weeks, my Brigade had 90 killed, and 186 wounded, with another 132 non-battle injuries, mainly trench foot and cold injuries caused by lack of cover in the South Atlantic winter, and broken bones, mainly the result of moving over the rough terrain at night when heavily loaded.

Ian Gardiner conveys this atmosphere and more besides with clarity, understanding and humour. He is well qualified to do so, having fought in the Dhofar for eighteen months, where he saw a great deal of action in a tough and at times extremely bloody war, about which very little is known to this day.

It is high time the story of 45 Commando Royal Marines in the Falklands was told, and Ian Gardiner is the man to do it.

Major General Julian Thompson CB, OBE

Acknowledgements

The human memory is a notoriously dodgy database, but, provided steps are taken to ensure accuracy, the passage of years does not necessarily do any harm. For instance, one of the best first-hand accounts of the Second World War by a private soldier was written by George MacDonald Fraser forty years later. I have used some of my contemporary writing as a basis and leavened it with the benefit of thirty years experience to digest the meaning of what we did. Those thirty years have also allowed me to discover the reasons behind some of the things that happened to us then, and which may have puzzled us at the time.

Another tome which has been of great value is *The Signals Troop Log*, a compendium of reflections of the men of Signals Troop of 45 Commando, gathered and compiled by Steve Parkin and Neil Gribby. Signallers served in every part of the Commando and their insights, when taken together, form as complete a picture of what happened as is likely to be found. It is a remarkable historical document and, reading it, I felt humble and yet proud of the humour, compassion, tenacity and professionalism that shine out from its pages.

I have been most fortunate to have the assistance of many who served in the Falklands War to do a lie detector test on my work. The more outrageous tricks of memory have been exorcised by their audit, and many of these men have been kind enough to add their perspective, thus enriching and deepening the book. In reality, it would have been no book at all without their help and I am most grateful for all their support so freely and readily given: then and now. My debt is all the greater since I know that in some cases the giving has not been without pain or cost to the giver. Those whom I have thus consulted, and who gave me their help are:

Major Graham Adcock RM
Major Gerry Akhurst MBE, RA
Colonel Peter Babbington CBE, MC, RM
Lieutenant Colonel Ian Ballantyne RM
Major Chris Baxter RM
Warrant Officer 2nd Class Charles Bell RM
Captain Brian Bellas MBE, RM
Captain John Brocklehurst MN
Keith Brown, Esq MSP
Ian Bruce, Esq
Lieutenant Colonel Alasdair Cameron RA
Christian Caröe, Esq
Major Pat Chapman MBE, RLC
Captain Mike Cole RM
Bob Colville, Esq
Lieutentant Colonel Martin Cooke RM
Lieutenant Colonel John Davies RM
Major Richard Davis RM
Brigadier Paul Denning OBE, ADC
Malcolm Duck, Esq
Clive Dytor, Esq MC, KHS, MA (Cantab), MA (Oxon)
Sapper Ray Elliot RE
Lieutenant Colonel Paddy George OBE, RM
Major Dennis Gillson RM
Lieutenant Colonel Mike Hitchcock OBE, RM
Assistant Chief Constable Andy Holt RD
Brigadier Rupert van der Horst CBE
Lieutenant Colonel Steve Hughes RM
Nick Iddon, Esq
The late Captain Mike Irwin RM
Surgeon Captain Rick Jolly OBE, RN
The Reverend Wynne Jones OBE, RN
Major James Kelly SG
Warrant Officer 2nd Class Hugh Knott RM
Charles Laurence, Esq
Lieutenant Colonel Paul Mansell RM
Lieutenant Colonel George Matthews RM
Commander John McGregor OBE, RN
Major Bill McRae RM
Warrant Officer 2nd Class George Mechen RM
Warrant Officer 2nd Class Frank Melia RM
Sapper Molly Morrison PhD, BSc, RE
Lieutenant Colonel Mike Norman RM

Warrant Officer 2nd Class Dave O'Connor MBE, RM
Captain Richard Passmore RM
Major General David Pennefather CB, OBE
Brigadier Andy Pillar OBE
Professor David Purdie MD, FRCP Edin, FRSSA, FSA Scot
Captain Dominic Rudd RM
Dave Russ, Esq
Geoff Russ, Esq
Harry Siddall, Esq MM
Warrant Officer 1st Class (RSM) Keith Simpson MBE, RM
Captain Andy Shaw RM
Colonel David Stewart OBE, MC
Major Alex Watson RM
Major General Andrew Whitehead CB, DSO
Major George Wiseman RM

I also received valuable practical assistance from:

Captain John Hillier MBE, RM, Editor of the *Globe and Laurel*
Brigadier Charlie Hobson, CEO of the Royal Marines Association
Lieutenant Colonel Ian Grant RM, Corps Secretary of the Royal
    Marines

I am once again grateful to Henry Wilson and Pen & Sword Books and
to Jan Chamier my editor, who while improving my work have allowed
me to write in a style which is my own. They are, one and all, a pleasure
to work with.

The photographs came from many sources and they are acknowledged
on the plates but special mention must be made of the freely given help
of Mr John Ambler, who assisted with the Crown Copyright from the
photographic collection of the Royal Marines Museum.

I also thank Alfred Music Publishing of California for permission to
print the lyrics of *Minnie the Moocher* by Cab Calloway as sung by him
in the film *The Blues Brothers* – the song and film that evoke the most
powerful memories for many Royal Marines who sailed to the South
Atlantic.

There are risks in singling out individuals. Nevertheless, I should like
to pay special tribute to Lieutenant Colonel Viv Rowe RM. He was the
Brigade Intelligence Officer in 3 Commando Brigade during the war and
I know of no one who has a more encyclopaedic, detailed, accurate
knowledge of what happened, what we knew and when we knew it.
This, combined with his own distinguished experience of command in
war, makes him a uniquely well qualified source. I have leant heavily

on his judgement and am most grateful to him for his assistance. Many books have been written about the Falklands War, but most of them would have been more accurate if the writers had consulted him.

Captain Michael Clapp CB, RN, also gave me more of his time than I could possibly have hoped for. My understanding of the maritime aspects of the war was given another dimension by his knowledge and wisdom and I am especially in his debt.

It would be difficult to overestimate the influence on me of the late Professor Richard Holmes. Ever since he was my tutor at the Staff College in 1984 he was a source of encouragement and inspiration. His openhanded assistance, his warmth and his example were always available when I needed them. My sorrow at his passing, just as this book neared completion, is matched only by my gratitude that I knew and enjoyed the friendship of such a man. Lizzie Holmes gave me permission to quote her late husband on the cover of this book and I thank her warmly for that.

I was thrilled when Major General Julian Thompson agreed to write the foreword. As the brigadier commanding the landing force during the most critical stage of the war, he, like Rear Admiral Sandy Woodward and Commodore Michael Clapp, could have lost it on his own. Every man in 3 Commando Brigade drew strength from Julian Thompson, either directly or indirectly, whether he met him or not. Not only did we know we were in good hands, but in its conduct of war under his command, 3 Commando Brigade practised what we now know as the modern war fighting doctrines of 'mission command', 'manoeuvre warfare' and 'intelligence-led operations' some years before these terms became all the rage in the British forces. I am humbly grateful for the foreword, and for the many, many other acts of support and friendship he has given me over the years.

Once again, my family scrutinised my work and improved it with their supportive, critical eyes. They, more than anyone, sniffed out inconsistencies and impenetrable jargon and I am most grateful to Louise, Catriona and Angus for this priceless service.

In spite of all the assistance described above, there will still be mistakes. There always are. All cock-ups and nonsense remain on my slop chit.

Finally, and most importantly: there rarely are any medals for wives when their husbands go to war; but my wife Louise most surely deserves one.

Introduction

Soldiers don't fight for big things. Queen, country, democracy, freedom, family: all these and many more may help to get people into the armed forces, and to the battlefield, but they are not the motivators which inspire a man or a woman to fight to the threshold of death, or to accept death with equanimity. Men and women ultimately fight for each other. A man doesn't want to let his friends down. He doesn't want his mates to think he is a waster. A soldier will endure to death itself in order to retain the good opinion of his fellows. It is this need for self-respect in the individual which binds together all men and women in adversity. It is this eternal truth which allows governments to embark on wars without the wholehearted support of the military or the populace, yet still rely upon their soldiers to fight. A soldier knows he can't choose his enemies. His enemies are the Queen's enemies and so he gets on with it because he is with his friends.

But if there is doubt or ambiguity about the validity of the cause, it can do long-term damage to the trust that must exist between the armed forces, the people and the government. In the long term, soldiers don't like fighting for causes that do not have the full support of their country-men. They know, even if only instinctively, that final victory always goes to the side that is most motivated, and if they feel that the people are not resolved to endure to the very end, then the war will ultimately be lost and the soldiers' sacrifices will be in vain.

Three decades ago, Britain and Argentina went to war over a small group of islands in the South Atlantic. Even today, the very idea has a whiff of absurdity about it. It was all the more remarkable because it was fought with the near wholehearted, patriotic enthusiasm of the popula-tions of both countries and it was evident right from the start that the government of one of those countries must fall as a result. The eyebrows

1

rise a notch further when one remembers that the British were prepared to risk the greater part of their navy and the lives of many soldiers, sailors, marines, airmen and civilians in pursuit of victory.

Moreover, in one respect it was a colonial war. Territory, prestige and resources were up for grabs, but the traditional imperial colonial power, Britain, was on the other side of the fence this time. It had hitherto been British policy to hand the Falkland Islands over to Argentina, provided a respectable means could be found of so doing. In the end, the British were forced to fight for the freedom of the Falkland Islanders from colonial oppression. It was Argentina, herself a former colony of Spain, that tried to impose an unwelcome, unrepresentative, foreign, colonial government upon the people who lived in the Islands. And so, irony joined absurdity.

The Argentine invasion was the work of deluded, murderous, immoral men, but they were also expressing the wishes of a society which harboured strange contradictions. However much many Argentines might have aspired to democracy and self-determination for themselves, the people who lived in the Falklands – or the Malvinas – were not to be allowed to choose their own government. The Argentine people in time turned against their evil, inept government; but not because in their wickedness they had murdered 30,000 of their own people, or because in their arrogance and ineptitude they invaded the Malvinas: only because their army was beaten. The British Government acted on behalf of a people who, once they discovered where the Falklands were, and were alerted to the issues, remembered just in time that if you are not prepared to fight for what you hold dear, sooner or later someone will take it away – you will lose it. If you value peace over freedom, you will lose them both. And if you value comfort, prosperity and peace over justice and freedom, you will lose them all.

Lawyers and diplomats trotted out rival sovereignty claims rooted in the eighteenth and nineteenth centuries and the fag end days of the Spanish empire, but politicians could safely ignore these. For the British people, the only thing that mattered was that all the inhabitants of the Falklands were British, and it was their declared and settled will unanimously to stay so. The question for British politicians was: 'Should we provide them with the security and protection that is the first duty of every government to its citizens; or do we abandon them to tyranny?' – a clear choice between principle and expediency. For the Argentines, British suzerainty over islands so close to Argentina was an offence to their national dignity and overruled all considerations of democracy and human rights. The affront must be expunged and national honour satisfied. So the British were fighting for their credibility: the Argentines

2

for their pride. When all is said and done, it was this paradigm which impelled the two countries to war in 1982.

In the end, it was indeed a matter of motivation. The Argentine move was based on the miscalculation that the British wouldn't fight. When it became clear that the British not only would fight, but were ready to risk so much to win, the Argentines' motivation failed them and, despite many individual heroic sacrifices, they lacked the heart necessary to beat the British. For those who were sent by Britain to fight, it was a source of great comfort that the country was soundly behind them. Many unknowns lay ahead but, since national motivation was clear, it seemed that any sacrifices might not be in vain.

The Falklands War has been described as an avoidable war. This idea is born out of wishful thinking. It is possible at some point along the road to every war to see, in retrospect, moments where if different decisions had been taken it might have been avoided. This conflict was no different and was no more avoidable than any other war. It has also been described as futile. If fighting for the principle of self-determination of peoples is futile, then it was a futile war, but we who fought did not think it so.

Much has already been written about the Falklands War, so why yet another book? History hangs on a thousand frayed threads, the breaking of any one of which could have diverted its course. In this case, had the Argentines delayed their invasion by a few short months, the amphibious ships, which were central to the British ability to recover their credibility, would have been either sold or scrapped. Britain would have been helpless to do anything about it. Of all the close shaves in the Falklands War, this was the most momentous. Moreover, the likelihood is that within a few short years, the Royal Marines, who were in the vanguard of the operation, would also have gone. This vital aspect of the war has mostly been obscured by the drama of the fighting and I have sought in some small way to bring it out of the shadows. But most importantly, in spite of the acres of words, it seemed to me that no one has properly covered the war from the point of view of the men who walked it – yomped it – and fought it. Historians, journalists, generals, admirals, sailors, soldiers, airmen and sundry others: all have had a go at telling the story; but no one at the junior levels who experienced the infantry war has fully given his perspective. Others have written first-hand accounts, but the story of the marine, the corporal, the lieutenant and the captain remains substantially untold. I was a captain when these events took place and I lived, walked, shivered, took risks and went hungry with some of these men, while being responsible for the lives and the performance of about 150 of them. This book is their story and

3

many of them have helped to write it. It is also representative of many others. It can never be the full story of course – no two people will ever paint the same picture of any one event. But I hope that those who were there will recognise this tale, and that those who were not there will enjoy it.

Ian Ritchie Gardiner   Edinburgh 2012

Chapter 1

Listening

Hey folks, here's the story 'bout Minnie the Moocher,
She was a low down hoochie-coocher.

Every war has its music. 'It's a Long Way to Tipperary' and 'Pack up your Troubles in your Old Kitbag' will forever be associated with British troops in the First World War. 'Lili Marlene' *(vor der Kaserne, vor dem grossen Tor ...)* was so pervasive in the Second World War that German troops who captured Tobruk found their British prisoners whistling the same tune to keep their spirits up. 'Lillibulero', which first seems to have been sung by soldiers on both sides in the Jacobite/House of Orange struggles in the seventeenth century, was more enduring still. Until recently it could be heard in the small hours of the night on the BBC World Service. The Romans, presumably singing in Latin, must have cheered themselves in song as they trudged across the known, and unknown, world, building and policing their empire. Did the Carthaginians sing the same tunes, but in Carthaginian? Did the Spartans at Thermopylae whistle some catchy refrain as they defied the Persian army? Did Alexander the Great's soldiers sing, hum or whistle while conquering Asia? It is inconceivable that they did not. Soldiers enduring boredom, privation and danger have resorted to music in some form or other for solace and good cheer since time immemorial.

For many, the hauntingly evocative 'Don't Cry for Me Argentina' sung by Julie Covington or Elaine Page, will trigger memories of the Falklands War, but not necessarily for the Royal Marines of 45 Commando. The music that diverted their minds from the realities confronting them was from the film *The Blues Brothers*. And it wasn't just the music. It was the entire sound track. Every ship in the Task Force had its supply of films to entertain those on board. Opportunities to resupply or renew stocks of films were few and far between in the South Atlantic, so films were shared with other ships. And once they had all been watched by everybody, they were recycled again. But some films got stuck in a groove. *The Blues Brothers* was one of those. On the Royal Fleet Auxiliary ship *Stromness*, in which sailed over 300 men of 45 Commando, it was theoretically possible – for those who had the time and stomach to do so – to watch it 24 hours a day. There was only one copy of the film on board, but when it had finished running in the embarked forces galley, it would then be shown in the NCOs' mess. Then it would appear in the crew's recreation space, then perhaps the officers' wardroom, and so on. And in the late, late hours, individual messes might have private showings. I don't know how many times I watched it: not as many as others, some of whom claimed to have seen it over twenty times. I can well believe it. There would even be sessions where the sound was turned down and men would take on the roles of the screen characters, eventually becoming almost word perfect. I don't suppose any one marine could recite the entire soundtrack, but between 300 of us, I'm certain we could have pieced it all together. The result was that marines could be heard talking to each other in soundbites from the film. The lyrics of the songs became a means of communicating. The random, absurd utterings of Jake and Elwood seemed to punctuate every conversation. Elwood: *It's 106 miles to Chicago, we gotta full tank of gas, half a pack of cigarettes, it's dark, and we're wearing sunglasses.* Jake: *Hit it!*

After the landings, of course, there was no opportunity to watch the film. For some this was a relief; for others, it was a minor bereavement. And on the way home afterwards, there were those who made up for lost time. But in the bitter winter march across the island, in the prelude to the battles, and in their aftermath, men could be heard lightening a shared predicament by whistling or singing 'Rawhide', or shaking a tail feather with Ray Charles, or 'thinking' with Aretha Franklin. Unlike 'Lili Marlene' or 'Lillibulero', I don't believe our music permeated to the other side. I don't know what the Argentines sang but I'm ready to bet it wasn't 'Minnie the Moocher'.

Music, like smell, is famous for triggering long-buried memories. For a certain small group of men, now mostly in their late forties and early fifties, the sound of John Belushi, Dan Ackroyd, Cab Calloway, Aretha Franklin and Ray Charles will forever trigger a very particular set of memories: memories of a long, wet, windy walk in winter when, as teenagers and in their early twenties, with their friends and comrades, they went to war and were watched with bated breath by the rest of the world.

Chapter 2

Leaving

She was the roughest, toughest frail,
But Minnie had a heart as big as a whale.

At five o'clock on the morning of Friday, 2 April 1982, like most other law abiding souls, I was at home; asleep in bed. When the phone rang, it yanked me from a distant other world. It must have been ringing for some time before it penetrated my oblivion. This was before the days of mobile phones or cordless handsets and I had to get up, out of bed, and go downstairs to where our phone resided in the hall. Even in my somnolent state, I was concerned. No one rings at five o'clock in the morning with *good* news. It was Maureen Morrison, our redoubtable telephonist who presided over 45 Commando's ancient telephone exchange in a bunker by the officers' mess tennis courts, telling me: 'The Commando has been recalled. Get into barracks as soon as you can, and be prepared to deploy on operations.'

A moment or two passed before this sank in. It was five in the morning, after all. Most of 45 Commando Group had just finished a busy and demanding three months' winter training period in the Cairngorm Mountains, on Rannoch Moor and on the Isle of Skye. One of our rifle companies, Yankee Company commanded by Major Richard Davis, was in Hong Kong, about to return from jungle training in the Far East. We were looking forward very much to going on Easter leave that very day. I was the commander of X Ray Company, one of the three rifle companies in the Commando. I had sent those men who had worked through the previous weekend off on leave already.

Maureen and I were well acquainted. Until three months before, I had been the Adjutant of 45 Commando and inevitably I had spent a great deal of time on the telephone. When you wanted to ring somebody, you picked up a handset and waited for Maureen to answer, and to put you through. The system was antiquated even for those days. Maureen, being the arbiter of whose request for a line was answered first, was a most important ally. She could make life easy – or not – for frequent phone users like me. I had never had to wait more than a few seconds for my phone to be answered, but I was conscious of how much I depended on her. And what if she was out feeding the cats, or taking in a quick burst of sunshine by the tennis courts? Well, business, urgent or otherwise, would simply have to wait ...

I must have been stunned into silence because she repeated her message. I didn't think Maureen was known for her practical jokes, but I couldn't be sure. 'But Maureen, April Fools' Day was yesterday.'

Weary of having been likewise challenged by everybody else whom she had rung, she came back with, 'Och no, it's for real – get yerself back into Condor Barracks now!'

As I plodded back upstairs, recollections of the TV news the day before began to dispel the sleep from my brain. We had heard of the illegal scrap merchants on South Georgia and knew that the Argentines were making aggressive noises about the Falkland Islands – but weren't they always doing that? Something must have changed. Perhaps they'd finally invaded. Was the British government really going to send us to the South Atlantic? It's just as well the Argentines did not invade the day before, April Fools' Day. Nobody would have believed it.

I dressed in the dark and, for the next hour, scratched around in the garden shed with a torch, gathering together my kit. This wasn't difficult. We had only recently come off exercise and we habitually kept our stuff more or less ready to go, either on another exercise, or in case a real operation materialised. By six o'clock, I was on my Triumph Bonneville motorcycle with my rucksack on my back, making the 11-mile journey into Arbroath in the gathering daylight, leaving my anxious wife alone and wide-awake in bed. It's a strange, eerie feeling being called to war from one's bed. Time has not dimmed the memory of the sensation.

The next few days were unreal, ethereal and highly charged. Having arrived in barracks in a great hurry, we company commanders and other key officers were gathered together in the Unit conference room. We were briefed by our Commando Second-in-Command, Major Rupert van der Horst, together with our Operations Officer, Captain Mike Hitchcock, and the Adjutant, Captain Mike Irwin. Our Commanding Officer, Lieutenant Colonel Andrew Whitehead, was in Denmark with key members of the staff of 3 Commando Brigade doing a reconnaissance for a NATO exercise. He arrived home that afternoon, but a number of important decisions had already been taken and the recall process was well underway. Not much information was available except a FLASH signal ordering us to prepare for operations in the South Atlantic.

It should be remembered that in 1982 we were in the depths of the Cold War. We had all been on exercises where the scenario had kicked off with a Soviet incursion into North Norway, or Yugoslavia, or some other potential trigger point. And it was often a FLASH signal – the highest priority – which had sent us on our way. We had done this so often that we had become rather blasé about it. I had even written imaginary FLASH signals to add what I supposed was authenticity to my own company exercises. Subconsciously, perhaps, we thought it was all theatre. The Cold War would never become hot. We played our parts on this stage enthusiastically and conscientiously enough, preparing for what might in theory be demanded of us, but surely that demand would never be made in earnest? So it was with some awe that we looked at this signal, the likes of which we had all heard of, but never seen for real.

45 Commando Group was unique in the British order of battle. It was based in an ex-Royal Naval Air Station, HMS *Condor*, near Arbroath in the county of Angus in Scotland. At its heart was 45 Commando Royal Marines, comprising three rifle companies, X Ray, Yankee and Zulu, which were the principal fighting elements of the unit, each of about 120 men. Each company was commanded by a captain or a major and had three rifle troops of about 34 men (a troop being comparable to an Army platoon), each commanded by a lieutenant or second lieutenant. Each troop broke down into three sections of eight to ten men, commanded by a corporal. Each section was divided into two groups – a rifle group of six or so men armed with 7.62mm self-loading rifles (the SLR) and a gun group of two or three men led by a lance corporal with a General Purpose Machine Gun (GPMG). Support Company comprised a mortar troop with six 81mm mortars, an anti-tank troop with 18 Milan anti-tank missile firing posts, and a reconnaissance troop which, together with a small surveillance troop, were the Commanding Officer's eyes and ears. We also had some assault engineers. Headquarters Company looked after all the administrative functions such as the quartermaster's stores, the motor transport troop, the intelligence section, the signal troop, a sick bay providing a regimental aid post in the field, the chaplain, the chefs, and clerical and financial support.

The men in the Commando were Royal Marines, supported by a small number of Royal Navy people who included the chaplain, the dentist, the doctor, an instructor officer, and their supporting staffs. Everyone wore the Green Beret, all having passed the Commando course at the Commando Training Centre in Devon. What set this unit apart was that it was also supported by a substantial number of British Army personnel who were integral to the Group. We had our own Royal Artillery battery,

9

7 (Sphinx) Battery, with six 105mm light guns. We also had our own Royal Engineers troop, Condor Troop, and our own Royal Marines helicopter flight, Montforterbeek Flight, with three Gazelle light helicopters. These men too had all passed the Commando course. We even had a Gaelic-speaking Royal Air Force Regiment sergeant, Jock Steele, attached to Zulu Company, thereby completing the representation from all three Services. All told, our commanding officer, assisted by his second-in-command, his adjutant and his operations officer, had operational command of some 1,000 men. United under our Green Berets, and geographically distant from our superior or parent units, we were a self-sufficient, tight-knit organisation. We were also a potent fighting force ready to be launched worldwide on amphibious or other operations, either as the Group alone, or as part of a larger formation. We shared the same messes, we trained together, lived together and drank together, and for the greater part we would fight together.

We were to serve in the Falklands under the command of 3 Commando Brigade Royal Marines. This formation normally comprised three Royal Marines commandos supported by its own artillery regiment, engineer squadron, helicopter squadron, air defence troop, reconnaissance cadre and logistic regiment. For the Falklands War, it would have a Rapier anti-aircraft missile battery and other elements attached to it. Two battalions of the Parachute Regiment would also join it in due course. The commander of 3 Commando Brigade was Brigadier Julian Thompson.

Some elements of our Group would be returned to their parent units, but 7 Battery, the battery commander and his forward observation officers, retained their intimate relationship with the Commando. Throughout the war, the battery commander, Major Gerry Akhurst, would never be more than a few paces away from our commanding officer, and the forward observation officers, Captains Derek Dalrymple and Alasdair Cameron, would be similarly attached to two of the three rifle company commanders. A third observation officer, Captain Jim Baxter, was eventually brought in from 8 Battery to work with the third company. Moreover, 7 Battery were short of men so about 20 marines and one Royal Marines officer, Second Lieutenant Steven Turnbull, were lent from the Commando and trained as gunners. They served and fought most effectively as gunners throughout the war.

It may be recalled that the Royal Marines and their core activity, amphibious warfare, had for many years been the subject of much uncertainty in the great defence debate. The survival of the fittest applies to defence just as starkly as it does in the commercial world. No regiment, ship, or squadron is owed a living or a continued existence by the country. Every organisation has constantly to look to its usefulness and relevance in the defence firmament. It was part of the hallmark of the Royal Marines that we should never rely upon one single role for our livelihood. Having played our part in the small wars that punctuated Britain's withdrawal from empire, we now specialised in making ourselves useful in a variety of ways. We called ourselves commandos and talked about, and practised, the raiding role, but in truth, the likelihood of conducting a raid as envisaged by ourselves was remote indeed. Amphibious warfare too looked an unlikely NATO contingency, although we had made a virtue out of it by selling its utility in the North Norway scenario. So we diversified.

The Royal Marines are an integral part of the Royal Navy, but our planners and our manpower managers made great efforts to meet every request for help from other Arms and Services. They never said no if they could possibly avoid it. So the Royal Marines manned the Special Boat Service to provide the Royal Navy with special forces. We manned the Royal Marines Band Service to make the Navy's music for them. We gave detachments of Royal Marines to the Navy to put in their ships to give them extra utility – and to fill gaps in their manning plots. We made ourselves the lead experts in maritime counter-terrorism and we protected the Navy's nuclear weapons. Royal Marines commando units played a crucial part in the Army's rota of battalions in Northern Ireland. We offered exchange programmes for officers and NCOs in the Army, the Royal Air Force Regiment, and the United States Marine Corps. We developed a very close operational relationship with the Royal Netherlands Marine Corps, thereby enriching our political and international credentials. Secondment for officers and NCOs to other countries' armed forces was encouraged and a solid quorum of Royal Marines had acquired serious operational experience in the Dhofar War in Oman.

But in those days, the British defence community saw only two spheres: NATO, and the rest of the world. They even referred to the rest of the world by its initials: ROW. And just in case there was any doubt about the relative priorities, there was another set of initials, OOA, which signified 'Out of Area'. The Royal Marines were both ROW and OOA, and the area we were out of was Germany and the North Atlantic: the vital ground, so to speak, of the Cold War. Recognising the importance of the transatlantic lifeline to NATO's survival on the European continent, we played our part in NATO plans to protect this lifeline from Soviet submarines operating out of northern Russia, and from a potential Soviet invasion of North Norway. Amphibious warfare had some utility here on the flanks of NATO and from this we developed our Arctic and mountain warfare skills and made ourselves *the* specialists in that most demanding of disciplines.

11

We had survived thus for about 20 years following withdrawal from empire, but successive defence reviews asked the same question again and again: were we providing value for money? We appeared to be expensive. Our basic training was longer than everyone else's. Why? The answer, that the resulting superior quality, flexibility and individual commitment were worth the extra cost, was impossible to quantify or measure. But our people tended to stay longer than their Army counterparts, so surely that made us cheaper, not more expensive? Maybe, but it still didn't look good to the accountants. The charge of 'élitism' or 'gold plating' always seemed to lurk near the surface in every argument. The Royal Marines themselves never sought to be élite troops – whatever these are – only properly trained ones. And maybe our training was gold plated, but war is a brutal, vile, utterly unforgiving business and, while one should always be mindful to husband resources, to send people to war without the very best preparation one can humanly give them is nothing less than betrayal. Any corner cutting during training would be repaid by unnecessary loss of lives during war.

The second-century Jewish historian, Josephus, said that the training for the Roman legions was so thorough that 'their exercises were bloodless battles, and their battles were bloody exercises'. While not many Royal Marines had heard of Josephus, we nevertheless aspired to the same results. We aimed at preparing officers and men who could take their full place on a battlefield the day they passed out of training, without being a liability to themselves or their fellows. Moreover, it seemed to us a self-evident truth that the better trained your troops are, the more options are open to you as a commander and planner. If your soldiers are comfortable working at night, or capable of crossing difficult ground in bad weather carrying heavy loads, the advantages you give yourself over the side that cannot readily do these things are manifold.

I had experienced at first-hand this philosophy, both from my own officer training and through being responsible for training recruits and officers for several years in the 1970s. It was to be triumphantly vindicated in the Falklands War, but these arguments did not cut much ice during the Cold War, when military thinking was dominated by the potential armoured battle on the North German Plain. There, NATO braced itself for the possible advance of the Soviet Motor Rifle and Tank Divisions sweeping towards Calais and Antwerp, and foot infantry skills would not be a predominant factor. Besides, the amphibious capability was costly and there were many who felt that amphibious operations in a modern high-intensity war would be untenable. For a Royal Navy under heavy financial strain, and under great political pressure to concentrate even more on anti-submarine warfare, it was increasingly difficult to see where the Royal Marines fitted into the long-term future.

Many Royal Marines perceived that the Navy would be happy to swap them for a frigate or two, and in the Navy there was a view that the amphibious role to which the Marines had nailed their colours was peripheral and unsustainable, and distracted people and resources from the core business of anti-submarine warfare. I served in a frigate for over two years in the 1970s. During the 1980s I worked in a Naval directorate in the Ministry of Defence for two years, and in the Fleet Headquarters at Northwood for a further two years, so I saw the Navy at close quarters. It was, in the main, peopled by high quality, dedicated professionals. Where the Royal Marines and Royal Navy worked closely together, a mutual understanding and respect would quickly develop, resulting in some powerful and most fruitful relationships. This was especially so in the field of amphibious warfare, where together we had generated a capability second only to that of the Americans, and could work seamlessly alongside them. The Royal Navy personnel who served in 3 Commando Brigade, and the units like the helicopter squadrons who worked with us, were among the most 'can do' flexible warriors one could hope to meet anywhere. However, during the Cold War, the central task of the Navy was anti-submarine warfare in the North Atlantic. Unsurprisingly, many of the brightest and best officers became submariners. That was where the action was. There was not much else going on and very few officers had any medal ribbons. If one ever saw a middle-ranking officer with a medal ribbon, the chances were that it was an OBE awarded for sniffing the backsides of Soviet submarines in the Kola Inlet.

The Royal Navy became extremely good at anti-submarine warfare in all its complexities, but many of the submariners themselves tended to disappear beneath the waves in their mid-twenties and re-emerge in their early forties, blinking from the unaccustomed daylight. This, combined with the naval approach to staff training which tended to treat attendance at Staff College as a drafting margin between appointments, meant that there was a broad band of very capable officers whose outlook and experience was rather narrow. And they tended to be the ones who got to the top. There was a significant school of thought which regarded the Royal Marines as something between bouncing clowns and pet rottweilers – an image which, it must be said, a fair number of Royal Marines did little to dispel.

By the early 1980s, the idea that Britain might ever operate on her own in any significant conflict without her NATO allies had been comprehensively abandoned. From now on, the components of an all round NATO capability would be divided up between the nations. The British would specialise in anti-submarine warfare, operating chiefly in the North East Atlantic. The Americans retained a large worldwide fleet and would fill the gaps her allies were unable to meet. Thus, for at least a decade, political and financial pressure, with some gratuitous 'help' from the Army and the RAF, the Royal Navy had been driven towards becoming a submarine-only navy. The large aircraft carriers which had provided an all-round worldwide capability had been scrapped. The Royal Marines had built a NATO role on the back of the residual amphibious capability, but this was looking increasingly at variance with British official defence thinking, and would have been scrapped in the foreseeable future. Significantly, while the British retained the command and control structures to operate their own submarines in support of NATO, it was not envisaged that Britain would deploy and command her own amphibious force. That would take place under the NATO, ie the American, aegis. Thus when the British government decided to deploy the amphibious force to the South Atlantic outwith the established NATO structures, the commander-in-chief at Northwood, Admiral Sir John Fieldhouse, widely liked and respected, was faced with command-ing a force and a capability with which he had no experience whatsoever. Neither did he have a staff which was able to advise or inform him. Joint warfare, namely warfare involving simultaneous integrated deploy-ment of land, sea and air assets had not been in much demand in the 70s, and what should have been part of the education of every officer had become the unglamorous specialisation of a few. I attended the Army staff college in 1983–4 and it is fair to say, incidentally, that the British Army in 1982, focused as it was on Northern Ireland and Northern Germany, was no better prepared for joint warfare than the Royal Navy.

But on 2 April 1982, joint warfare suddenly became the only thing that mattered. The call went out immediately for officers with appropriate expertise to supplement the staff at Northwood and, within a few days, Admiral Fieldhouse was being advised by some of the best qualified people in the business, including Major General Jeremy Moore and many of his staff. But in that heady, fast moving first weekend of April 1982, the question of command and control of an amphibious force was not one of the issues that forced itself to the front of the queue. Finding the ships and deploying them was the wolf nearest the sledge. Besides, the 8,000 miles of sea between home and some islands which looked ever so small on the map, may have seduced some into believing that they were about to conduct a chiefly maritime operation. And yet, before victory could be claimed, the largest British amphibious landing since World War Two would have to be successfully achieved, and a land battle fought and won against a well equipped enemy who out-numbered our forces by at least two to one, and who had had time to consolidate on ground of his own choosing.

By the time the implications of this became clear, a number of important decisions had been taken, and could not easily be reversed. For instance,

Rear Admiral Sandy Woodward had been made the operational commander. Woodward was a submariner with no experience of air or amphibious warfare. A better qualified choice in the eyes of many would have been Rear Admiral Derek Reffell who had serious amphibious experience, had the appropriate staff and was currently commanding a flotilla of ships. But it was now too late to change commanders. Instead, on 9 April, Admiral Fieldhouse took back overall command and made the amphibious group commander Commodore Clapp, the land commander Brigadier Thompson, and the carrier group commander Rear Admiral Woodward, each answerable directly to him at Northwood. Command of all submarines remained with Fieldhouse at Northwood throughout.

Given the successful outcome of the war, it is self evident that Admiral Fieldhouse learnt very quickly and he and his expanded staff did remarkably well. But having such a narrowly focused mainstream Navy had done the British no favours. That they had an amphibious capability at all was only because the Royal Marines, with the help of a small number of believers, had managed to retain it. Had the Royal Navy understood better the tool they had in their hands, they would have been able to use more readily and quickly the amphibious doctrine which had been hammered out from lessons learned from the First and Second World Wars, the Korean War, the Suez operation, and many exercises since. They would have used the agreed command and control arrangements which had proved to be the most durable and flexible. They would have understood from the start something of the manifold complexities of amphibious operations. And, crucially, Admiral Fieldhouse might not only have appointed a joint operational commander with the necessary background and relationships to coordinate and lead an amphibious operation and support a land battle a long way from home, but also he would have placed him in-theatre, so that he would be able to see what was going on and be in a position to put things right when they went wrong. That these things were not on Northwood's radar that weekend was to lead to a number of misunderstandings in Northwood, the Ministry of Defence and in the South Atlantic, which compounded the normal friction of war.

Luck plays its part in any war. But how lucky were Britain and the Falkland Islanders, not to mention Margaret Thatcher herself, that the British were able to deploy successfully an amphibious capability that their Naval Headquarters had no experience in deploying, and that their government had had every intention of consigning to the scrap heap in the very near future.

In 1979, the new Conservative government led by Margaret Thatcher, while being welcomed with a huge sigh of relief by many individuals in the armed forces, was greeted with caution by those who remembered that, historically, Labour governments are often more generous to 'defence' than Conservative ones. So it was to prove. It is easy to forget that Margaret Thatcher's love affair with the armed forces began only after they had saved her bacon. In 1981 her Defence Secretary, John Nott, had announced a review which envisaged savage cuts in the Royal Navy's surface fleet. This included the disposal of at least one of the new small aircraft carriers, and the amphibious ships, *Fearless* and *Intrepid*, were in the frame for sale too. The withdrawal of the Antarctic patrol vessel HMS *Endurance* was also planned. No announcement was made about the future of the Royal Marines, but it seemed that if the amphibious capability which remained at the heart of our *raison d'etre* were to be discarded, our days must surely be numbered. Indeed, having subsequently served in the Ministry of Defence and read a number of the internal papers that were written at that time, it seems clear that the Royal Marines would not have survived much beyond the mid 1980s, had not events intervened. Paradoxically, one of those events was the IRA's attempt to kill the commandant general of Royal Marines, Lieutenant General Sir Steuart Pringle. In October 1981, they put a bomb under his car outside his home in Dulwich, but although he was grievously injured, they failed to kill him. Whatever plans Secretary of State John Nott may have had regarding the future of the Royal Marines, the banker John Nott was sufficient of a politician not to make these public while General Pringle was still recovering in hospital from the attempt on his life. By the time Pringle had recovered enough for cuts to be decently placed on the agenda again, events in the South Atlantic had changed the political landscape beyond recognition.

So, while no one in his right mind ever wants, or looks forward to war, it was with a certain thrill that we absorbed the implications of this FLASH signal. Here was an urgent, direct instruction from the highest authority to us Royal Marines in far away Arbroath. After years of feeling like an endangered species, we were suddenly in demand. The Rest of the World, Out of Area and amphibious warfare were now the only things that mattered. And how much further Out of Area could one get than 8,000 miles away in the South Atlantic? We were wanted at last and they needed us to get them out of a hole – right now. The world had been turned on its head and, for the time being, we who survived at the lower end of the food chain were now at the top. Thus, while great risk and uncertainty beckoned, so also did opportunity and hope.

But we could not allow ourselves the luxury of such musings for long. We had to get down to business and prepare for whatever might come our way. Those men still in barracks had had a rude awakening

16

that morning by the provost staff going through their accommodation shouting 'turn to in your company lines – the Falklands have been invaded'. The average reaction was similar to my own: 'Is this a late April Fools' joke?' But gradually the truth sank in. Not all of those who had been roused from their beds at 4.00 am had been told why. Captain Nick Pounds expressed the relief felt by many when he eventually found it was the Argentines who had disturbed his sleep. 'Thank God it's not the Russians.' About 30 men of X Ray Company were conducting adventurous training in Northumberland. They were due to arrive back that day and to go straight on leave. They were in for a surprise. Men who had been sent on leave already were quickly recalled. Some had managed to get a long way in the 24 hours since they had left, and there were tales of people interrupting their weddings in America. Lieutenant Paul Mansell, with men from Zulu Company, was hang gliding in the Brecon Beacons. They watched amused as the overweight local police-man cycled a mile and a half up the mountain, eventually to stammer in the broadest Welsh accent, 'Lieutenant Mansell you've to get back to Arbroath, Boyo ... the bloody Argies have invaded the Falklands!' Lieutenant Malcolm Duck was in the South of France rock climbing and cycling with his men. Captain Mike Cole, Zulu Company Commander, had great fun ringing the landlady of the YMCA guesthouse in Marseilles where they were staying and, in his best French, explained to Madame that he would like to speak to Monsieur le Duck. They got back in time, as did those men freefall parachuting in Devon. The two corporals who were skiing across the Hardangervidda in Norway did not get back in time to sail, but were able to join their company in Ascension Island.

On 2 April, the men of Yankee Company, commanded by Major Richard Davis, were enjoying some rest and recreation in Hong Kong after their jungle training in Brunei. That evening Richard heard a rumour that Argentina had invaded San Salvador and thought little of it. The delights of Hong Kong beckoned. The following morning, one of his corporals told him that he had heard on the BBC World Service that the Argentines had invaded the Falklands. He was convincing enough to persuade Richard to forgo that day's entertainment – a trip to Sea World – to try and find out what was going on. On a Saturday in Hong Kong this was easier said than done. He couldn't find anyone to enlighten him until the Wrens in the Royal Navy communications centre gave him access to all recent incoming messages. Eventually, in among the routine stuff, he found one which warned a number of ships and units off for 'operations in the South Atlantic'. Among the addressees was 45 Commando Group. This was presumably the same signal that we had read with awe the day before. Richard knew now he would be going to war, but couldn't do much about it until he saw his men again late in the afternoon. Feeling very lonely walking the waterfront on his own in Hong Kong, he sat down with a coffee and started making a list of all things he would need to do to get his company back to Scotland at the rush.

There was a happy buzz on Yankee Company coaches returning from Sea World that evening. A Saturday night in Hong Kong lay ahead. Runs ashore were being planned, building on the experiences of the previous night and, in some cases, promises made. Thoughts were also turning to going on leave. The coaches were met by Richard, who explained that the Argentines had invaded the Falkland Islands, and that a Task Force had been formed with 3 Commando Brigade, including 45 Commando, providing the landing force. 'In short, Gentlemen, we are off to war.' After a stunned silence, a hand went up. 'Excuse me, Sir, can we have an advance of pay?' 'Yes' was the reply. At which smiles broke out as run ashore planning was ratcheted up a few more notches and they set about partying with the purposeful vigour of young men who didn't know when the next run ashore might be – if ever.

Richard, his second-in-command, Lieutenant Steve Hartnell, and Company Sergeant Major George Mechen, then went to see the representative of the Soldiers, Sailors, Airmen and Families Association (SSAFA), who was a charming, helpful lady, with one of the few direct phones that could be used for overseas calls. While she supplied tea and cakes, Richard phoned Arbroath. He got hold of the Commando second-in-command, Major Rupert van der Horst. The conversation was short. 'Hello Richard, can't stop and talk now – just leaving to go south to join the Task Force. See you *en route*.' Having arranged the flights, there was little else for Yankee Company to do except enjoy Hong Kong for the next two days.

Shortly before they left, Richard received a telephone call from the duty staff officer of the General Officer Commanding Hong Kong, wishing Yankee Company well and asking if there was anything the GOC could do? 'No thank you', was probably the right answer but Richard had an inspirational moment. 'Actually there is. We are due to land at Brize Norton and then do a ten hour coach journey to Arbroath. It would really be appreciated if we could land at RAF Leuchars instead, just an hour from Arbroath. This may need the GOC to sign the signal ...?' The GOC did his stuff. The RAF cabin crew, who were presumably based at Brize Norton, were not exactly over-friendly, but that was a small price to pay for landing so close to home.

Among the many diverse tasks that the Royal Marines had taken on was the provision of the garrison on the Falkland Islands. Sergeant Ian Davidson in Yankee Company had served in the garrison and was able to tell his company a little of what might lie before them. Most

Royal Marines knew where the Falklands were – but not all. On hearing that he had been recalled because the Argentines had invaded the Falkland Islands, at least one man assumed that he would be engaged on operations off the west coast of Scotland. We didn't think to ask him where he thought Argentina was. He was in good company in his confusion. When the First Sea Lord, Admiral Leach, told the Prime Minister and her cabinet colleagues that it would take three weeks to sail the Task Force to the Falklands, he was met with the incredulous response 'surely you mean three days?' Thereafter, he saw to it that there was a map on the wall of the War Cabinet Room.

Equipment that had seemed hitherto to exist only on paper, or in some civil servant's imagination, suddenly started to materialise at our base in Arbroath. Twenty-four hours after we had been called from our beds, thousands of rounds of artillery ammunition appeared in trucks, having made a 400-mile journey from the south of England. It was met by the duty officer, Lieutenant Andy Holt. With some trepidation, he sought out the warrant officer in charge and asked if he would mind turning the convoy round and driving 500 miles back to Marchwood near Southampton, where it was due to be loaded on to our ships. After receiving a smarter salute than the deliverer of such a request had any right to expect, the warrant officer asked if it would be all right if his lads got a cup of tea before they started their return journey. This was typical of the positive and helpful responses we received from every quarter.

Much thought went into deciding what to take; issuing kit lists, packing, unpacking, repacking, and checking stores. Each unit or sub-unit has its own logistic organisation. At our level, we had our company stores run by the arch-fixer Colour Sergeant Dave Scanlon. There are various choices that can be made regarding what type and quantities of stores should be held, and at what level. Should we go light, or should we go heavy? The temptation to take everything, just in case, was strong. We had no idea where operations might take us, and 45 Commando Group was equipped and trained for Arctic warfare. Should we take our skis and our Arctic scales of kit? The Falkland Islands have a temperate 'Atlantic' climate, rather similar to the Outer Hebrides. But we might well be required to go to South Georgia, and the terrain and climate there is distinctly mountainous and Arctic. We would look pretty stupid if we were deployed there and were found not to have brought Arctic kit. So we packed it just in case. That decision was undoubtedly the right one although we never used the equipment. However, later, the precautionary principle was carried too far. When our headquarters issued a kit list for our march across the Falklands, it included many Arctic items. The Falklands are neither mountainous nor Arctic but perhaps we were sidetracked by our Arctic experience. Items such as toe covers and

Map 1. War at the Other End of the World – not everyone knew where the Falkland Islands were ...

tent sheets soon found themselves left behind in the bottom of trenches or tucked under rocks. It was also clear by then that the Argentines were not going to gas us, so quite a few respirators joined them. Doubtless many are still there as part of the detritus of war which can still be found on the Islands.

And what about vehicles? Were there any roads on the Islands? Should we load our heavy stores in our vehicles? If we did, and there were no roads, we might never see our kit again. Tents, cookers, defence stores, engineering equipment, heavy machine gun mounts, spares of every sort: all these and more would be urgently required if we found ourselves in a static or defensive posture for any length of time. So we packed it all in containers ready to be broken out into helicopter loads. As it happened, we were about to fight the only campaign since the invention of the internal combustion engine where widespread use of wheeled transport was impossible. It wouldn't have mattered where or how we packed our heavy stores. We were destined not to see them again until after the war was over. We were to fight with what we carried and little else.

In the midst of these preparations, I was dispatched to the home of a marine who lived in Glenrothes in Fife. This man had been part of the team of Royal Marines that had resisted the Argentine invasion of South Georgia. We didn't know what had happened to him but, although he was missing, we believed he was alive and had been taken prisoner. It was my duty to explain to his parents what we knew about him, and to offer such official comfort as I could. The job of informing the next-of-kin of people who have been killed, wounded or taken prisoner can be a very difficult one and I had never done this before. But these people in Glenrothes were wonderful. They were very grateful to me for coming and for giving them what information I had. The father made my job easier by telling me proudly that he had flogged his way through the Burmese jungle with the 14th Army during the Second World War. They were quite confident that their boy could look after himself and that he would turn up sooner or later. Meanwhile, the mother made me a comforting cup of tea, almost as if I was the one in need of solace, rather than them. In any case, they said, whatever had happened to him, they were deeply proud of what he had done. They made it abundantly clear that they supported any attempt to recover the Islands, and the sooner we got going the better. Knowing I was one of those who would probably take up the business where their son had left off, they sent me away with their hopes and prayers for me and my marines. So, having gone to give information and comfort, I myself came away from this visit, touched, humbled and encouraged.

21

This was not to be the last time I drew strength and encouragement from those whom I was supposed to be helping. Their son did indeed turn up unharmed a few days later, repatriated with others of the garrison who had been taken prisoner, removed to Argentina, and flown home. But I sensed that the attitude of these good people living in Glenrothes was fairly representative of the general mood in the land. If the government really wanted to send us to fight for the Falklands, it would surely have pretty solid public support.

Within 36 hours, from a very flat start, the Commando Group proudly announced that we were ready to deploy anywhere with all our people, weapons and equipment. We had been dispersed around the UK, Europe, America and the Far East. Many men had been on leave, and the remainder had been preparing to go on leave. Our normal notice period for operations was a week rather than hours, and now we were ready in a day and a half. By any standard, this was a remarkable achievement.

As the situation developed, it became clearer and clearer that we would actually deploy. The debate in the House of Commons on Saturday, 3 April, set the political scene. We were sorry that the Foreign Secretary, Lord Carrington, had resigned. In a previous government, he had been a respected Secretary of State for Defence and we felt that, while it might be the honourable thing to do, he was being made a scapegoat while there were others more culpable. We were equally sorry that John Nott's offer of resignation had not been accepted and considered that the cuts that he had announced in the Navy had at least in part precipitated the crisis.

This question of political leadership is an interesting one. Once, while I was serving at the Commando Training Centre, Enoch Powell had been invited to talk to the officers under training about leadership. Powell had been one of the youngest brigadiers in the British Army during the Second World War and we were sure he would have something useful to tell us. However, he declined the invitation, his letter of reply saying something to the effect that, so far as he was concerned, leadership had no part to play in politics. Whether he really meant that or not, I am certain he was wrong. It was of great importance to us that we felt that our politicians knew what they were doing. Even down to the most junior level, men had a sense of whether their political masters were up to the job or not. We had faith in Margaret Thatcher, who provided such a different leadership from the invertebrate governments of the 1970s. 45 Commando had completed a tour in West Belfast the year before and we had watched her stand firm while ten IRA men had starved themselves to death, eight of them on our watch. However, this need for leadership did not simply apply to the Prime Minister but extended right across the spectrum of power. John Nott, our Secretary of State for Defence, on the other hand, did not fill us with confidence.

The background, and the lead up to the Falklands War have been described in many other fora, and this is not the place to rehearse the arguments about sovereignty, or the sequence of events in detail. For us, the issues were ultimately very simple. Professional soldiers cannot choose their enemies. Their enemies are the Queen's enemies, and Her Majesty is not in the habit of consulting those whom she sends to war. When one joins the armed forces, one makes a kind of Faustian bargain with the Devil, the Devil in this case being the Queen. This bargain on the one hand provides you with a marvellous, fulfilling career which you share with agreeable, dependable fellows but, on the other hand, when HM The Devil calls, she reserves the right to demand your body and your soul in unqualified commitment to Her business. Professor Richard Holmes talks about the 'contract of unlimited liability' that servicemen and women tacitly sign up to when they join the armed forces. He says: a serviceman or woman agrees to go at no notice to a place one can't find on the map; and can't pronounce when one does find it: to risk life and sanity fighting with barely adequate resources, against an enemy whose politics one has no strong feelings about; with a plan one doesn't think much of; alongside coalition partners whom one does not hold in high regard.

We understood and accepted the terms of that contract completely. You shouldn't have joined if you can't take a joke. However, it is only natural that we should be concerned about the validity of the purpose for which we were about to risk our lives, and we were of course interested in the justice of our cause. We were not especially interested in the historical, legal, geographical arguments that were trotted out by both sides to justify their case for sovereignty over the Falkland Isles. The whisper that there might be oil to be found in these waters didn't much impress either. What mattered to us was that the people who lived there seemed in every discernable way to be as British as the people on Arran, Mull or the Isle of Wight, and had been for as long as the islands had been inhabited. It was manifestly clear that they did not want to be Argentine. They wanted to remain British, under a British government. By force of arms, their country and home had been invaded and occupied and they had been made subject to a government most patently not of their own choosing. And when we looked a little more closely at that government, we saw a thoroughly unpleasant, military fascist dictatorship which felt in no way bound by the rule of law and seemed to have no scruples about eliminating dissent in the most violent and terminal way. This was enough for us and, judging by the near unanimous agreement in Parliament, it was enough for most other

23

people in Britain too. If we were not prepared to deploy our armed forces to protect our own citizens, then why did we bother having any armed forces at all? It was not about territory, resources, prestige or power. It was about people. The fact that there were only 1,800 of these people, and their islands 8,000 miles away, changed nothing.

It is possible now to see how the vacillation, prevarication and mealy-mouthed, flaccid behaviour of successive British governments over the previous decade or more might have led the Argentines to suppose that we might not fight. The final straw seems to have been the decision of the Thatcher government to withdraw the ice-patrol ship HMS *Endurance* from southern waters. The Argentines undoubtedly thought that we would protest and whine loudly, but that we would eventually accept the *fait accompli*. No doubt if there had been a trapdoor through which the government might escape and accept the situation, they would have weaseled their way through it, just as their predecessors had done when the Argentines had placed a so-called scientific station on the Southern Thule group in the South Sandwich Islands in 1976. Bad behaviour, if rewarded or let to pass unremarked, is usually followed by more bad behaviour. So it was in this case. No doubt influenced by the junta member, Admiral Jorge Anaya, who had been the naval attaché in London in the 1970s and had formed a low opinion of British resolve, they assumed that invasion would be met with a supine response. But the Argentines had miscalculated most gravely. By flying so outrageously in the face of everything we stood for, they had ensured that we simply had to do something about it.

Besides, there were other geopolitical considerations beyond a small group of islands a long way away with an imprisoned population. The international system can be compared to an unruly children's play-ground. If a bully threatens to take an apple from a small boy, the boy might resist the bully and fight. By so doing, he may lose the apple, and he may be hurt, but, if he can hurt the bully in return, then the next time the bully comes, he is likely to go for a less prickly target. This is why most sensible dogs avoid actually fighting cats. But if the small boy supinely lets the bully have his apple, then the next demand is likely to be for his trousers. The lesson of the playground is that if you are not seen to be prepared to fight for what you value, someone is likely to come and take it away. If you behave like an invertebrate, you will get squashed. Britain was a major player in the North Atlantic Treaty Organisation established as a defence alliance to protect Europe against the Soviet Union. NATO's strategy was based on deterrence which at heart depends on convincing the other side that you are willing and able to fight for what you think is yours. Deterrence depends on credibility.

24

It was never thought likely that the Soviets would launch an outright invasion without a prelude. Long before the application of overwhelming force, the Soviets would apply pressure on weak spots like Berlin, North Norway or the Balkans to test our will, and our credibility. Depending upon NATO's response, the Soviets might raise the temperature and take things a stage further, or they might back off as they did in the Cuba crisis of 1962. We were in no doubt that our response to the Argentine invasion would be watched, noted, and taken into account in our future relationship with the Soviet Union. Deterrence had failed with the Argentines. When deterrence fails, you either fight, or you surrender and lose credibility. A failure to fight the Argentines would send all sorts of dangerous messages to the Soviets. And how would the Americans react? Would they back up their so-called closest ally, or would they fold their arms and turn away? Peering through this long-range, wide-angle lens thus, it was possible to see the greater security of Britain and her allies at stake in this squabble between Britain and Argentina over some remote under-populated islands.

Margaret Thatcher and her government took huge risks in sending the Task Force to recover the Falkland Islands. As well as her own political life, she risked the bulk of the Royal Navy, the Royal Marines, the Merchant Navy and the lives of many soldiers and airmen. But she did so because she knew that the risks involved if she did *not* send a Task Force were even greater still.

This much we were aware of from the beginning. We were also aware of the fact that, in some ways, we were poorly equipped for operations in the South Atlantic. Our Navy had been configured to fight alongside our NATO allies and it was assumed that these allies would cover certain gaps in our capabilities. Chief among these shortcomings was airborne early warning. We had no means of detecting the approach of enemy aircraft beyond the range of the radars and aircraft of our own ships. This would give the Argentines an important advantage in the air. In particular, it would potentially allow their aircraft to approach the target with the purpose of launching Exocet missiles and to remain undetected until the missile was on its way. There was no easy way of overcoming this. The nearest runway that might have supported airborne early warning aircraft, assuming we had them, was at Ascension Island, nearly 4,000 miles away from the theatre of operations. South Georgia was mountainous and even when recaptured it would provide no obvious area where a runway might quickly be prepared. But in spite of this, the Chief of the Naval Staff and First Sea Lord, Admiral Sir Henry Leach, advised the Prime Minister that the Navy was ready to sail and recover the Islands. Indeed, it is understood that she asked him, 'Do you think we can do it?'

'Yes we can', he had said, 'and what's more, I think you must do it. If you don't, then in a few months we will be living in a different country whose word will count for little.' I believe he later went on to say, 'If we fail, I shall no longer be your First Sea Lord.'

'If you fail,' she replied tartly, 'I shall no longer be your Prime Minister.'

But Henry Leach knew what he was doing. He was aware the risk was great and the price we might pay for our lack of capability could be high; but he also assessed that the shortcomings in early warning would at least in some small part be balanced by our Sea Dart and Sea Wolf missiles. The Sea Harrier aircraft was untried and we had only a very few of them, but Leach knew it was potentially a very powerful weapon. He also knew plenty about his own Navy. Above all, he didn't see the conflict through the eyes of the technocrat who measures only capabilities. He saw the human side too and was keenly conscious that the tradition of his Service was one of fighting and winning against the odds. He knew that, somehow, his people would find a way of cutting and pasting; of improvising; of masking weaknesses and playing to strengths. In this he turned out to be dead right. Leach also knew plenty about war at sea. He had been a young officer commanding a four-gun 14-inch gun turret in the *Duke of York* when she sank the *Scharnhorst* in the Arctic Ocean in December 1943. Moreover, he had good reason to understand keenly the penalties of having inadequate air cover. Off the coast of Malaya in 1941, the battleship *Prince of Wales* had been sunk by Japanese aircraft. Among the 327 officers and men who went down with her was her commanding officer, Captain John Leach, young Henry's father. The only reason Midshipman Leach was not sunk in the same ship was that his posting to the *Prince of Wales* was changed, when his father was appointed as her captain.

I was lucky enough to meet Admiral Leach at a dinner a few years later when he told us something of what I have described above. There can be little doubt that his leadership and decisiveness at this critical moment was of momentous importance.

The Chief of the Defence Staff, Admiral Sir Terence Lewin, was another senior sailor who had first-hand knowledge about what we might be getting into. At the time of the invasion, he was on official business in New Zealand, but returned home within a day or so. But he had served in a destroyer on the Arctic convoys and on Operation Pedestal, the convoy which, with epic gallantry and heavy loss, fought its way through to save Malta in August 1942. That the Navy and the Defence establishment were being led by men who had such heavy-weight maritime war experience was a real bonus. It meant that there should be no illusions at the highest level about what might realistically be achieved, and what it might cost.

There was of course no contingency plan to recover the Falkland Islands. Indeed, the Task Force sailed without any of the directives or instructions that are usually associated with amphibious or expeditionary operations. It has been said, only half jokingly, that the planners reached into the cupboard and took out the NATO plan for re-enforcing North Norway. They deleted Bardufoss and inserted Ascension Island, and they said to the Navy, 'When you leave Portsmouth, instead of turning left, turn right; and keep on going.' True or not, that is essentially what happened.

When ships are loaded for amphibious operations, it is normal for those things that you are likely to need ashore first to be loaded last. But that presupposes that you have a plan. And a plan presupposes that you have a mission. We had none of these. Consequently, in the hurry to sail the Task Force and to demonstrate our political will, ships were loaded with whatever turned up on the dockside in the order that it appeared. Based on some intelligent assumptions, a loading plan had been made and promulgated, but as more and more ships, people and equipment joined the order of battle, it was rapidly overtaken by events. This inevitably led to some pretty muddled loads and it simply wasn't possible to unscramble them all before we landed on the islands. This in turn was to lead to difficulty and delay when the landings started and presented our commanders and their staffs with some complex and dangerous problems; but more of that later. It is disingenuous to say that the ships could have sailed a week later with the loads in a much more logical order. That may have been true, but the imperative at that moment was to get a force, however chaotically loaded, on its way. This was not simply as a demonstration, but also to get them away while the political will to do so held good.

Zulu Company drove to Dundee and embarked in RFA *Resource*, Commando Headquarters and Support Company were dispatched to Portsmouth by civilian coach, to embark in RFA *Stromness*. This was the first occasion when elements of the Commando Group were exposed to the novel experience of well-wishers lining their route, waving flags and cheering them on their way. One officer's wife plus their four children and a handful of neighbours presented themselves on the Arbroath Road, all waving their hastily purchased union flags. While not such a surprise in home territory, similar demonstrations of support were evident all the way to Portsmouth. Even when they sailed, the word had spread and crowds along the Solent cheered them on their way.

RFA *Stromness* had already been sold to the USA and she was on the point of transfer of ownership. She was therefore empty and in tip-top condition. Presumably we asked the Americans at the last moment if we could just hang on to her a little longer. In a matter of days the ship had to be fully stored and equipped for the dual role of troop carrier and fleet resupply at sea. Throughout the night of 45 Commando's arrival and right up to the moment of sailing there was a constant buzz of activity as HM Dockyard personnel embarked troops and the ship's crew loaded stores and made modifications to the ship. Even as *Stromness* pulled away from the dock and sailed, on 6 April, more vehicles loaded to the gunwhales were arriving – only to be greeted with the universal international gesture of outstretched hands and a shrug of the shoulders. We never knew what we had missed.

When she sailed, the Commando lined the decks as she passed through Portsmouth Harbour. Other ships blew their horns in salute and the marines and sailors on HMS *Victory* saluted them with bugle and drum. It was a lovely spring evening and the people of Portsmouth came out of the pubs to cheer as *Stromness* passed. Lieutenant Martin Cooke, the Commando signals officer, could not help thinking of all the other ships that, through history, had passed this way as they sailed to war and an uncertain future, and of the men who had manned those ships and lined their decks. He felt their ghosts at his shoulder whispering, 'It's your turn now, lad!'

Montforterbeek Flight, 7 Battery and some others meanwhile drove to Marchwood near Southampton and embarked in the RFAs *Sir Percivale* and *Resource*. *Sir Percivale* had been due for a refit and her Hong Kong Chinese crew had been paid off and were waiting at Gatwick airport for their flight home. As members of 45 Commando Group drove down to Marchwood to join her, her crew were turned round and returned to the ship.

Major Gerry Akhurst, the Commander of 7 Battery, driving in an open Landrover through the night in filthy weather, was also astonished and heartened by the numbers of well-wishers who had turned out to cheer them on their way. Other merchant ships, which at that moment were elsewhere in the world's oceans, were taken up from trade and ordered to converge on Ascension Island.

Not all the necessary shipping was in home waters. So X Ray Company – soon to be joined by Yankee Company from Hong Kong – remained in Arbroath awaiting flights to Ascension Island, with a view to joining shipping there in due course. Virtually the entire command and administrative structure above us had gone. The Commando Base organisation commanded by the wise and experienced Major John Ingram was still there to cover our backs and to open doors for us, and Captain Dennis Gillson, who had been allowed to remain long enough to bury his father-in-law before he went to war, was there to coordinate the eventual movement of our companies. The stalwart Lieutenant Brian Bellas, our motor transport officer, ex-regimental sergeant major and veteran of the Suez and Kuwait landings, was also there to lean on, and to help with training. Soon we were joined by Major Richard Davis and Yankee Company who were keen to find out what was going on and trade in their jungle greens for Arctic warfare clothing. This began to create a strong bond between the two companies who were to fly and live together on Ascension Island to await the Task Force. From there they sailed south together on RFA *Stromness* and at the end of the war returned together as far as Ascension from where we flew home.

After the frantic activity there was now a lull, but we didn't waste our time. We set about conducting a most active and valuable training programme. Live ammunition, which hitherto had been issued with Scrooge-like thrift, suddenly appeared in quantity. Both companies spent part of every day on the firing range at Barry Buddon. Shooting, zeroing and other forms of training were given an extra edge with the knowledge that the next time we fired our weapons, it would probably be for real. We visited the RAF station nearby at Leuchars where the Royal Air Force readily told us everything they could about the Argentine aircraft that we were likely to come across. I was also lucky in having as my second-in-command Lieutenant Phil Witcombe. He had served on the Falklands a few years before, and his knowledge of the climate, the terrain and the people was a huge boon. The Royal Marines of the Falkland Islands detachment which had been captured during the Argentine invasion had by now been repatriated. We were briefed by a corporal from this detachment who, together with his fellows, had been sent round the assembling Task Force to give us as much useful information as they could. His quiet, understated description of the battle and his experiences were listened to with great interest.

The Royal Marines on the Falklands had been put in a very difficult situation. The Argentine invasion had happened during the handover between two garrisons. I knew well both the outgoing commander, Major Gary Noot, and the incoming commander, Major Mike Norman. They were there to deter invasion, but by 1 April, it was quite clear that deterrence had failed. They knew they couldn't repel the invasion, but it was important that the Argentines should not be able to claim that they had taken the Islands peacefully: it was vital that the British should not be seen to have simply handed the place over. If the Argentines were going to take the Islands, they must be forced to commit a demonstrably aggressive act. They must be forced to fight. So, three days into the job, Mike Norman had a very delicate balancing act to perform. He had to position himself and his men so that they would not be bypassed, and he had to ensure that they could not be overwhelmed without meaningful resistance. They had to inflict sufficient casualties on the invaders to make the point. No doubt many in Britain would have wished that he and his men had staged a glorious last stand where they fought to the last man, but ultimately his purpose was to give British diplomats in the United Nations and elsewhere around the world sufficient ammunition to press the British case. It is a moot point how much Argentine and British blood would need to be shed to achieve that aim. In the end, in spite of poor communications, order, counter-order and the fog of war, they, and their comrades on South Georgia led by Lieutenant Keith Mills, did brilliantly. They destroyed a tracked amphibious vehicle and they made the enemy pay a price in blood when they captured Government House. On South Georgia, a small frigate was damaged and a helicopter destroyed. One Royal Marine was wounded on South Georgia, but no British lives, civilian or military, were lost in either place. We didn't know precisely how many Argentines were killed in the invasion. They only ever admitted to one death, but it seems highly likely that others were killed or wounded on South Georgia and on the Falklands themselves.

With Phil Witcombe's knowledge and experience at our disposal, and with the information which this corporal from the original Falklands detachment gave us, we gained a very clear idea of the nature of the country and climate where we were about to spend our second winter in six months. We were going to a barren, treeless landscape, where the wind would be our constant companion. There were no roads to speak of and all land movement would be on foot. For walking the terrain would be rather like Dartmoor, only worse because of the tufted tussock grass which invited a twisted ankle or worse at every step. The weather would be highly changeable and we could expect rain, sun, snow and hail – sometimes all within half an hour. Summer was over so we should expect the weather to get colder and wetter as the weeks advanced; there was every chance we would be there in mid-winter and there was no Gulf Stream to moderate its effects.

It all sounded pretty grim, but we were not at all dismayed by any of this. All Royal Marines start their training on Dartmoor. Moreover, for us in 45 Commando Group, based in Scotland and training in North Norway and the Scottish Highlands and Islands, it sounded like home from home. Besides, Norway had taught something more than simply how to survive in the Arctic. Living and operating at minus 10° or minus 20° Celsius requires special skills and knowledge, but once acquired it can be relatively pleasant, provided one has all the right food and equipment. But in coastal Norway, the temperature can go from minus 10° to plus 5° overnight. Ice melts, one gets wet; then it drops to minus 10° again. This makes it one of the most testing environments on the planet and coping with it requires something extra, and most of us had learned that too. From the environmental point of view at least, it was going to be business as usual.

However, marines in Yankee Company, who had just returned from Brunei, took some good-natured ribbing along the lines of 'how useful to have just spent six weeks training in deep jungle only to be going to a place with no trees'. In fact it had been of great value. They had put aside the urban counter-terrorist tactics required for the tour of duty we had just completed in Northern Ireland and had become well versed in working in larger teams in a conventional war setting. They had been able to carry out training and exercises in a demanding environment and returned as a well worked up team. The company did, however, need to return to base and re-equip themselves for a somewhat harsher climate. They were lucky that they did just that. Someone in 3 Commando Brigade Headquarters had aired the idea that being in Hong Kong, they might be geographically well placed to take part in the capture of South Georgia. Brigadier Thompson wisely killed that one at birth.

The atmosphere and morale of our people was superb and this was an exciting, exhilarating time. Half the Commando had gone and it was certain we would go soon as well. But it was unsettling too. A soldier going to war has to set himself apart from normal life. The routine things that ordinary people enjoy by way of home and family perforce are now relegated to a nostalgic corner of the soldier's mind: not far away, perhaps, but his chief preoccupation must be the task in hand. When we were not training at night, many men embarked on yet another final run ashore. Those with families went home in the evening. It is not easy for yourself or your family, to say farewell in the morning, not knowing for sure if you will come back in the evening. And if one did not come back in the evening, would one come back at all? It was nearly two weeks after our initial recall when we eventually flew off. A fortnight is a long time to say goodbye.

The strain under these circumstances is far greater for those left behind than for those who go. The warriors are buoyed up by what they might encounter in the near future. However dangerous and un-comfortable it might be, they will be with their friends, doing what they volunteered for and what they have been trained to do. And during the hostilities, they at least know what is happening to them and have some control, however little. The prospect of death or injury does not loom large in the minds of young, active, well-led and well-trained young men in these circumstances. But their families did not volunteer. At best, they accept the career of the man they love. All being well, their man will come home again in one piece, but he will have survived an experience which he will find impossible to share with his people. And the family may find it difficult to explain to him the true nature of the many burdens that they have carried while he has been away. A barrier can be erected between them. The potential for misunderstanding is great. A soldier faces the prospect of losing his life, but the family faces the prospect of living without their beloved soldier. Is it too much to suggest that, in some ways, the families have more to lose? They certainly have nothing to gain.

In our society, where conscription no longer exists, very few people have any conception of what it is like to be a serviceman or woman. Notwithstanding new conflicts elsewhere in the world, even fewer still know what it is like to bear any burden of war whatsoever, beyond a theoretical financial one. We have out-sourced the fighting of our wars to a tiny fraction of the population. The reality is that virtually nobody in our country suffers when we go to war: nobody, except the families of those who go. While our soldiers on active service must have our encouragement and support, it is their families who carry the real burden of war and who are far less likely to receive the help and succour they need and deserve.

Neither should it pass unremarked that among those families who bore the true burden of war in this case was the one living in Buckingham Palace. By allowing no exception for their second son, who flew helicopters in action, the Queen and the Duke of Edinburgh were spared none of the agonies and anxieties of this war. This was a singular instance of leadership by example, the equal of that of Her Majesty's parents when they insisted on staying in Buckingham Palace during the Blitz.

There were also some difficult decisions to take. When it became clear that we would fly to Ascension Island, we started finalising our flying manifests. Going to war by air rather than ship, one is much more constrained. In a ship, weight is rarely a consideration and one can almost always find space in a corner for extra kit, or extra people. Not so in a Royal Air Force VC10. We were allowed a very strictly limited number of passengers: I was given fewer seats than I had men in my company. The tension in the barrack blocks was intense. No one, young or old, wanted to be left behind. All wanted to be part of whatever was to come and to be there for each other. No one volunteered to stay. This meant I had to decide who would be left behind. I chose those men who were due to be discharged in the very near future, at the end of their service. This was a bitter blow for men who had served nine or twelve years during the Cold War only to be left out when things looked like getting interesting. The alternative was to leave the most newly trained people behind, but I felt that it would be wrong to say to a young marine at the beginning of his career, 'we don't trust you or the training we have just given you', especially when it was not true. Our trust was not misplaced.

One day I was approached by a corporal section commander who said he was very concerned about our weakness in the air. He felt it was madness that we should be heading into a war where we were so ill-equipped, and so vulnerable to enemy air attack. I got the impression that he had discussed his fears with his section of eight or ten marines. We all knew that this was a point of concern, but most of us accepted that there were others who were employed to worry about that. Our job was to look to our people and see that we and they were fully able to carry out the jobs we were employed to do. I discussed it with him for a while, but eventually I said, 'Look, there is nothing you or I can do about it. You and I must put these concerns aside and concentrate on giving our men the leadership and support they need.'

'Yes, but ...' He clearly wasn't getting the message. We were about to go to the shooting range, so I told him to come back and see me in the afternoon and tell me that he was now ready to go to war with a smile. Meanwhile I discussed it with his troop commander and my company sergeant major, Warrant Officer Second Class Charles Bell, and Major John Ingram. We agreed that the possibility of someone with this attitude spreading his concerns in the hold of a ship in danger of being bombed or hit with a missile was a risk we did not want to take. If he hadn't sorted himself by the afternoon, I would sack him. That afternoon when we met again in my office, after further conversation it seemed clear to me that he still hadn't understood what his priorities should be, so sadly I told him he would stay behind. He was of course flabbergasted. He was an intelligent, educated, able man and, in every other respect, an excellent corporal. But it is the ultimate duty of every leader to give his people hope. If the leader himself spreads gloom and despondency, then all is surely lost. The leader must be the banker of hope. At that time, in that place, I was not confident that he could be that banker for his section. It is with some unease that I now reflect that I, for my part, had been unable to give him the hope that he needed then.

Happily we next saw this man in Port Stanley. He had managed to wangle himself an attachment to another formation when we had gone and his subsequent career showed no signs of having been held back by this unhappy little episode.

Meanwhile, we were now one corporal down. The section second-in-command, Lance Corporal 'Roscoe' Tanner, could take over, but it would be good to get as many experienced NCOs in the team as possible.

Corporal Hugh Knott was recovering from a broken leg and had just had the plaster removed. Would he be fit enough to come? I didn't ask the doctor. I asked Corporal Knott if he was up for it. Of course he was. To prove it we told him to do a four-mile run in less than 35 minutes. In this he succeeded with the encouragement of numerous friends. So he came with us and had a successful war.

Other companies had a similar experience. Most men wanted desperately to be with their fellows, but not all. Two men went absent without leave from one company, although one came back and deployed. One marine from Lieutenant Paul Denning's troop in Yankee Company was serving time in the cells for some misbehaviour in Brunei. Paul had a chat with him about where he found himself. He asked to be allowed to deploy with the Commando. It was clear that he had learned his lesson, and it was felt that he was a good professional marine at heart, so he was sprung from jail and went to war with his friends.

My wife Louise and I lived in a cottage in the village of Newbigging between Monifieth and Monikie in the county of Angus, and we enjoyed a very friendly relationship with our neighbours, Gracie and David Malcolm. David had been a regular soldier and had served in armoured formations during the Second World War and I knew they would look after Louise as well as they could while I was away. They too were never quite sure if I was still there, or whether I had gone. One Sunday, Gracie, who played the organ in the local kirk, came and told us that they had said prayers for my safety in the morning service. At the time I had been planting cabbages in the garden. It was high time I went.

Chapter 3

Pausing

She messed around with a bloke named Smokey,
She loved him though he was cokie.

In the year AD 1501, a Portuguese sailor called João da Nova sighted land on the horizon where he was probably least expecting it: in the middle of the ocean between Africa and America. The Genoese adventurer, Christopher Columbus, had established the reality of a new world away out to the west a mere nine years before, and João da Nova must have wondered what this new sighting presaged. But as he approached, he found nothing but a barren, rocky, conical outcrop which offered little in the way of shelter or succour. We don't know whether he landed there, but if he did he would have found little to encourage him. There appeared to be no fresh water. Seabirds could be hunted for their meat, and enormous female turtles might be found laying their eggs on the occasional sandy beach. But otherwise, it offered little of value. He didn't even bother to give it a name.

Two years later, towards the end of May 1503, another Portuguese navigator, Alphonse d'Albuquerque, journeying to India, sighted the same volcanic outcrop. Coincidentally, he carried among his crew a certain Amerigo Vespucci, the man who would achieve immortality when his name was given to the continent that Columbus had encountered eleven years before. Alphonse d'Albuquerque felt inspired by the date to give this hitherto anonymous peak a name. In the calendar of the Roman Catholic Church the day was Ascension Day, when according to Christian doctrine Christ's body ascended to Heaven.

Four hundred and eighty-one years after da Nova discovered Ascension Island, I sighted it under very different circumstances. X Ray and Yankee Companies of 45 Commando Royal Marines had finally taken off in a

35

VC10 from RAF Leuchars in Fife on 13 April 1982. After a brief stopover at Dakar in Senegal on the West African coast, we were inbound for Ascension Island. The captain of the aircraft had kindly suggested that I come up to the cockpit and sit in the back seat while we approached and landed. For many miles there was nothing but the blue-grey expanse of the Atlantic Ocean, but then, perhaps a hundred miles away, there was a discernable cloud-covered spot on the surface. Spot and cloud grew as we approached and from about 30 miles out I had a spectacular view of a stereotypical volcano, apparently complete with smouldering summit. Neither João da Nova nor Alphonse d'Albuquerque would have seen the peak like this. It was only after successive visitors started planting on the volcano that the micro-climate of the 3,000 ft (914 m) high mountain began to change. The higher reaches of the hill are no longer barren. Rather, they are now as lush and green as any Devon valley. Today it's even called Green Mountain. The clouds which sit on top of the island for much of the time add to the Devon effect. So, one can bake and burn by the sea as if in southern Italy, but a short trip up the hill will take you back to the south of England. There are even Guernsey cows to complete the illusion.

We were taken in coaches to the north side of the island and billeted in huts and tents at English Bay. It seemed very warm after Scotland in early April. We spent over two weeks living here and continued the training programme we had started in Scotland. Yankee Company had just come out of the jungle which, although superb low-level tactical training, was very different to what was now required. What we do as infantrymen is in essence not very difficult, but to succeed it has to be done extremely well and, most importantly, as part of a team. Constant practice is the only way to develop and retain the cohesion and corporate fluency necessary to win battles and save lives.

The 3,000 ft volcano on our doorstep was the scene for daily mountain races and the adjacent beach was a magnet for other recreational purposes. It was something of a challenge to stop the marines from overdoing the sun tan and burning themselves. The simple cure was some robust physical training conducted on the abrasive sand. No one got burned twice. But it was a strange irony that when we flogged across the Falklands in midwinter a little over a month later, some men were still suffering from sunburn. Others were recovering from venereal diseases they had picked up in Hong Kong.

Tucked away on the northern side of the island, we were largely isolated from the feverish activity that was taking place by the airfield, as servicemen of every shape and condition converged on Ascension Island; all competing for space and resources, all convinced of the essential nature of their role, all demanding to be given priority. There was an inevitable air of confusion, and Richard Davis and I were very happy to be left to our own devices with our men in our own little corner. Soon we were visited by the officer placed in command on the island. I was delighted to find it was Captain Bob McQueen Royal Navy. I had served in the frigate HMS *Diomede* some years before, and Bob McQueen had been our much respected and well-liked commanding officer. To him had now fallen the unenviable task of controlling and managing the incipient chaos on Ascension, and by all accounts he succeeded very well with charm and a firm hand. It was indeed good to see him, and it was even better when he handed over a supply of surplus whisky that didn't seem to have any other home. But I was a little dismayed when he said to me, 'You'll go through the Argentines like a knife through butter, Royal'. I know he meant to be encouraging, but it was not a point of view that I shared, and certainly not one that I wanted to encourage among my marines. One of the greatest crimes a soldier can commit is to underestimate his enemy, and it is a crime of which the British have on occasions been notoriously guilty. I was determined that neither I nor my marines would fall into this trap.

We felt that, in spite of the efforts of Captain Bob McQueen and his team, Ascension always seemed to have a whiff of confusion and chaos about it – we were in fact, quite deluded. The operation of Ascension Island was one of the unsung masterpieces of the war. From a standing start, in a few short days, this hitherto unknown tiny spot became the forward operating base for movement, supply and training for the largest force Britain had sent to war since Suez. In a fast changing situation of ever growing complexity, it is inevitable that some things may not work quite as smoothly as one would like. But through the leadership, the brains, the nimbleness, the flexibility, the goodwill and the sheer Herculean effort of all involved, Ascension provided the required service for all who needed it. Without Ascension, the Falklands would probably still be in Argentine hands. But there is a tendency, when looking up the chain of command, to sneer at the efforts of one's superiors when they stumble. How easy it is to accuse the bosses of bungling, when you yourself have no notion of the many demons that are clinging to their backs. I confess we were guilty of this on more than one occasion.

Before thousands of British servicemen invaded their space, Ascension Island was home to a few American airmen and some British radio technicians. The latter ran and maintained a BBC radio relay station, the aerials of which were next to our camp. They also had their own small bar tucked underneath the cliff with a fine view of the sea. They were a hospitable bunch and shared their limited supply of beer with us with open hands. The bar was an attractive spot, but there were indicators that life on station here could be something of an endurance test. It had become the custom, before finishing one's tour on the Island, to leave a name plate with an inscription of one's choice on the wooden panels in the bar. The only one I remember was, 'I came; I saw; I fell over', but there were others of a similar sentiment.

The island is home to turtles and to crabs. The turtles confined themselves to the beach but the crabs tended to wander, and those wandering on the road tended to get run over. Marine Neil Gribby of the Signals Troop captured one of these creatures the size of a dinner plate in a sack. When he returned to his tent, he enquired of those within if any of them liked crabmeat. 'When the reply was "yes", the contents of the sack were launched into the tent just seconds before the contents of the tent launched themselves out of it.'

Notwithstanding our heavy training programme and the prospect of war that faced us, it was difficult not to feel something of a tourist on this island. Small though it was it had an interesting history and evidence of our forebears could be seen in the old Royal Marines barracks, on the memorials in the church, and the Royal Marines' Globe and Laurel crest on what was now being used as a piggery halfway up the mountain. There was a bar on the road up, which was most convenient, and banana trees and open fields at the summit. At the very top is a bamboo jungle with a pond complete with goldfish. As the vegetation is slowly encroaching down the mountain, we wondered if one day it will be lush green all over. It would have been difficult to find a spot more dissimilar to the one to which we knew we were going. And while we expected the South Atlantic to be sore on us and our equipment, it was unlikely to match the way that the knife-sharp lava on Ascension was ripping our boots to shreds. This attrition on our boots became a concern. We knew we would be needing good, well-worn-in boots before long, and from now our chances of resupply were pretty slim. So we took care so far as we were able to confine training to ground that was kinder to our footwear.

We converted a suitable piece of real estate into a firing range and took the opportunity to fire weapons we had not used before. The American 66mm hand-held anti-tank weapon was in our inventory. Each launcher held one missile, and one discarded the empty launcher when it had been fired. We had practised the drills with 'empties' but the real thing was on such limited issue that we had never had a chance to fire it. There was a helicopter squadron on Ascension which was being used to ferry stores around the island and from ship to shore. We persuaded the squadron commanding officer that our need for these weapons was greater than theirs. He kindly let us have their allocation to play with. We let two or three men from each section fire a live weapon on our improvised firing range. It was a most useful exercise. These weapons were probably too light to be of much use against modern tanks, but against strong points and bunkers they were to prove invaluable. The live practice that X Ray and Yankee Companies got with the 66mm meant that, in battle, the first rounds we fired were mostly on target and we didn't waste time and ammunition learning about the weapon. I hope the helicopter squadron commander didn't live to regret his generous decision. But his weapons were put to good purpose, and probably saved Royal Marines' lives.

Not all our training exercises were so productive. We found, in one of our older training manuals, guidance on how to shoot down aircraft with machine guns. Given our lack of airborne early warning, perhaps this might come in handy? 'Approachers', 'chasers' and 'passers' were all addressed. This manual told us, with a straight face, that when shooting at a passing high performance jet aircraft flying within range of our machine gun, we should aim at a distance of some thirty times the length of the aircraft in front of its nose. Quite apart from the difficulty of estimating the distance, we didn't think we would find pilots who were willing to let us practise on them. However, when we got to San Carlos Water, we realised those old pamphlets were not so daft after all. Even high performance aircraft are vulnerable to a skilled man willing to stand up with a machine gun.

By now, the ships of the Task Force which had deployed in such a hurry in early April were arriving daily. The carrier group arrived, followed by the key amphibious ships. Admiral Fieldhouse, who had flown out from Northwood, held a council of war aboard the carrier HMS *Hermes*, where many of the key players met each other for the first time. The carrier group then continued south, as did the formation of ships and men destined to recapture South Georgia. After nearly two weeks on Ascension we were able to meet up with the remainder of the Commando. It was good to see them. Their experiences had been rather different to ours – the Bay of Biscay and the North Atlantic had been their lot, while we had been conducting ourselves to our own satisfaction in the sun. Their journey hadn't been without its lighter moments though. To comply with tradition, King Neptune boarded the *Stromness* as she crossed the equator on her route to Ascension, and held his court where he tried sundry felons for their misdemeanours. The commanding officer, Andrew Whitehead, was found guilty and duly punished for 'failing to get his unit on Easter Leave'. Space and accommodation on Ascension was at a premium, and so we handed over our little health resort by the sea and embarked on our various ships.

No single ship was able to take the whole Commando and our logistics were scattered throughout the fleet, but mainly in MV *Elk*, RFA *Stromness* and RFA *Sir Percivale*. *Elk* had been a North Sea ferry until pressed into our service and was notable for her enormous rise and fall in the South Atlantic swell and her near constant rolling. If *Elk*'s bow doors were down, it was relatively easy to board and remove any necessary items to whatever boat was available. At other times, access to the ship was via an open hatch halfway up the side. Boarding then became a leap of faith taken at the height of the swell. Some likened the experience to playing a game of 'chicken'. Once we left Ascension and landed on the Falklands, despite many briefings advising our logisticians that *Elk* would be approaching shore for an opportunity to offload stores overnight, she was never sighted again by them during the war. There was a move to commission a T-shirt with the logo 'The South Atlantic Elk is a Myth' but they soon had other more pressing things on their minds. One hastens to add that the captain and crew of *Elk* were always very 'can do' and with the large quantities of fuel and ammunition that she carried, they were constantly at risk of a sudden and spectacular demise. Moreover, she did enter San Carlos Water and she did unload large quantities of ammunition. But there had been no tactical consideration whatsoever with her loading and to get at the landing forces' stores much else would have had to be moved, then put back again and lashed down safely for sea before sailing. It all took so much time. Her visits were necessarily brief, because if she had been hit she would have gone sky high and probably taken other ships with her. This was typical of the problems facing the amphibious staffs, and the risks that the Merchant Navy crews took without complaint in spite of the fact that they were civilians.

Zulu Company commanded by Captain Mike Cole embarked on *Sir Tristram*. Lieutenant Colonel Whitehead with Headquarters Company commanded by Captain Dennis Gillson, Support Company commanded by Captain Ian Ballantyne, Yankee and X Ray Companies, were all embarked in the Royal Fleet Auxiliary ship *Stromness*. The guns of 7 Battery went to *Sir Percivale* with Montforterbeek Flight, although the battery commander, Major Gerry Akhurst, embarked in *Regent*.

The Royal Fleet Auxiliary is a strange, hybrid creation. RFA ships are manned by civilian sailors and for legal purposes they are not warships. Many of the crews in 1982 were Hong Kong Chinese. As a rule, the ships have no offensive weapon systems, although they may be mounted with close-in self-defence weapons from time to time. But they are very plainly the logistic vessels for the Royal Navy, without which the Navy could not operate, and they share all the risks of the Service they support. This certainly applied in the Falklands where they bore all the burdens and hazards of war without flinching or hesitation. Their ambiguous status can be very convenient and there are occasions where countries and ports around the world will not accept the entry of a British warship, but will allow the entry of a 'civilian' RFA vessel. Moreover, not being warships in the conventional sense they tend to be built to much more comfortable standards. By the lights of the 1980s, *Stromness* was a very comfortable ship. Although comparatively new she had been earmarked for disposal in the 1981 Defence Review and eventually was sold to the American Navy, where she started a new career as the USS *Saturn*. Meanwhile, she was to be our home for the foreseeable future.

Stromness was a stores ship. She had four holds. Three of them were full of prodigious quantities of fresh, frozen and dried food, plus what appeared to be half the fleet's beer ration. Although she did not carry weapons or ammunition in any quantity, in pallets and in containers she had every imaginable item of clothing and equipment for men going to war. She carried spares for all sorts of machinery and equipment for ships and aircraft. On her decks were lashed down aluminium planks ready to be reassembled into a landing strip for the vertical take-off Harriers, whenever and wherever the appropriate moment came. She was a cornucopia of untold treasures for scrounging marines, an Aladdin's cave: the provider of all things to all men. In the few days before she had sailed from the UK, her fourth hold – the after hold – had been converted in great haste into accommodation for 300 Royal Marines. Dockyard workmen were still on board when she sailed and marines were still finding welding rods in odd corners for weeks afterwards. This accommodation took the form of metal racks with bunks four levels high – nothing too grand, but for marines who are used to being stuffed into cramped corners in warships built to economise on every space, while living according to strict Naval discipline, it wasn't half bad. The ship herself was spacious and offered many opportunities both on her flight deck and inside for physical exercise and other training.

The ship's officers, led by Captain Barrie Dickinson, were helpful and cooperative to a man. Their normal routine was following the fleet plying the world's oceans and replenishing warships; a demanding enough routine, but during the Cold War a reasonably predictable one. To find themselves hosting over 300 Royal Marines, who had strange habits like running up and down the flight deck carrying heavy loads and shooting at floating targets, and cluttering up every corner in their ship, must have been somewhat disruptive for them. But they entered into the spirit of their new role as troopship and, as it eventually transpired, amphibious assault ship, with great enthusiasm and élan.

We ate like kings. The purser, Second Officer Denning, apart from being the son of a lieutenant general and the nephew of Lord Denning, the Master of the Rolls, was an expert chef and an *aficionado* of Chinese cooking. With him and his Chinese cooks, we could not have eaten more authentic or better Chinese food anywhere. Some men fished from the stern of the ship as she progressed southwards. The catch, whatever it was, went straight into the wok; although some men's ambitions were perhaps greater than was good for them. Andy Holt found two marines fishing for an eight-foot shark, with a large piece of meat on a stevedore's hook on the end of a length of rope. It had not occurred to them that if it really went for the bait, it might be they who were eaten by the shark. But to find ourselves in this capacious vessel with a civilian crew who treated us as welcome guests was an unprecedented and most agreeable experience.

The purser very kindly gave us a Merchant Navy flag – the 'Red Duster' – which we adapted and made into the X Ray Company flag. 'We will fly this in Port Stanley,' we said. It was carried all the way across East Falkland and duly made its appearance as promised.

We made good friends with many of the crew and both they and we considered ourselves very lucky with such a harmonious partnership. We came to think of *Stromness* as a great grey mother who provided us with all we needed. We grew to love her. When we were ashore in the Falklands, we saw her being attacked unsuccessfully and later we heard rumours that she had been bombed. We were greatly concerned, not only for those of our number whom we had necessarily left on board, but for the ship and the crew that had treated us so well. It transpired that she had indeed been attacked by Mirages and Skyhawks and claimed one kill with her machine guns. One bomb exploded 150 yards from the ship and ruptured some plates. There were no casualties. Two more bombs apparently hit the water very close to the ship, one forward and one aft. They did not explode. One hesitates to speculate on the damage they might have inflicted if they had. We were similarly concerned for *Sir Percivale*, where Bill McRae and his team were based with much of our logistics. But although she had an exciting war, *Percivale* too avoided the bombs.

One day at around midday, while in *Stromness* at anchor off Ascension Island, I was told by Colonel Andrew Whitehead in a somewhat breathless meeting, to get X Ray Company prepared in one hour's time with mountain and Arctic kit, ready to be deployed by brigade headquarters. That was all. This flew in the face of all my expectations and was quite impossible to do properly. But I issued what I thought were the necessary orders and I think we might just about have met the deadline. Very soon after this order I was asked how soon my company would be ready, because helicopters were on the way to pick us up. I indicated that they had better send them away again and call them in when we were ready, which they did. I was then informed that mountain and Arctic kit would not be necessary. On receipt of the first order, I had wondered if perhaps we were going to deploy to recapture South Georgia; now I was baffled and didn't know what to think. Soon after I had passed this new instruction on to my men, I was told the whole thing was off and I could stand down. In all, the whole performance had taken 45 minutes from beginning to end. It transpired that an Argentine freighter had been seen near Ascension – indeed I had seen it myself – and we had been sparked up as a contingency against sabotage parties being sent ashore – not an unreasonable notion. Eventually Yankee Company was sent ashore and thrashed around the side of Green Mountain for some hours and found nothing.

This episode worried me and it disturbed my marines, to whom the confusion had been perfectly obvious. I harboured black forebodings, and hoped earnestly that this was not a presage of things to come. It has been said that there are three, and only three, types of military operation: the Adjustable Military Fuck Up (AMFU); the Semi Adjustable Military Fuck Up (SAMFU); and the Complete Military Fuck Up (CMFU). This is a rather cynical acknowledgement that nothing in war ever goes to plan, and there are so many unforeseeables, so many uncontrollables, so many unknowns, that the only thing one can expect at every turn is the unexpected. I was a new company commander having only been in post for three months, but I had learned about the chaos of war eight years before, while commanding a company of Omani soldiers fighting Marxist guerrillas in the Dhofar War. From this point onwards I determined to make a positive effort to teach my marines to expect nothing and to be ready for anything. War is the province of the unexpected and we had better get comfortable with that. This, the first practical lesson, was a good grounding.

South Georgia was retaken on 25 April. We heard of this with as much pleasure as the Prime Minister plainly received it although, unlike her, we were not privy to the nail-biting situation on the glaciers that had preceded the successful landings. We were pleased also because it simplified our task. We could rule out the possibility that we might be dispatched to recapture this mountainous Antarctic island. We could now concentrate on the Falklands.

The airfield at Ascension Island is said to have been the busiest in the world for a few days during this period. This was no surprise to us who were able to observe it from the side of the mountain (Green Mountain) which overlooked the runway. We had never seen so many aircraft and so many different types. Not long after we arrived, we saw a number of Victor tankers land and take their place on the increasingly crowded airfield apron. About ten days later, we noticed they had been joined by two Vulcan bombers. Victors could be used to refuel a variety of aircraft and aroused interest but little speculation. Vulcans however were different. I had been fortunate a number of years before in visiting an RAF station where a Vulcan had been sitting in a hangar. My RAF host had shown me round this huge manta ray-like aircraft. I clambered around the cavernous bomb bay and sat in the cockpit like an excited small boy. I was struck by the contrast between the size of the aircraft and the cramped space of the cockpit. I was also surprised at the restricted vision of the pilot. Like much else in the way of ships, aircraft and capabilities, the Vulcan was due for the scrapyard when the crisis blew up. And yet here they were sitting on the pan at Ascension. This could only mean one thing: we were going to bomb something. I don't think we thought in any depth about what the target might be, but the following day we found out.

That evening, 30 April, we were conducting a night navigation exercise on Green Mountain. We saw that there was substantial air activity on the runway and heard and saw a number of Victor tankers taking off. Then it was the turn of a Vulcan bomber to take to the air. I had not heard a Vulcan take off until then, but the distinctive, eldritch, banshee howl of its engines as the pilots piled on maximum power remains with me to this day. In the morning we discovered we had been watching the launch of the first Vulcan raid on Stanley airfield; Operation Black Buck One.

Operation Black Buck was a series of raids, each flown by one Vulcan bomber flying for 16 hours supported by eleven Victor tankers, to bomb Stanley airfield and the radar installations around it. Some of these raids were conducted in conjunction with attacks by our Sea Harriers in the Carrier Group which was by now in the theatre of operations. The story is told fully elsewhere, but it was a remarkable operation, and involved considerable gallantry. It wouldn't have taken much to have gone wrong in the way of fuel miscalculations or machinery malfunctions – not to mention interference by the enemy – to put any one of these huge aircraft down beyond help in the South Atlantic. The results were controversial then, and to this day are a matter of debate. The investment in fuel alone to put one aircraft over target, was prodigious, perhaps even profligate. The results were modest and the missions of preventing the use of the airfield to high performance aircraft and destroying radars were never conclusively achieved. It also seems that one stick of bombs failed to explode because of an oversight in the aircraft. Since we had publicly declared that we did not intend to use this capability to bomb Argentina, it is doubtful if we even persuaded the Argentines to redeploy aircraft which could have been used to attack us. The Royal Air Force under-standably made much of this feat of airmanship, although the Harrier pilots flying from the carriers were taking similar risks several times daily and nightly. But in a sense, the material damage that Black Buck may or may not have inflicted was less important than the psychological effect. We in the Landing Force were encouraged and buoyed up by this action which might help to limit the air power of our adversaries. For the Argentines on the Islands, the message clearly was: 'We are coming to get you.' And for the Argentine junta it was, together with the sailing of the Task Force and the recapture of South Georgia the week before, yet another factor which would dislocate their expectations. It would be followed by quite a few more.

Ascension Island has a fine airfield, some pristine beaches, but no harbour. A small concrete jetty served the needs of the local community, but large vessels – and that meant all the ships of the Task Force – had to anchor off the island. A steady traffic of landing craft and small boats between ship and shore used the beaches and the jetty, and while we lived on board *Stromness* we came ashore frequently by day and night to continue our training programme. We practised helicopter assault drills, we clambered up and down our home-made nets on the side of the ship, in and out of landing craft, by day and by night. The staff of 3 Commando Brigade was also able to exercise the planning and conduct some of the elements of both helicopter and landing craft borne assaults. However, there was no time to put all these constituent parts together and conduct a full rehearsal, an exercise which might have helped to iron out the many wrinkles associated with bringing together so many men who had no experience of amphibious warfare, with so many ships which were designed for anything but amphibious warfare.

At the end of one of these Brigade exercises – a route march along the island ending up at a beach – I found myself sitting in the sand next to a lieutenant colonel in the Parachute Regiment. I recognised him. Two months earlier, I had commanded X Ray Company acting as enemy on an exercise with the Army brigade, 5 Infantry Brigade, at Thetford in Norfolk. I had seen this officer at various meetings during this exercise. He did not recognise me. It was probably just as well. During the course of the exercise, one of my fighting patrols had destroyed his battalion headquarters. While going through the tents, my marines had found a large catering-sized open tin of tomato ketchup. It was just too tempting. A lit thunderflash was planted in it and the resultant mess must have been a realistic simulation of an artillery shell landing in a crowded room. The reaction to my apologies the following day had indicated that the hilarity with which the rest of X Ray Company had greeted the news of this escapade had not been shared by the other side.

I introduced myself and he looked rather fiercely at me. The rivalry between the Royal Marines and the Parachute Regiment is well enough known – although it has suited the media to make more of it than any Para or Royal Marine would recognise – and perhaps he thought I was about to try and make some scoring remark. When it became quite clear that I had no ambitions in that quarter, his 'north face' quickly mellowed and we passed the time in pleasant, inconsequential conversation. This was the only time I spoke to Herbert Jones whose name was about to become a household word after the Battle of Darwin and Goose Green. I'm glad I met him properly.

It would have been good to have been able to rearrange and re-stow our higgledy-piggledy hastily loaded ships. Much useful information on the whereabouts of items had been gathered by the simple expedient of placing one man from the Commando Logistic Ordnance Squadron on each logistic ship with a clipboard and pencil, who spent the journey from UK to Ascension Island crawling through the holds of his ship, making a record of what it carried. A certain amount of re-stowing did take place, and Captain Alex Watson managed to concentrate most of our logistic assets in RFA *Sir Percivale*, but without dockside space, and anchored as we were in a near constant Atlantic swell, we were never going to get very far unscrambling this tightly bound Chinese puzzle. Besides, our planners had to be mindful that helicopter hours were precious. Spare parts and repair facilities were limited, and profligate use of helicopters at Ascension, transferring stores between ships, could have disastrous effects on helicopter availability in the operational theatre. Notwithstanding all these constraints, helicopters buzzed the sky like hornets while all types of small surface craft, from inflatables to landing craft, criss-crossed the water in scenes reminiscent of Istanbul harbour at peak commuting times.

We remained based on board *Stromness* for the rest of our time at Ascension, and from her we watched the rest of the fleet assemble and prepare to sail south. Of particular fascination were the Sea Harrier aircraft based in *Atlantic Conveyor*. *Conveyor* was a civilian container ship requisitioned to carry aircraft and stores and she was an impressive vessel. We provided a number of working parties for her during our voyage south and we got to know her quite well. At Ascension, she was anchored close to us and we were able to watch at close quarters the Harriers operate from her. These extraordinary aircraft, which eventually turned out to be war winners, would take off vertically from the deck of *Conveyor*, buzz around the anchorage at high speed, and land again. As they came in to land, they would slow down, stop, and hover behind the ship's mast which the pilot used as a reference point. Then they would sink down to the deck with a controlled slump. It seemed such an extraordinary thing for a high performance jet aircraft to do. Once landed, the aircraft would be trundled aft, to the well created by the walls of containers built up on either side of the ship to protect them from the weather. It was a remarkable performance. Harriers, with their short wings and stumpy bodies, reminded me of penguins. We saw every type of aircraft deployed by our own fleet during those days, which was

46

a very useful exercise in aircraft recognition. At least we would know which ones not to try and shoot down with our machine guns.

While lying at anchor off Ascension, we heard that the Argentine cruiser, the *General Belgrano* had been sunk by one of our submarines. Given the large number of sailors who were killed and the fog of war which led to some inaccurate reports by the authorities in London, it was only to be expected that some people would smell a rat. A Peruvian peace proposal was in the air and it was suspected that Prime Minister Margaret Thatcher had ordered that *Belgrano* be sunk in order to forestall it. But there was no rat. The Argentines had taken the Falklands by force and we had responded by sending a fleet of warships. We had fought for and recovered South Georgia and disabled the submarine *Santa Fe* while doing so. The day before *Belgrano* was sunk, our ships had bombarded Argentine positions on the Islands. The Argentines had bombed and tried to sink our ships with Mirage aircraft and we had bombed Stanley airfield with a Vulcan bomber. Their ships were at sea manoeuvring to attack ours: each side was trying to sink the other. We were manifestly at war. The *Belgrano* group of ships was a potent force. The *Belgrano* herself had fifteen 6-inch guns with a range of 13 miles and her escorts carried Exocet missiles with a range of 30 miles. The possibility of an attack coordinated with the Argentine aircraft carrier group to the north presented a real and present threat to our ships. If we didn't sink them first, they would sink us. *Belgrano* was indeed outside the Total Exclusion Zone when she was sunk and she was heading westwards to Argentina when the torpedoes struck. However, the Argentines had been warned through Swiss diplomatic channels that any approaching warship which amounted to a threat would 'encounter the appropriate response' regardless of whether it was inside or outside the Total Exclusion Zone. The direction in which she was sailing was irrelevant. *Belgrano* could have changed direction at any time in an instant. Most importantly, at a moment's notice, she could have turned north towards the British ships across the shallow waters of the Burdwood Bank and wiped off the shadowing British submarine, which would have had difficulty following her. Indeed, one could argue that not to try and sink her at this stage would have been irresponsible. One wonders whether those who persistently complained about the sinking would have preferred that we had left her and her escorts to sink a British ship, for that would have been the most likely outcome.

We, of course, didn't know these details at the time. But we felt the natural satisfaction that comes to those whose own side had scored a hit, although this was tempered by the knowledge that a large number of sailors had lost their lives. Living on board a ship which was about to sail into the same theatre of war, we felt a certain solidarity with those who had lost their lives at sea while exposed to the violence of the enemy – regardless of which side they were on. Indeed, when initial reports suggested 400 sailors had gone down with the cruiser, a certain *frisson* went through the fleet. The final figure was 321, but by any standards this is a high butcher's bill. Notwithstanding this, and the reservations expressed in certain quarters at home, it did not occur to us to regard the *Belgrano* as anything other than fair game. And the notion that we should have stayed our hand because she might have been on her way home was absurd. The German battleship *Bismarck*, in the Second World War, was on her way home to Brest when she was sunk, but that didn't make her less of a threat.

It has since become clear that the Argentines shared this understanding of the nature of the hostilities. Both Captain Hector Bonzo, the commanding officer of the *Belgrano*, and Admiral Gaulter Allara, the flag officer commanding the force to which *Belgrano* belonged, are on record as saying that the attack was legitimate and that they knew what they were doing and accepted the risks. In 2007, I had the pleasure of meeting Captain Carlos Castero Madero, the Argentine naval attaché to the United Kingdom. He was lecturing to the British Advanced Command and Staff Course, together with Captain Chris Wreford-Brown, the captain of HMS *Conqueror*, the submarine that sank *Belgrano*. The attaché had been a midshipman in the *Belgrano* and, as well as losing a number of his friends, he himself spent a couple of days in a life raft before he was rescued. It was a moving moment seeing these two – the sinker and the sunk – meeting each other. Captain Castero made it absolutely clear that *Belgrano* was indeed seeking an opportunity to strike the British fleet and that he and his comrades understood and accepted their fate as a legitimate act of war

Even before Midshipman Castero had been pulled from his life raft, he and his friends had been avenged. The sinking of HMS *Sheffield*, on 3 May, was as much a shock to us as it was to those at home, but it merely intensified our wish to get stuck in and sort the business out. Years later, I met Captain Sam Salt, the Commanding Officer of the *Sheffield*. He told me that soon after his rescue, when he was waiting in HMS *Hermes* with other survivors to be taken home to the United Kingdom, a special forces soldier approached him. This man had said how sorry he was that Sam had lost his ship and asked him how many men had been killed. Sam told him that 20 men had gone down with the ship. The soldier sympathised and disappeared. Two days later, he reappeared. He had just returned from taking part in the spectacularly successful special forces raid on Pebble Island where 11 Argentine aircraft were destroyed on the ground. He came up to Sam and said quietly, 'We've squared the account, Boss.'

Chapter 4

Sailing

He took her down to Chinatown,
And he showed her how to kick the gong around.

We sailed for the South Atlantic on 7 May. The intense training period had left the marines itching to get on with things. It was therefore something of a relief to sail, although this was tinged with curiosity and perhaps anxiety, at the unknown – but at least it would be an unknown for which we felt we were well prepared. Setting off from the equatorial balm of Ascension Island, knowing we were going to war in the sub-Antarctic, produced a rather disjointed sensation but, as we progressed south, the weather slowly began to match our expectations. *Stromness* was a relatively large ship with a deep draught but, in heavy weather, even she moved around. When doing physical jerks on a ship that is rolling or pitching, the unpredictable movements can be dangerous to knees and backs. Those with previous leg injuries were particularly vulnerable and some with missing cartilage found their knees began to swell. So great care had to be taken to ensure that we didn't knacker our bodies before we even got there. We acquired our sea legs fairly soon, but very few stomachs were immune to the really heavy stuff that the South Atlantic can throw at you in winter. We watched the smaller, shallower draught vessels rolling like sows and we felt for them. Mike Cole and Zulu Company on the other hand were by now enjoying the relative comfort of the P&O cruise liner *Canberra* and her rather camp but very hospitable stewards, and had struck up a good relationship with 40 and 42 Commando and 3 Para who were also on board. We were all now fully committed to the idea of landing and fighting and, weather permitting, our training programmes once more reflected this.

49

Notwithstanding the obvious constraints, much valuable military training can be done while at sea, and with our naval experience we were expert at maximising the opportunities. Every available space was used to practise (in between showings of *The Blues Brothers*): communications, weapon handling, aircraft recognition, disembarkation drills, map and procedural exercises, and so on – all by day and by night. First aid was practised with especial interest. If wounded, you could live or die depending on the ability of the man next to you to use a first field dressing, apply a tourniquet, or insert a saline drip. Weapons were fired day and night and the targets were anything that would fly or float. The officers and crew of the *Stromness* remained very patient while hundreds of marines ran hundreds of miles carrying hundreds of pounds around the flight and upper decks, and when the weather worsened, the internal stores deck.

Charles Laurence of the *Daily Telegraph* and Ian Bruce of the *Glasgow Herald* had joined us at Ascension. Both journalists were to come with 45 Commando throughout much of the war, sharing with us many discomforts and dangers. Charles Laurence opened his dispatch of 11 June 1982 by writing ' "Yomping", they call it in the Royal Marines,' thereby giving to the English-speaking world a word that the Royal Marines had hitherto kept for themselves. Both Charles and Ian yomped. Charles's health broke down, but he rejoined the Commando at Bluff Cove Peak and accompanied Headquarters Company for the Two Sisters battle and the advance on Sapper Hill. Ian succeeded in being one of that small group of journalists who were among the first into Stanley. The dispatches of Laurence and Bruce were written with the authority of men who were really there and, reading them again today, I can confirm they pass the test of time. At the beginning, we had to prepare the correspondents with equipment and training sufficient for them not to be a liability to themselves and others on the battlefield. They were ready students.

We also brushed up our mortar and artillery fire control drills. Each company had a Royal Artillery Forward Observation Team attached to it. X Ray's team comprised Captain Alasdair Cameron, Bombardier Barry Ingleson and Gunners Howell and Jones. No self-respecting soldier ever does anything without artillery or mortar support. Alasdair was my adviser on all matters of artillery and he and Ingleson were also the means of supplying it when required. So they were key members of the team. We had worked together before on exercise and we had got on very well. I was very glad to have Alasdair, not only for his guns, but for his good fellowship and sound advice. Corporal Andrew Foster was also attached as my mortar fire controller. As my advisor, and my link to the Commando's troop of 81mm mortars, he performed a similar

50

function to Alasdair. He too was a critical player and before long, we would be most grateful for his coolness and professionalism. During the land campaign, I never went anywhere without these two. Between them they ensured that every man in the Company had the skills to call for artillery and mortar fire if required. This would indeed be put to good use in the battles to come.

A fleet at sea is an impressive sight. I had served in a frigate for a couple of years and yet only now, for the first time, did I really understand what the term 'ocean going navy' means. *Antrim* and *Antelope* had not been replenished since leaving Gibraltar some weeks earlier. Both ships had run out of many of the staples of food and were low on other basic items. For several hours, they steamed alongside us, one on either side, taking on tons of stores by means of the cables slung between the ships. And this was all done at night while all ships were blacked out. I had seen many replenishments at sea, but none as impressive as this, and none with such important portents.

One of our problems was lack of information. Our only source of news was the BBC World Service and as we got further south reception got worse. Sometimes we couldn't receive it at all. Rumours were rife. This became a point of some concern because inevitably there was still speculation that either the Argentines might withdraw, or the British might compromise. It is most important that men who are going to war have their expectations shaped closely to the realities of what they might actually face. Any notion that they might not have to fight, or that no one will get hurt, can be very damaging when unpleasant reality intrudes.

While we were at Ascension Island, we had listened with much interest to the news of the negotiations being conducted between Britain and Argentina, via General Al Haig. We discussed among ourselves what it all meant. For some men, it seemed unlikely that our two countries would actually resort to fighting each other. Surely the Task Force had been sailed as a political gesture only? Maybe the Argentines will withdraw under international pressure? However, I went to some pains to dispel any residual notion that there would not be a war. Negotiations can only ever succeed when there is some overlap between the absolute minimum requirements of both sides. There was no such overlap in this case. Having 'recovered the Malvinas' to much popular acclaim, the Junta could not possibly give them up again peacefully and survive. Why would they withdraw? They had possession. On the other hand, by dispatching the Task Force the British had declared that they were willing to fight to recover the right of the Falkland Islanders to choose their government. The idea that the Islanders would willingly accept any form of Argentine suzerainty was cloud cuckoo land. To bring the Task Force home without achieving its goal would result in a crippling

51

loss of credibility and could only mean the end for Margaret Thatcher. So, no possible common ground; no negotiable settlement. We were going to war. We would win, but we would have to fight and we must get into that frame of mind immediately.

Now, in the South Atlantic, I made a point of hunting out the news from the BBC World Service and from such military and naval broadcasts that were available, and disseminating it to my company regularly each day. I was adamant in telling the men that whatever they might think they had heard, they should be in no doubt that we were going to war. They should harbour no notion that some political or diplomatic fudge might be found. Neither was this a bluff. We would have to fight, and we would win. Nothing other than this should be entertained. A government was going to fall: theirs or ours, and we would surely see to it that it was not ours. But we would not be allowed the luxury of a Dunkirk. We had to get it right first time.

I was lucky. I had been to war before. Together with a small core of British officers from all three services, I had been seconded to the Sultan of Oman's Armed Forces for nearly two years during the Dhofar War. There we had commanded Arab and Baluch soldiers fighting in the mountains against Marxist insurgents who were a wily, hardy and determined enemy. It had been a low intensity war, but on occasion the action had been fast, furious and bloody enough. Officer training at the Commando Training Centre had been as good as peace time training can be, but nothing can substitute for the real thing. I had learned my craft, so to speak, in Oman; I had a first-hand idea of what we might expect. As well as experiencing AMFUs, SAMFUs and CMFUs, it was there that I had learned about the importance of attitudes and expectations. Men who think that they may not have to fight are very vulnerable when it turns out that they do have to. Men who are not prepared for the worst can be unbalanced when the horrors of war impose themselves unexpectedly upon them. The greatest single difference between peace and war is the unexpected. No matter how realistic an exercise may be, one always knows that it will end, it will end soon, and it will end well. In war, no one knows when it is going to end, or what is going to happen next. Only those soldiers who are trained to expect the unexpected will flourish in war. Many hours were spent discussing the physical and moral aspects of what we were about to do, thereby further fostering knowledge and understanding of what to expect in the inevitable confusion and uncertainty that would follow. When training soldiers, one is trying to shape a very special type of person. One is trying to breed constructive cynics, optimistic sceptics: men who, when you tell them what the plan is and what you think is going to happen, look at you and say, 'Nice plan Boss; we know that whatever happens it won't be that: but we know what you are trying to do and why you are trying to do it, and between us we'll make it work.' The most resilient soldiers are those who revel in their ability to flourish in what appears to others as chaos, but for them is normality.

People must also expect to take casualties, and they should prepare themselves mentally for this. Leaders get killed and men must be ready to take over from commanders one level, even two levels up during the battle. I had tried to get this across in training my company and I now placed extra emphasis on it. I sat each of my rifle troops down on the quarterdeck of the ship and told them that, not only would we have to fight, but that we would also take casualties. I asked each man to think what he was going to do when the man next to him dropped. I didn't want to hear the answer, but I wanted them to think themselves into that possibility now. I wanted each corporal to think about what he was going to do when the troop sergeant dropped. I asked Phil Witcombe, my second-in-command, to think about what would happen when I dropped. Where would he be? How would he get enough information to take over from me? What would be the first thing that he did? Only by thinking about this now would he be able to withstand the shock when it happened, and effect a seamless takeover. I pointed at one marine and said, 'What are you going to do when *you* drop? Are you going to scream like a Dervish and unnerve the man next to you, or are you going to die quietly like a soldier?'

Someone started laughing and said, 'He'll probably be screaming before he's shot.' More laughter; which was precisely the effect I was hoping to achieve. If my marines could understand fully the awful potential that faced them, and yet laugh at it, then they would be all the more able to withstand it when the shock came. I also impressed upon them that when the shooting starts it is not personal. Just stick your head up and you will see the rounds are hitting somewhere else.

When Winston Churchill was forced to leave the Admiralty as the Gallipoli adventure descended into disaster, he gravitated to France and Belgium and wangled for himself the command of the 6th Battalion of the Royal Scots Fusiliers. He would frequently be found in the trenches at the front line, talking to his soldiers, smiling and laughing and bolstering their morale. His soldiers thought very highly of him, and were sorry when he left. 'War', said Churchill 'is a game to be played with a smiling face.' I had not yet read Roy Jenkins' biography of Churchill where all this is described, but there can be no doubt that Churchill was dead right. Humour is our sabbatical from reality; the blacker and more macabre the humour, the better. Men facing even the most dire of prospects can find comfort in humour.

While we were at Ascension Island, we were able to receive and send mail through an efficient British Forces Postal Service. Now that we were at sea, all that changed. There were two air drops of mail and other essential supplies to *Stromness* from a Hercules flying out from Ascension. On one of these drops, we were all watching expectantly as the aircraft flew over the fleet when, out from the back, came a bag which promptly burst open and loose paper floated down into the sea. We were appalled at the thought of our precious, long-awaited mail being thus lost to what we assumed was the incompetence of the RAF. Our despair turned to relief, then gales of laughter when, having amused themselves at our expense with a sack of waste paper, the aircrew dropped the real mail in a waterproof bag which was picked up safely by a cutter.

I received a pair of windproof trousers sent by Louise at my request, for which I was very grateful. Ian Ballantyne was less impressed by the application for life insurance that his wife had kindly sent him, asking him to complete the form and send it back to her. Ian thought that it was probably a bit late for that, and no doubt the insurance company would have thought so too if he had filled it in, but his men enjoyed the joke. The last mail drop was on 10 May. We were not to know that the next mail we would see would be a month later, just before we captured Stanley.

There were occasional reminders of the wider implications of what we were doing. It was clear that the Soviet Union was intensely interested in what we were up to. A Soviet spy ship attended the Fleet at Ascension Island and for part of the journey south, no doubt listening in to all radio transmissions, and as we proceeded south we regularly saw Soviet reconnaissance Tupolev Tu 95 'Bear' aircraft – the Bear in the air – flying high above us. The Soviets wanted to know if we would fight. The fact that we were apparently able and willing to go to war for 1,800 people living on some barren islands 8,000 miles away was not what they had expected of the decadent, flaccid West in the early 1980s. We knew that our conflict was one small but significant part in the Cold War and there can be little doubt that our eventual victory played its part in bringing it too to a successful conclusion. It was almost as great a pleasure to dislocate Soviet expectations as it was to beat the Argentines.

One day, one of these large four-engined Bear aircraft came down and did a graceful, slow pass at mast level, presumably taking photographs. Many marines were on the upper deck watching the performance. Unanimously and spontaneously they dropped their trousers and 'mooned' the Russian. Doubtless there are some charming snaps somewhere in the Moscow archives ...

Plans were now being made for the landings. We received new 1:50,000 maps of the Falklands. They looked pretty good maps, although it was a trifle disconcerting to see occasional spots which were annotated as 'obscured by cloud'. We wondered why this should be so with a territory that had been British for 150 years. We didn't know the half of it. The original maps that 3 Commando Brigade were presented with had no grid lines on them, and they were made from air photographs taken in 1956 and printed in 1961. This meant that no grid references could be given or received, thus seriously limiting their utility for military purposes. The story of how these maps were given accurate grid lines, printed in sufficient quantities and delivered to us in time to fight with them is yet another extraordinary unsung saga of people on the Brigade Staff and elsewhere working frantically behind the scenes to overcome incipient chaos. Later, we also received 1:25,000 maps of the environs of Port Stanley. They were excellent and were very up-to-date, having been printed in April 1982. In fact, so up-to-date were they that the Royal Marines barracks at Moody Brook, which had been destroyed by the Argentines during their invasion, was marked as 'derelict'. A nice touch that, we thought. We were to see no air photographs of the Falklands at any stage during the campaign.

The Argentines used the original ungridded 1961 maps, reproduced illegally from Crown Copyright. Their forces being largely static, grid references were not so important to them. Instead, they used a series of numbered reference points. They directed their artillery by registering points on the ground by fire, and once fired, observers could correct from the fall of shot. But their inability to use grid references was another limiting factor on any mobile operations they might have planned. Unbeknownst to us, we had much to thank our mapping staffs for.

Naturally we were not involved in the decision making process for the landings, but we were well pleased when it was decided that we should land at San Carlos. There was a strong American influence in the Argentine military culture. Partly because of the resources at their disposal, US amphibious doctrine was far more direct than ours and accepted the possibility of opposed fighting landings. Therefore, we judged that the Argentines would expect us to land near Port Stanley. That would almost certainly involve a degree of opposition, and probably to quite a high degree. However, so far as the British were concerned, it was always better to land where the enemy was not. The act of trying to get ashore is usually the most vulnerable phase in an amphibious operation and trying to get ashore in the face of violent opposition makes it all the worse. Long gone were the days when we had the hardware necessary to conduct landings in the face of well equipped opposition. San Carlos was unlikely to be heavily defended. It was the opposite side of the island from Port Stanley, our final objective, so we might have to fight our way across the island. But once ashore, we would have a number of options. If we couldn't get ashore, or were badly mauled in trying, then we could forget about the rest.

As we approached the islands, Brigadier Julian Thompson, the commander of 3 Commando Brigade, visited us in *Stromness*. It was good to see him. It was a happy coincidence that he had been the chief instructor in the Officers' Training Wing at the Commando Training Centre when I and several others of the Brigade company commanders and staff officers had gone through training 14 years before. He had proven himself as the commanding officer of 40 Commando, and had led the Brigade successfully during the two most recent winter deployments in Norway. We knew he was an experienced, highly capable officer. He brought with him his chief of staff, Major John Chester. John had very recently been a company commander in 45 Commando Group and we knew him extremely well. He too was a known and highly regarded operator. The coincidences did not stop there. Our own commanding officer, Lieutenant Colonel Andrew Whitehead, had been one of the instructors in Officers' Training Wing at the same time as Thompson, and the boss of the Wing had been a certain Major Jeremy Moore, who as a major general, on 12 May while still at Northwood, was appointed the commander responsible for the entire landing force. This pattern was repeated throughout the Brigade – wherever one looked: on the Brigade Staff; the supporting Royal Artillery, or Royal Engineers; the Brigade Air Squadron; the Logistic Regiment; in the other Commandos, even further afield among the Royal Navy officers in the warships: there were men whom we had served with before, and whom we knew and trusted. Trust is of course the glue which holds together all human relationships, but in the civilian or business world it is not always a salient feature. In the military world, it is essential currency. No military organisation can flourish unless there is a high degree of trust: upwards, downwards, and sideways. In 3 Commando Brigade, we trusted our commanders and we trusted each other. The Headquarters was a repository of years and years of amphibious experience. We knew we were in good hands; indeed, within the courtesies of age and rank, many of us were friends. Trust was also key among the marines. Many men in the Commando had been with the unit during the recent tour in West Belfast. This had helped to engender a high degree of trust, cohesion, reliance and mutual respect within the rifle sections. Inscribed in the Gaelic language on the memorial to the 51st Highland Division at Beaumont Hamel on the Somme battlefield are the words: *Là a' Bhlàir s'math na Càirdean* – 'Friends are good on the day of battle.' Wise words indeed.

Brigadier Thompson told us two things during his visit. When men became casualties in Northern Ireland, the normal procedure was immediately to devote all one's effort and resources to attend to them and save their lives. He said that this must not apply here. If men went down during an assault, they were to be left for those following up to attend to them. The momentum of the battle must be maintained. We understood this well enough. He also advised us to sharpen our bayonets. We would need them, he said: and indeed we did.

The Royal Marines are unique in the United Kingdom in that they train all their officers, NCOs and marines at the same place. For Royal Marines, there is no Sandhurst, Dartmouth or Cranwell where officers are trained in isolation from the men and women they will lead. At the Commando Training Centre at Lympstone near Exmouth in Devon, all Royal Marines are trained together. There are separate wings devoted to the training of each group of course, but a recruit under training will see young officers on parade and hear them being shouted at by their instructors. He will see them going through the same gruelling Commando tests to earn the same Green Beret; except he will know that the officer has 10 per cent less time in which to complete the tests. In turn, the young officer under training will meet and exercise with marines under training. Very early in his apprenticeship, he gets a feel for the temper of the men for whom he will be responsible later on. This tends towards a shared understanding and respect between all Royal Marines which starts from very early in one's service. Officers and men join the Royal Marines from every sort of background, but there is a classlessness in the Corps which not every British military organisation shares. Officers do enjoy privileges not given to other ranks, but in the professional field, no quarter is given. Neither do the Royal Marines see themselves as 'exclusive'. Men from the Army, Royal Navy and the Royal Air Force who serve in the units which support the Brigade also do the Commando course at Lympstone, and are included in this brotherhood. The only thing that matters is: can you do your job? Thus 3 Commando Brigade, comprising as it did of men of all three services who had won the Green Beret, enjoyed an especially strong sense of cohesion and spirit. When we were joined by two battalions of the Parachute Regiment, a regiment which brought with it a similar ethos and a fighting reputation second to none, we knew that provided we got ashore, we were going to win.

A great deal of work was going on elsewhere to ensure that we would get ashore. Special forces started landing on the Islands from 1 May onwards, gathering information on the ground and the enemy. Naval gunfire observation teams also went ashore and the Royal Navy ships in the vicinity of the Islands began a programme of shore bombardment which was intended to erode the morale of the Argentines and destroy their installations. Amphibious doctrine requires that local air superiority is achieved over the amphibious operating area before any landing is attempted and we knew the Sea Harriers were trying to engage the Argentine Air Force, hoping to draw down their substantial superiority in numbers.

Although we knew that all this would be going on, we had no part in it. We knew in outline that a number of plans had been postulated and that a final plan had been settled upon. In 45 Commando, we concentrated on preparing ourselves and our men for the job of landing and fighting when the time came. Ammunition and rations were issued and we packed and repacked our kit. For most men, this was the first time they had ever been issued with live ammunition before a disembarkation. In addition to his own ammunition, each man would carry four 81mm mortar rounds to drop off at the mortar pit when he got ashore. Live ammunition weighs more than exercise ammunition, and the extra weight was something of a surprise. Our burden was further increased because we had more than twice the normal number of machine guns.

Rifle companies in Commandos equipped for Arctic warfare had two scales of 7.62mm machine guns. The normal scale was ten GPMGs. But this was a belt-fed weapon and in the Arctic the ammunition dragged in the snow and jammed the breech mechanism. The solution was to issue a parallel scale of magazine-fed machine guns. The weapon used was the Second World War Bren Gun re-barrelled to fire 7.62mm ammunition. We called it the Light Machine Gun – the LMG. All three company commanders decided that, since we had these extra weapons, it seemed foolish not to take them all.

British infantry tactics at that time tended to treat the rifle group and the machine gun group within each section as interchangeable in the attack. One would support the other as they moved forward. But in Oman, I had learned about the real importance of machine guns. I had discovered that the only thing that really matters is the weight of automatic fire that one directs at the enemy. It was only by bringing to bear a greater weight of fire, either from artillery, or aircraft, or machine guns, that we won our fights in Oman. I had been at the receiving end of machine guns in Oman, and had seen what ours did to the other side. They were the main armament at my disposal. Consequently I thought of my company not in terms of 120 men, or three troops or nine sections, but in terms of nine GPMGs. Together with a 50-round belt of ammunition, a GPMG weighs nearly 14 kg, so being a GPMG gunner was no sinecure. But the kudos that came with being chosen to carry this powerful weapon was often reward enough for the men who were burdened with it. A GPMG could chew its way through brick walls, trees, and sand bags. Nobody moved if you suppressed them with machine-gun fire. So when we were ordered to prepare for operations in the South Atlantic, the company commanders in 45 Commando were unanimous in their decision to take both scales. We all took every machine gun we could lay our hands on. Consequently, instead of nine, we each had nineteen 7.62mm machine guns in our company. By doing so we gave ourselves a substantial weight and logistics problem, but when it came to a fight this would pay handsome dividends, helping us to win battles and save British lives. The GPMG, after a temporary absence from front-line service, has been brought back to the fore and is currently used extensively in Afghanistan as effectively as it was in 1982.

We regarded the kit list produced by Commando Headquarters with some scepticism. It seemed to be a catch-all which took little account of the extra weight of live ammunition. The assumption was that we would conduct our major movements by helicopter. On the occasions when we might march, we would only carry fighting order. Our rucksacks with our sleeping bags, spare clothes, spare food and so on would move by helicopter and be brought up to us in the evening. This was a reasonable enough assumption in peacetime, but I was not alone in suspecting that in war there might not be enough helicopters to fly our rucksacks around the countryside after us. 'Put ye not your faith in princes and helicopters' and 'Don't get separated from your kit' were saws constantly repeated by instructors at the Commando Training Centre, and now it seemed that we were going to disregard them both. In fact, had the container ship *Atlantic Conveyor* not been sunk with most of the heavy lift helicopters, there might well have been enough helicopters. So in the event, I was right, but not for the reasons I had supposed. The result, however, was that to begin with, when we carried our packs we were overloaded. And when we left them behind to be brought up to us, we went hungry and cold because they rarely materialised when hoped for. However, we quickly learned our lesson and soon no man walked anywhere without the essentials on his back.

As seen from the point of view of the individual marine or soldier, an amphibious landing is pretty simple. The man musters at the appointed time in the appointed place with his weapon and equipment. When ordered, he shuffles with his comrades along the passages in the ship, often lit by a gloomy red light so as not spoil his night vision. He emerges on to the flight deck to board a waiting helicopter, or climbs down into the well-deck of the ship and boards a landing craft. When all is ready, he either flies or sails off. His work only really begins when he lands on the enemy shore. It becomes slightly more complicated when his mother ship is not a specialised amphibious ship. In this case, he might be required to board his landing craft by climbing down the ship's side on a ladder or a net, or out through a hatch in the ship's side. If there is a swell running, the landing craft will be moving up and down, and he needs to time his final step carefully to avoid jarring his knees and back. But it is still pretty simple. Most types of vessel can be made useful in an amphibious landing provided there is a quorum of specialist ships at the core of the operation. The stores ship *Stromness* was not conceived for the amphibious role, but she made a valuable contribution as such in the Falklands. The *Norland* was a North Sea ferry but, using specialist landing craft, she successfully launched the Parachute Regiment to war. In fact, the soldiers of 2 Para emerged through a door in the ship's side that was normally used to tip the rubbish into a skip. Since a landing craft looked to them much the same as a skip with an engine on it, they naturally called it 'skip-jumping'. Dead easy. But that is where simplicity stops.

Ideally one wants to get as many men ashore as quickly as one can in as good order as possible. It is essentially a time and distance calculation. Variable factors to be taken into account include the enemy threat, mining, beach gradients, available landing sites, weather, tide, currents, wind, hours of darkness, distance from objectives, number and size of helicopters and landing craft, number of landing spots and embarkation points, availability of fuel, and fuelling points and so on. And then you have to think about getting guns, artillery ammunition, and other essential stores ashore. With ships designed for the purpose, the planning staffs have a good knowledge of how long it should take to do what. With properly loaded ships, they know where things are. With well worked up ships and with troops who have rehearsed their disembarkation drills by day and by night, things can go more or less as planned. Nevertheless, it is at the best of times a delicately balanced evolution, and everybody has to be ready for a change in plan.

In the Falklands landings, the staffs had the worst of all worlds. Many of the ships were merchant ships. Crews were willing and able enough, but had no military or naval experience of any kind. Some had had flight decks welded on to them only a few short hours before they sailed from UK. In the hurry to sail the Task Force, stores had been loaded as they arrived in the dockyard without any consideration for the order in which they might be required ashore. Two out of the five assault units had no amphibious experience whatsoever. Some units were split up among several ships. The Brigade Staff was not helped by the fact that their superior headquarters at Northwood in overall command of the war, eventually 8,000 miles away, was almost entirely devoid of amphibious expertise. This meant that they had little idea of the constraints the staffs of the Amphibious Task Group Commander, Commodore Clapp, and

3 Commando Brigade were working under and therefore couldn't understand why things took so much longer than they expected. They also made demands, like the attack on Darwin and Goose Green, which took no account of the logistic realities on the ground.

On the journey south, the Amphibious and Brigade Staffs had made huge strides in finding out what was where and at Ascension Island they had made a gallant effort to bring some logic to the random stowage of stores. An intense training programme had been carried out to ensure that every unit had at least one daylight rehearsal disembarking from their ship. But in the case of some units, that was all. There had been no time to do a complete Brigade rehearsal. And yet, somehow, as if in a masterclass of improvisation, the Amphibious and Brigade Staffs made sense of all these manifold complexities, and produced a workable plan to support the Brigade Commander's design for battle.

All the unit commanding officers and their key staff officers gathered in HMS *Fearless* on 13 May, to hear the Brigade Commander deliver his orders for the forthcoming landings. On return to *Stromness*, Lieutenant Colonel Whitehead prepared his plan for 45 Commando. A day or so later Colonel Whitehead and his Headquarters planning team then delivered his orders to the company commanders and key Commando staff.

The Commando intelligence officer, Lieutenant Richard Passmore, told us about the ground and the enemy forces. On the face of it, it appeared that the Argentines on the Islands outnumbered us by at least two to one. This bald statistic meant very little because such numbers always include non-combatant staff and in any case we, the attackers, would have the initiative and would seek to achieve local superiority in our battles. It was reported that Argentine morale appeared to be low, although quite how this information was gleaned was not clear. However, the Argentines were well equipped. In virtually every area, their equipment was the match of ours and in some it was better. They had 155mm artillery which out-ranged ours and packed a bigger punch. They also had 120mm mortars while we only had 81mm. Their machine guns included the .5 inch Browning – the Fifty Cal of the movies –which was a formidable beast and packed a greater punch, out to a longer range than our 7.62mm weapons. They had an assortment of vehicles, some of which were armoured, but since they all seemed to be wheeled and there were hardly any roads on the Islands, this was unlikely to affect the balance. However, they might be able to use them to support their defensive positions around Port Stanley. Subsequently we discovered that they had excellent night vision equipment, but it seemed that they did not know how to use it properly.

The Argentine soldiers were a mix of professionals and conscripts. It is usually a mistake to assume that conscripts will fight less well than volunteers. I don't recall that the conscript armies of Britain or Germany in two world wars fought any less well because they were not professionals. Leadership, motivation, training and the national mood are much more important – and judging from the hysterical crowds of people screaming on TV in Buenos Aires, they did not appear to be short of national support. But again, one could not draw too many conclusions from that. Whether that would translate into motivation, or whether they were well led, remained to be seen.

The words 'young' and conscripts' have somehow become inextricably linked. All armies comprise young soldiers. War is necessarily a young man's business. A British serviceman had to be 18 to serve in Northern Ireland, but for operational service elsewhere, the minimum age was then 17. The average age in the Royal Marines rifle companies was probably around 21. Some had served in Northern Ireland, but for most their personal experience of war was nil. Marine Keith Simpson, one of my key signallers, had his eighteenth birthday in Port Stanley three days after the Argentine surrender. Much to his relief, Marine 'Flo' Nightingale was able to come with us because he had celebrated his seventeenth birthday just before we left Scotland. In Oman, some of my soldiers may have been as young as 14. With good officers and NCOs, most ordinary young men can achieve extraordinary things. We would find out soon enough whether this applied to our adversaries. Meanwhile, what was clear was that the Argentines had had time to consolidate and entrench themselves in easily defended positions on ground of their choosing and there was every prospect that sooner or later we would have a real fight on our hands to get them out.

Colonel Whitehead personally explained his design for battle and gave each of us our missions. The commander of 7 Battery from 29 Commando Regiment Royal Artillery, Major Gerry Akhurst, and our support company commander, Captain Ian Ballantyne, covered artillery and mortars. The operations officer, Captain Mike Hitchcock, went through the many coordinating instructions and timings, followed by Lieutenant Martin Cooke, the signals officer, who covered communications. Finally, and critically, the second-in-command, Major Rupert van der Horst and Captain Alex Watson, our quartermaster, dealt with logistics. Everything was backed up by a written operation order. I don't recall there being many questions. By the end of it, we had the clearest possible idea of what was required of us, and why. There was only one critical element missing. The date and time for landing was not yet set, but it would not be before 21 May.

At Northwood's insistence, the entire operation was to be conducted in Greenwich Mean Time (GMT). This looked to us as if the tail was wagging the dog. Having everybody involved in conceiving, planning, supporting and conducting operations working in the same time zone may have seemed a sensible thing to do. However, for virtually nobody involved in the operation was this the time zone in which they were really living. The UK was on British Summer Time which is one hour ahead of GMT: no great problems there perhaps, for those whose place of work was a desk in Whitehall, or a bunker 100 feet under Middlesex. But the Falklands were four hours behind GMT and five hours behind UK Summer Time. So for us who were living and working permanently out of doors and whose lives were regulated by the rising and the setting of the sun, it wasn't so straightforward. Every question of time brought with it the consideration: would it be dark; would it be daylight; and how many hours would it be before it changed. Dawn in the Falklands was around 6.30 am local time, or 10.30 am GMT. Last light was around 4.15 pm local, 8.15 pm GMT. This four hour dislocation from 'real' time was a pain in the neck for those like me whose mental arithmetic was less than fluent. I solved my problem by wearing two watches: my own watch on real time and my service issue watch on GMT. But I never really got used to it. It was an extra irritation which I could have done without.

But at least I only had two time zones to cope with. Not every ship felt constrained to work to the directive from Northwood. Some of them seemed to live domestically in a time zone all of their own which did nothing for the digestion or the sanity of those who had to move from ship to ship. Incidentally, the Argentines had imposed Buenos Aires time on the Islands, which was GMT minus three hours, but everybody except the Argentines ignored it.

The Brigade was going to land in the sheltered waters of San Carlos Water. This would afford protection from air launched Exocet missiles and submarines. It would also make things difficult for attacking aircraft. Special forces would carry out a diversionary raid at Darwin and Goose Green concurrent with the main landings. 40 Commando would land at San Carlos Settlement, 3 Para would take Port San Carlos, and 2 Para would secure Sussex Mountain. 45 Commando's initial objective was to take the disused meat refrigeration plant at Ajax Bay. X Ray Company's objective was to secure the buildings themselves, Yankee Company was to take the ground immediately to the north, and Zulu Company would land behind in reserve. Upon securing the beachhead, the Commando was to deploy to the high ground to the west and dig in on the reverse slope. The Commando was also warned off to be ready to conduct raids after the landings.

The Commando landing force, with three rifle companies and the commanding officer's tactical headquarters, would embark in four landing craft and land about two hours before first light. There was a small enemy force reportedly in the region of Fanning Head, but measures would be taken to suppress it before the landings. No other opposition was anticipated. We might expect to meet some Special Boat Service people on the beach. If they felt the need to get in touch with us, they would indicate their presence by an agreed signal with a red torch. It was also plain that we would not have the air superiority that we wanted, but provided we got ashore in darkness, we should be fine.

The company commanders in turn took all this away and prepared their plans for delivery to their troop commanders. My three troop commanders were lieutenants in their early twenties. James Kelly, Christian Caröe and David Stewart were young officers who had either been with the Company when I joined it three months before, or had joined soon afterwards. They were inexperienced, but we had all been on exercise together in the Scottish mountains and in Thetford, and I was entirely happy that they would be up to the challenges that faced us all. Moreover, each one had as his troop sergeant and helpmate a non-commissioned officer of proven ability. Sergeants George MacMillan, George Matthews and Pete Jolly were highly skilled, intelligent, experienced men. Under them, I had a quiverful of corporals and lance corporals who had my complete trust, and the trust of their marines. Whatever the difficulties and unknowns that lay in front of us, I knew that my command team was of the most sterling quality.

For my own part my plan was simple enough. Notwithstanding the intelligence to the contrary, we would assume that there were enemy holding the buildings. There was a small jetty on the shore adjacent to the meat packing plant. Tempting as it was to use the jetty, any enemy would surely have their weapons lined up on it. X Ray Company would move in one of the four landing craft and land a couple of hundred yards to the north of the jetty. Staying silent until we were fired upon, we would sweep up the buildings from the side. If there was any shooting, we would be firing away from Y Company who would be behind us. One troop would secure the outside, one troop would go through the buildings, and one troop would remain in reserve. On completion, we would reorganise and carry on up the hill as planned. Everyone was reminded that the landings were merely a means to an end, not the end itself. The goal was to secure the beachhead from which we could develop operations to remove the Argentines. I consulted my Royal Artillery officer, Captain Alasdair Cameron, and my mortar fire controller, Corporal Andrew Foster, and we tied up details for the use of indirect fire: not that there would be much available in the initial stages,

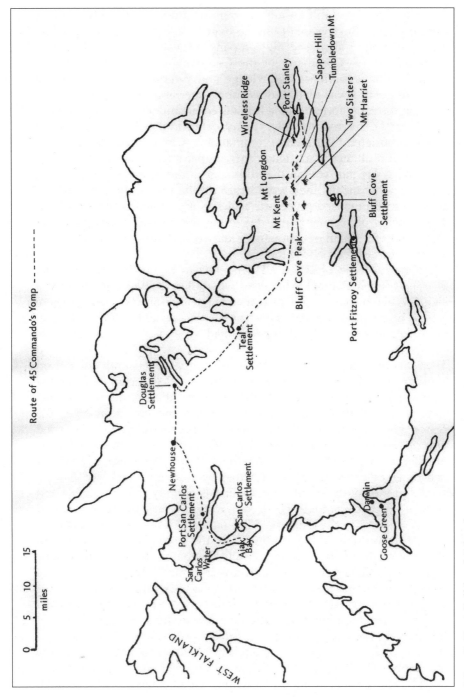

Map 2. East Falkland Island

because there wouldn't be any mortars or guns ashore until we had done our stuff. But in case of dire necessity, we would be able to call on a ship for help. I also used my company sergeant major, Mr Bell, as a sounding board. Command of the Company was my responsibility alone, but his experience, knowledge and reservoir of commonsense was a resource I was glad to draw upon over and over again.

Using the same format as the Brigade commander and the commanding officer, I delivered my orders to my team and they in turn made their plans and briefed their section commanders, who briefed their men. At the end of it all, every marine in my company knew what I knew and knew what his part was in the fulfilment of the Brigade commander's intent. By this means they would turn all the preparation into action. It was a well practised procedure which every company would follow. This process of receiving and delivering orders and preparing plans right down the chain of command – known as 'battle procedure' – was all part of our bread and butter.

On the morning of 20 May I happened to be on the bridge of the *Stromness* when Colonel Whitehead was called to the bridge to read a signal. When he had read it, he turned to me and said, 'We're off.' There was no more to be said. All plans had been made, all briefings given, all kit packed and checked. All that remained was to issue the ammunition.

Then, at this very late stage, Northwood intervened and insisted on a major redistribution of troops around the fleet prior to final disembarkation. This was not going to be easy and the planning staffs must have wished that they had had more notice and had been given the reason why. They might then have had a chance to explain to Northwood why it wasn't necessary. Cross-decking at sea can be achieved by a number of means depending on the weather: by landing craft, by helicopter or by winching men across by rope on a jackstay. During winter in the South Atlantic, no method is entirely safe or reliable and all take up precious time. The troops who now had to move included Zulu Company, in the *Canberra*. They had to cross-deck to *Intrepid* to be ready to board one of her landing craft and marry up with the rest of 45 Commando for the landings. Zulu Company arrived in their new berth via landing craft after a rough crossing, but safely. Not so fortunate were 22 men of the Special Air Service, who were killed when their Sea King helicopter crashed at night in transit between *Hermes* and *Intrepid*. I met the surviving pilot of this aircraft a few months later. He had been flying along normally and suffered catastrophic engine failure. It is not really known why. Perhaps a seagull or an albatross got ingested into the engine. The helicopter hit the water and started going down very quickly, and he was going down with it. He managed to kick through the windscreen and get himself out but he was being held back by his seat pack containing his safety equipment. The pack was trapped inside and he was struggling outside: there was a strong strap connecting him to his pack. He heaved and heaved on this strap to no avail and, consciousness fading, felt himself being pulled down to his death. He gave one final mammoth heave and the strap came away. He floated to the surface and was rescued. He was not a large man, yet *in extremis* he had somehow broken the strap. Ordinarily, it was strong enough to hang an elephant. The loss of these men was a terrible blow and saddened the entire Task Force. Moreover, many of those who died had taken part in the highly successful raid on Pebble Island and their hard won experience would be missed.

The Amphibious Force had been poised out of range of the Argentine Air Force for some days. Now we were steaming in at speed, well within range of air attack. For that final day, fortune blessed us with a bank of misty foul weather, protecting us from enemy aircraft just when we needed it. The threat of submarines had always been present and as we approached that threat became more real; the convoy zigzagged its way towards the Islands. For the Navy, the optimum time for landing would have been dawn, thus giving maximum time in darkness to approach the disembarkation point. But dawn was just when an enemy might expect a landing. The landing force needed to be established in the beachhead by first light and wanted maximum darkness to achieve this. An equitable compromise was reached, and the precious hours of darkness were shared out evenly between them.

Eventually the time came early in the morning for us to muster at our assault stations. This was probably one of the most tense moments of the campaign. We had heard of the action on South Georgia, we had heard of and seen newspaper pictures at Ascension of *Belgrano* and *Sheffield* sinking. We knew about the battles for air superiority too, but hitherto it had all been academic. We had been conveyed in considerable comfort and good cheer from Ascension and the most we had done was talk about it. Now we were about to make the transition between comfort and discomfort, safety and danger: from certainty to the complete unknown. Uninvited into my head came the thought of what it might be like to be trapped inside a sinking, burning, capsizing ship in the dark, a fate which had already befallen the sailors in the *Belgrano* and *Sheffield* (and unknown to me then, still awaited a number of soldiers and sailors in the Task Force). Had *Stromness* been bombed or torpedoed at that point, it seemed to me that not many of us would get up the single ladder out of her fourth hold alive. I mentioned it to nobody and quickly dismissed the thought.

67

The last fifteen hours of peace passed very calmly. Many men now wrote a final letter to their next-of-kin to be left on board and delivered only if they were killed. I wrote one to my wife, Louise, and one to my parents. Keeping them simple and to the point, I found them surprisingly easy to write and I sensed they served more than one purpose. One hoped that they would provide some shred of comfort to the recipients, but they also helped to put us in the frame of mind that the world of family and home was now behind us. When a man goes to war, he sets himself apart from the world of normal people. Family, children, mortgages, broken washing machines, noisy neighbours: all these fade into the background as he enters a new, more immediate, much starker and simpler reality. His world is now his weapon, his rucksack and his mates: these are the only things that matter. The process of moving to that world had been taking place ever since we left Arbroath, but I found that, by the exercise of writing these letters, it was now complete. Not everyone found it so easy though. Martin Cooke thought it was the most difficult thing he had ever done. He found the experience intensely emotional and extremely upsetting. It wasn't so much the difficulty of accepting his own death that was so troubling; it was the intense grief of not ever seeing again his wife and son, or ever meeting his unborn child. It was as though they had died to him. His morale crashed for a short while, and it took a stiff whisky and the support of his friend Mike Hitchcock to restore it.

I slept a bit and I ate a lot, not being entirely sure when I might have an opportunity to eat my next meal. I wandered around the ship speaking to my men. Contentment was what I identified. We had set them up in every way to go and do a job – now they had been given that job.

Down in the hold that evening, the atmosphere was not unlike a rugger changing room before a big match. No white lights, only red in order to preserve night vision. Each man going about his business; preparing himself, dressing, putting camouflage cream on his face and hands, packing, loading magazines. Quiet determination was evident everywhere – and humour. Marine 'Blue' Novak was to be seen parading with a bra and stockings on over his combat clothing, declaring that he'd be OK because the Argentines would not want to shoot women. I saw another marine examining his face closely in a mirror. He let out a plaintive call: 'Keith!'

'Yes, mate?'

'I can't possibly go ashore!'

A concerned 'Why not?' issued from somewhere in the dim, red gloom.

'I've got spots!'

Chapter 5

Landing

She had a dream about the king of Sweden,
He gave her things that she was needin',

The appointed time for our disembarkation into landing craft on 21 May
came and went. It was a clear, starlit, moonless night. From the deck of
Stromness, we could see the dark bulk of the other ships in the anchorage.
45 Commando was to be part of the second wave of landings. The
objectives of 40 Commando and 2 Para were further away from the
entrance of San Carlos Water, so they had gone in before us. We were to
use their empty landing craft upon their return. One of the returning
craft was to collect Zulu Company from HMS *Intrepid* and then, with the
other three empty craft, join us by the *Stromness*. One hour late: no sign
of Zulu, and no sign of the landing craft. We could see machine gun
tracer from the fire-fight between the Special Boat Service and the enemy
post on Fanning Head and we could hear the guns of HMS *Antrim* as
she fired in support. For many of us, this was the first visible sign of
war. Still no sign of landing craft. I went to the ship's operations room in
search of news. It was at this point that communications between ships
had chosen to break down. Colonel Whitehead was there too, desperate
for information. I felt for him. He told me that the whole operation had
been delayed because a soldier from the Parachute Regiment had fallen
between the landing craft and the *Norland*, and had been crushed. So
'skip-jumping' was not so easy after all.

Two hours late, two landing craft appeared. We climbed over the guardrail down the scrambling net – a net incidentally that the Commando
had had to make themselves as *Stromness* had had nothing suitable. This
form of disembarking is not as easy as it appears in the films and in the
South Atlantic at night, in a heavy swell, carrying all one's fighting order

and more, with the landing craft rising and falling several feet, it can be a delicate, time-consuming operation fraught with hazard. Then Zulu appeared in a third craft. Further delay waiting for the fourth craft: delay, wait, delay, wait: no sign of it. It had broken down somewhere. Back alongside *Stromness* we had to cram the remaining people into three landing craft. Further delay. At last, fully loaded – more like overloaded – our landing craft sailed round the bow of *Stromness* and another sailed round the stern. Then we heard the cox'n in our craft shout, 'STANDBY – BRACE, BRACE, BRACE!' Initial thoughts were that we were under attack, but no: we were merely about to crash into each other. A barrage of curses was hurled at the cox'ns as we all struggled to stay upright. Eventually we sailed. The sky was getting grey. No plan survives first contact with the enemy. Ours had not even survived that long.

All our plans had been based on the assumption that we would be landing in darkness. We were not expecting strong opposition, but had there been any opposition at all, things would not have gone well with us. Here was the greater part of 45 Commando, perhaps 600 men, crammed into three small boats sailing up a sea loch surrounded by unsecured land. It needed just one machine gun or a lucky pilot and we would have taken a hammering. However, there was simply no way to change the plans now and the intelligence people had got it right. Only Fanning Head was occupied and the enemy were in the process of being sorted out by the Special Boat Service supported by *Antrim*, although the withdrawing Argentines were later to destroy two helicopters with their Parthian shot.

I had brought my mouth organ with me. It would have been nice to be able to say that I serenaded our assault but, in truth, I did not have the heart for it just then. Later, when we sailed in landing craft across San Carlos Water to start our yomp towards Stanley, I did produce my instrument and X Ray Company had a good old sing-song to set us up for our exertions. But now, my stomach knotted with anxiety, I was too preoccupied with the need to get ashore.

We approached the derelict meat factory. There was no sign of occupation, but then there wouldn't be, would there? Closer in: still no raking fire into our exposed, crammed-full landing craft. Any self respecting Special Boat Service man would long have scarpered by now. The landing craft cox'n tried very hard to get us in close enough to jump on dry land, but not quite. We still had to wade ashore. Royal Marines are used to christening their feet at the start of amphibious exercises. This was no different, except this time our boots would not get dry again until we entered Stanley, 26 days later. Each man dropped his mortar bombs on the beach and the first marines swept along the shore, groups of men covering while others moved forward in short sprints – this is called pepperpotting. They entered the buildings, cleared every corner, then out the other side. I followed with my headquarters. Having secured our objectives, we quickly deployed up the hill. For the first, and not for the last time, fortune had smiled upon us. It was a beautiful morning. We now had our first sight of the Islands we had come so far to liberate. They appeared bleak and rocky certainly, but they were also hauntingly beautiful. As we looked around, it was almost possible to believe that we had not left Scotland. San Carlos Water looked for all the world like the Northern Isles or the Outer Hebrides. Was this real? Was this not one glorious, elaborate, massive practical joke? Could we be sure that we hadn't arrived on yet another exercise on Orkney or the Isle of Lewis?

The sense of relief as we stepped ashore – to face we knew not what – was almost tangible. Whatever hazards might lie unseen before us, it would be better than being a helpless passenger in the hold of a ship exposed to torpedo or air attack. Now we were in control of our own destiny. Of course, that was not really true, but the illusion was comforting. At least this was our natural habitat. We tramped off, feeling a great deal better.

As we neared the top of the ridge to the west of Ajax Bay, the first of many Argentine aircraft arrived. This was an Aermacchi MB339 and it whipped along the ridge line very close to James Kelly and me. Instinctively we all hit the deck. In a split second, he was gone. Mike Cole and Zulu Company were just putting their feet ashore when this happened and their feeling of utter exposure to enemy air attack made it a very speedy landing. But the pilot had missed his chance. We were ashore. Soon someone shouted that the Union Flag was flying at San Carlos Settlement across the water. I looked through my binoculars. Sure enough, there it was as smart as you like in the breeze. A brief thrill went through me and a small cheer went up from the Company. We started digging our trenches. We were to spend a very chilly night in them. Our rucksacks with our sleeping bags didn't turn up until the following day.

According to the Brigade plan, X Ray Company was to have a Rapier anti-aircraft missile detachment at the top of our hill. This had been due to arrive at first light as an underslung helicopter load around the time we should have been digging in. Because everything was late, it didn't arrive until three hours later. But even that didn't solve the anti-aircraft problem. The Rapier was an untried, sophisticated, delicate weapon system. The firing posts had been buried deep inside a ship to protect them from the weather on the way down. There they had been subjected to heat and vibration and plans to get them out and test them at

Ascension had had to be abandoned. The gunners who were to man the Rapier were not helped by their base support people in UK who, when asked to send out essential spares to Ascension, recommended they buy the parts locally. Such a suggestion might have been reasonable enough back at home, but in Ascension it was ridiculous and indicated a poor level of understanding of what was involved. It took time to bed the system in and calibrate it. Its generator also consumed quantities of petrol and it always seemed to be in need of more. One of our scarce helicopters had to be earmarked permanently for resupply. We did our bit to relieve the logistics problem by humping jerry cans of petrol up from the beach head. Our marine signallers, with long experience of making dodgy generators work under difficult circumstances, were also able to lend a useful hand. Rapier was to have a disappointing war. Sited on the hills around the anchorage, it was not easily able to engage aircraft flying below it nearly at sea level. It was yet another piece of equipment designed for a vehicle-rich army, operating in a relatively benign environment. Whatever the reasons, when the Argentine Air Force attacked in strength later that morning, Rapier was certainly not ready to protect the beachhead.

Soon four Mirages flashed over our hill. They were so close we could see the pilots' faces. Some said they saw the rivets on the fuselages. But they weren't interested in us. Indeed, I doubt if they even saw us, by now tucked away like little chameleons in holes in the ground. They were after ships. However, a hail of rifle and machine-gun fire erupted at them from 45 Commando in their trenches. It was an utterly instinctive reaction. Everyone felt the need to shoot back with whatever he had. Marine Keith Brown, a signaller carrying a short range sub-machine gun, threw his weapon to his shoulder and pulled the trigger, but by the time he had remembered to release the safety catch, the planes had gone. Marine Dave O'Connor, a famously good shot, poured a hose of GPMG tracer into the belly of one Mirage, which disappeared over the ridge. Down they went out of our sight and attacked HMS *Ardent* in Falklands Sound. One plane was reportedly shot down, claimed by a ship – or was it O'Connor's? – but the attack on *Ardent* was pressed home. 'Our' Rapier fired a missile but it failed to respond to the controls. The missile went wild and speared into the peat some 50 metres beyond our trenches. Life was getting interesting. I hurried up to the top of the hill and received the description of the attack from the Rapier crew. *Ardent* had limped out of sight but I could see smoke and the irregular pattern on the water's surface where bombs had exploded. Later, Alasdair Cameron, who had established his observation post on top of the hill, gave me a chilling real-time description on the radio of *Ardent* burning and sinking stern first. It was almost as vivid as seeing it for myself.

When I next joined him, she had disappeared beneath the waves and I could see her abandoned life rafts bobbing along the coast. The reality of actually being at war was beginning to sink in. I was to see things in the next few days that I never thought I would live to see, and hope never to see again.

The serious bombing in San Carlos Water started on 22 May. Incoming raids were usually announced by ships' horns sounding off. Several times throughout the day, Skyhawks appeared and tried to bomb the large number of ships anchored there, unloading their stores into the beachhead. On one occasion, we saw a Rapier missile pursuing an aircraft. In a moment it would surely have hit it, but an instant before impact, the aircraft flipped over the ridge on the far side of the water and the missile exploded on the hillside. Several other aircraft disappeared trailing smoke and couldn't have got very far. The ships were putting up so much flak that they and we were in as much danger from our own people as we were from the aircraft. By now, the Commando Logistic Regiment had established the Brigade maintenance area in and around the meat factory down below us. When enemy aircraft flew over them they opened up on them with everything they had. But the aircraft were so low that they flew between them and us, and on several occasions we had to take cover as the Commando Logistic Regiment's fire ripped into the parapets of our trenches. To be fair, they hadn't quite realised where we were and when we asked them politely to temper their enthusiasm, their fire control got better. We were lucky compared to others, who were on the receiving end of the 40mm Bofors guns fired by the ships in the anchorage.

At the time, we couldn't understand why so many valuable ships were crammed into that small stretch of water. There seemed no need for them to be there. While San Carlos Water was easy to defend against submarines, it seemed to me that the ships couldn't manoeuvre and the surrounding land screened their air defence radars. Furthermore, they couldn't fire at will for fear of hitting us and the numerous friendly helicopters ferrying stores and equipment around the anchorage. And we were likewise restrained for fear of hitting them. We feared greatly for the safety of our logistic ships. The loss of a frigate or a destroyer would be bad enough, but to lose a ship like *Canberra* or *Stromness* could unbalance our campaign. If one of the ammunition ships like *Elk* or *Fort Austin* blew up, it could take the neighbouring ships with it. Indeed, the captain of RFA *Fort Austin*, the redoubtable Commodore Sam Dunlop, told his men, 'If we get hit, we won't go down with our ship. We'll all go up with it.' But why, I thought, couldn't they remain at sea and come in at night and unload as required?

I was guilty of making judgements in ignorance of the facts. The concentration of ships was to a large degree a knock-on effect of the hasty stow. How nice it would have been to bring in the Brigade logistics, item for item to order. The trouble was that very little logic had been applied to the loading and items had been spread around several ships, or were stowed behind kit that was not wanted that evening. The idea of bringing ships in and off-loading at night was considered but *Elk*, for instance, had all her ammunition on palettes lashed to the deck. To get stuff out meant she had to be in calm waters, then unlash and shift palettes to reach the ones we wanted, get them to her stern ramp, re-stow and lash down before attempting to sail. This left too little time for her to sail in or out safely in darkness. It was the same for the others, but ammo was more critical. *Elk* had been stowed with petrol next to bombs and other munitions below decks. There was no time at Ascension Island to re-stow her properly. After a couple of days wrestling with this quandary, it was decided that the quickest way was to bring the ships in and simply disgorge them as quickly as possible.

Moreover, the Harriers and the ships in open water exacted a steady attrition on enemy aircraft approaching the Islands, so the ones we saw in San Carlos Water had already run a formidable gauntlet. Those aircraft were forced to come down low to avoid Sea Dart missiles and to take advantage of the screen provided by the land. Furthermore, the commander of the Amphibious Force was Commodore Michael Clapp. Having been an observer flying in naval Buccaneer aircraft, and the commander of a bomber squadron, he himself was experienced in conducting ship attacks. He knew precisely the problems that the Argentine pilots were facing. He knew how difficult it was to attack ships in an enclosed anchorage. An aircraft entering the anchorage at low level would see the ships only at the last moment. Finding himself presented with an array of targets, the pilot would have a very few seconds to decide which one to attack. He had to choose one which was nearest to his line ahead; and he would only get one chance. A second pass would almost certainly be fatal. Calculating carefully the likely lines of approach, Commodore Clapp saw to it as best he could that the ships on those lines were not logistic ships. The Argentine Air Force has been criticised for attacking only warships. This is unfair. Several logistic ships were attacked in San Carlos Water, but they were either missed, or the bombs failed to explode. In this we were lucky, of course, but by forcing the aircraft down to below mast height – so low that mechanical bomb fuses would not have time to operate – and by denying the Argentine pilots a free opportunity to select the most valuable targets,

Commodore Clapp gave luck the best possible chance to work in our favour.

We should of course have kept the fact that bombs were not exploding to ourselves. This was important intelligence which the other side could use. Our handling of public information seemed to have been bungled in a number of areas, and this was one. The news got out into the UK media and – surprise, surprise – the Argentines started to use bombs with parachutes and electronic fuses.

On the evening of 23 May, two frigates limped in to San Carlos Water. HMS *Argonaut* was shepherded in, steered by two or three landing craft. She apparently had sustained damage to her steering mechanism, but otherwise she looked pretty healthy. I watched her with especial interest. A few years before, I had spent two and a half years commanding a Royal Marines detachment in her sister ship HMS *Diomede*. I had made many friends in the Royal Navy and learned much about its ships. HMS *Antelope* came in under her own steam a little later and anchored adjacent to our positions above Ajax Bay. During my time at sea, I had visited *Antelope* and had been given an extensive tour of her. Some marines from 45 Commando Signals Troop had sailed south in her and we all knew her medical officer, Surgeon Lieutenant John Ramage, who had been our Commando medical officer a short time before. She was now making smoke, rather dirty wispy smoke, which I thought unusual for a frigate powered by Olympus and Tyne engines. She had a hole forward on the port side and another in her starboard side below the funnel, just about where the engine room would be. We guessed these might be unexploded bombs. Perhaps she had also some trouble in the engine room. I noticed too that the top of her mast was bent over. How could that have happened? Had an aircraft flown into it? Otherwise she seemed sound enough. Her 4.5 inch gun traversed, depressed and elevated, so she seemed to have power enough to fight. I continued watching her while I boiled my tea and prepared my evening meal.

Presently the crew of *Antelope* began to gather on the upper deck, all wearing their orange once-only immersion suits, but I was completely unprepared for the huge explosion that erupted soon after sunset. A large lump of superstructure flew through the air as the explosion ripped through her, just forward of the Sea Cat radar, aft of the funnel. From the magnitude of the explosion and the rapid spread of the fire that followed, it soon became evident that there was no saving her. The fire was so great that those on the upper deck in front were separated from those aft and this cannot have helped command and control. Although the sun was down by now, all was as bright as day. A number of helicopters had taken off from *Fearless* or *Intrepid* and were illuminating the ship with their lights. Much bravery was done that night. A number of secondary explosions was taking place and yet helicopters continued to fly above the ship, illuminating it while landing craft, disregarding their own safety, came alongside and started taking people off. Through my binoculars, it all looked very orderly, with people queuing to go down ladders and nets. Soon everybody appeared to be off. The landing craft pulled away and the ship aft of the funnel was well ablaze. Suddenly about a dozen men appeared on the port waist aft of the bridge. One landing craft cox'n, seeing them, returned to the ship's side and took them off from a ladder. It was a most impressive rescue. No one even got their feet wet. A second explosion comparable to the first went up about half an hour after this rescue. Two weeks later, five of the crew of this landing craft, including their gallant cox'n, Colour Sergeant Brian Johnston, were killed when it was attacked by Skyhawks in Choiseul Sound.

In fact, *Antelope* had been hit by two bombs, neither of which had exploded. The first killed a seaman as it entered the ship forward on the port side. The aircraft which dropped the second bomb was shot down and crashed into the mast as it passed over the ship. This bomb went deep inside her. Staff Sergeant James Prescott of the Royal Engineers had been trying to defuse it when it had gone off. He was killed and his boss, Warrant Officer John Phillips, lost an arm. This pair had already defused one of the bombs in *Argonaut* the day before.

However, when presented with an unexploded bomb in *Antrim* on 21 May, Fleet Chief Petty Officer Mick Fellows, a clearance diver more used to disposing of mines and underwater obstacles, took advice from the UK. The recommendation was that rather than trying to defuse it, he should try to lift it out and lower it overboard. With much skill and gallantry, and by cutting a hole in the flight deck, this was successfully achieved. Thereafter, both naval clearance diver teams dealt with unexploded bombs in this way. Lifting out was of course easier said than done. Some bombs ended up several decks down and there was no easy way to get them out while not tilting them from the angle at which they had come to rest. Much ingenuity and bravery was applied to this formidable, blood-chilling problem in several ships, including *Argonaut*, *Antrim*, *Sir Lancelot* and *Sir Galahad*. *Argonaut* had been hit by two bombs on 21 May, one in the boiler room and one in a magazine which detonated two Sea Cat anti-aircraft missiles and killed two sailors. The bombs themselves did not explode and she lost the power to steer and move until her boiler room was brought back into commission. The boiler room bomb had been defused by Prescott and Phillips on 22 May, before they tried unsuccessfully to do the same in *Antelope* the following day, but it took a team led by Lieutenant Commander Brian Dutton a week to remove the second one. There was no question of evacuating

Argonaut while the second bomb was dealt with. She was a useful warship still able to move and fight and, more importantly, to control aircraft. She remained in San Carlos Water for a week, performing valuable service as the air defence control ship directing Sea Harriers; the air battle raging above her and the battle against her bomb proceeding quietly and patiently deep inside her.

Sir Lancelot and *Sir Galahad*, which had both been evacuated, each had an unexploded 1,000lb bomb deep inside them. These bombs were removed by Lieutenant Bernie Bruen and Chief Petty Officer 'Piggy' Trotter, mine clearance divers with no experience of anything bigger than a 10lb anti-handling device. They were assisted by Commander John McGregor, a nuclear submarine marine engineer with no experience of ordnance at all. Assured by Bruen that 'if it blows up, you won't feel a thing', McGregor and his volunteer team of engineers and shipwrights used cutters and chains to make holes through several decks and lift the bombs out, while Bruen and Trotter then took them away in an inflatable dingy and sank them. At one stage, a bomb was protected only by an asbestos cloth, while an acetylene flame was directed onto it, as Mechanician Gordon Siddle cut through a metal ladder. These actions allowed the two ships swiftly to be used again. One is left gazing in wonder at the insouciant gallantry of those who fiddle with bombs in this way.

I watched fascinated as *Antelope*'s destruction went on throughout the night. I had been in her, I knew people in her, and here she was, a British ship, exploding, burning and sinking before my eyes. How could something made of metal be so combustible? I can well understand why sailors, and particularly captains, get emotional about their ships. However, although we were all shocked, this did nothing to affect our spirits or our conviction that, sooner rather than later, we were going to sort this business out. The fires and explosions on *Antelope* continued until soon after first light her back broke and, folding like a deck chair, she sank quite slowly in a cloud of smoke and steam. Her bow remained visible for some hours, still anchored to the bottom. When that finally disappeared, there remained one solitary life raft attached to the sunken hull, as if as a marker buoy to indicate the wreck below.

The Ajax Bay Air Show continued without let up on 24 May. For the first time they attacked ground forces. Out of a wave of four Skyhawks, two attacked the ships and two headed for the beachhead. One bomb exploded harmlessly on open ground some 1,000 metres down our hill. A second bomb landed very close to the corner of the meat factory. We were at this stage being supplied with hot meals by our Commando chefs from their field kitchen by the meat factory and half of X Ray was down there getting their meal. They all returned in one piece, fully laden with goodies grabbed as the opportunity presented by the air raid allowed, but hot stew and bread by the meat factory rather lost its attraction after that.

We did watch with wonder the conglomeration of men, equipment, stores and artillery ammunition around the meat factory. The buildings themselves were now being used as a field dressing station and yet no red crosses were in evidence. Sooner or later, enemy aircraft were going to get lucky and we were going to take serious losses. However, again, we were unaware of the constraints that were being imposed upon the logisticians. It had originally been planned to keep the bulk of the Brigade logistics afloat and only put supplies ashore where and when they were needed. This is normal amphibious procedure and allows great flexibility and economy of effort. But this is only possible if you have the air superiority that the doctrine stipulates. In view of the risk to the logistic ships, and the haphazard stow, the safest course in this instance was to offload much of the stores at Ajax Bay. Again, in these circumstances it would have been normal to disperse them over a wide area, but to do that one needs roads and hard standing. There were no roads, and the only hard standing was immediately adjacent to the meat factory. So that is where the stores and ammunition had to go. As for red crosses, they could only be used if there were no warlike installations within a prescribed distance of the medical facility one wished to protect. So our dressing station had to share the same risks as everything else. It was not long before our fears were realised.

Somewhere on the hillside above all this, Colour Sergeant Bill Eades, the Commando provost sergeant, had constructed a centralised latrine known as the 'bog of the planet' where one could do one's business while watching the Fleet being bombed – 'the best laxative known to man,' he declared. Unfortunately the straining bar broke on one occasion with disastrous results for at least one man.

Meanwhile, the air attacks continued. Again, waves of Mirages and Skyhawks came barrelling down San Carlos Water. We saw two aircraft crash this day. We watched a Mirage being hit by a Rapier missile. It immediately started trailing smoke and then crashed into the side of a hill on the other side of the water. I saw no parachute. Parts of smoking, burning aircraft were spread over a wide area. A cheer went up from the troops on the hillside that would not have been out of place in a football stadium. But it was nothing to the roar of approval as a Skyhawk, coming in very low over the water and in full view of us on the hill, was struck by something – it could have been any one of a number of projectiles – flipped over on its back and plunged into the water with an almighty splash. Ironically enough, it ended up very close to the spot where *Antelope* had disappeared two or three hours before. How the pilot had time to eject is hard to imagine, but we saw his parachute coming down into the water. The pilot, whose name was First Lieutenant Ricardo Lucero, became something of a personality in the hospital at Ajax Bay. We watched him being rescued. A fast raiding craft reached him first and then transferred him to a landing craft. The raiding craft cox'n, in his enthusiasm to help, ran him over and nearly drowned him, giving him burst eardrums to add to the dislocated knee he had suffered on ejecting.

I did wonder at the morality of feeling elated when one sees aircraft with men inside them crash into hillsides. Did I like myself feeling like that? Not really; but I suppose that men whose lives are threatened are entitled to express their relief when they see those who would kill them get their come-uppance.

This was a gladiatorial contest of the highest order that we were watching. Those pilots were very brave and skilful. Whatever propaganda they may have been fed, one presumes they were intelligent men and they came back again and again even though they saw their comrades being shot down, and in full knowledge of the hazards they were running. They pressed home their attacks with vigour, skill and determination and achieved a number of notable successes. They could have won the war for Argentina, had it not been for the outstanding performance of our Harriers, and the Royal Navy ships, which stopped many aircraft from getting as far as us and our logistics. We understood well the scale of the Navy's achievement.

All the marines had been to sea, even if it was only to sail to the South Atlantic. But many had much more sea service than this. I, together with many other Royal Marines officers, had served for some years on board frigates and destroyers. I had manned radars, guns and missiles in the frigate *Diomede* and was a qualified bridge watch keeper. We knew only too well the limitations of the weapon systems and we had a fair idea what it must be like at sea, trying to fight the weather and a determined air force simultaneously. We were conscious of what the Harrier pilots and the sailors of the Royal Navy had achieved for us and the risks they were running on our behalf, and we felt very warmly towards them.

We also felt for our helicopter pilots. Rarely did they get enough warning of an air attack for them to land or take some kind of evasive action. This would usually mean either landing as quickly as they could or, as in the case of one naval Lynx under attack from Skyhawks, diving down to our hillside and hovering with its nose up against a rock. It became quite normal to see enemy aircraft swooping in along the water, past helicopters with underslung loads going about their routine business. This had unexpected benefits. Hearing an air raid was coming, one helicopter made a rapid release of its underslung load so that it could make an emergency landing to avoid the attention of the Sky-hawks. The load ended up adjacent to our rear echelon trenches. After the air raid, the marines examined the jettisoned object, which turned out to be a pallet of cigarettes. We in the rifle companies were to go short of a number of things during the subsequent campaign, but thereafter we never went short of cigarettes. I don't know who they were intended for, but we certainly put them to good use. Not everyone was so fortunate. Rupert van der Horst was desolate when the supply he had scrounged for the Commando from the ships was destroyed in the bombing at Ajax Bay, and he and others in the Commando Headquarters did not get a smoke again until we liberated supplies from the enemy.

We watched the waters around *Stromness* being ploughed up by bombs, but each time the spray subsided there she was, serene and untouched. We were very concerned for the whole ship, but especially for the administrative party we had left on board in the charge of Lieutenant David Pendleton who, incidentally, was holding all our 'last letters'. How ironic it would be if we were to survive, and he and all those letters were to be lost. David was our Imprest Holder, or pay-master. Before he had left Arbroath, on his own initiative, he had drawn a quarter of a million pounds in cash from the bank and taken it with him to the South Atlantic in his briefcase. With this money, he thereafter acted as unofficial paymaster to the amphibious force. He went around the ships using the daily helicopter mail service and advanced pay to anyone who needed it, irrespective of their parent unit or ship. In this way, he provided 'cash flow' to the force and it was because of him that people could buy beer, tobacco, chocolate and other sundries from the NAAFI during the war. This was only one of the many unsung backroom services which David and his team performed, and which contributed so much to the efficiency and well being of us all. By the end of the war his briefcase was nearly empty, but needless to say, his paperwork was in perfect order.

The same could not be said for the paperwork of the Regimental Institute Fund of which I was the fund supervisor. This was a non-public fund which ran a field shop supplying writing paper, toothpaste, cigarettes and other sundries which make life more pleasant for men on active service. Sergeant 'Spot' Watson, who was in charge of this fund, was badly wounded when the logistic base at Ajax Bay was bombed on 27 May and the books for the fund were destroyed. Another NCO took over the duties and the supply of these items to us all continued seamlessly. After the war, I tried to reconstruct and audit the fund and was baffled when, whichever way I looked at it, it seemed to hold some

Royal Marines in HMS *Fearless* shortly before the assault on the Falklands. At times like this, the ship was heavily overloaded and space very short indeed. (*Trustees of the Royal Marines Museum*)

Landing craft coming ashore from *Fearless* laden with men and stores. Together with the helicopters, these craft were the principal movement assets in a campaign where wheeled transport was virtually useless. (*Trustees of the Royal Marines Museum*)

3. HMS *Antelope* was attacked by four aircraft on 23 May. She was hit by two 1,000lb bombs, neither of which exploded. One bomb came through the port side near the bow and killed a sailor. The hole where the other entered is visible here below the funnel. *Antelope* shot down the second aircraft that bombed her but it hit her mast as it crashed into the sea. The bent mast above the funnel can be seen here. (*Trustees of the Royal Marines Museum*)

4. One of the bombs in *Antelope* exploded as attempts were made to defuse it. Many people saw the explosion, but no one photographed it. This photo shows the second major explosion and is probably a magazine going up. Her surviving crew had been successfully taken off her twenty minutes earlier. (*Trustees of the Royal Marines Museum*)

5. *Antelope* burned all night and, her back broken, she folded like a deckchair and sank after dawn the following day. (*Trustees of the Royal Marines Museum*)

6. The Argentine Air Force pressed home their attacks with perseverance, skill and gallantry. But the British choice of amphibious landing site forced them to fly low and constrained their freedom of action. In this photo a Mirage is caught framed between the foremast and mainmast of HMS *Fearless*. (*Trustees of the Royal Marines Museum*)

7. Our 'great grey mother' the RFA *Stromness* survives a near miss in San Carlos Water. (*Trustees of the Royal Marines Museum*)

8. Mechanician Gordon Siddle and the unexploded bomb he helped remove from RFA *Sir Lancelot*. The volunteer team of engineers and shipwrights of which he was a part spent forty-eight hours cutting a hole through several decks, then the bomb was lifted out and dumped at sea. (*Gordon Siddle*)

9. In this action-packed shot, to the right HMS *Fearless* and HMS *Plymouth* survive near misses. The splash on the left is a crashing Skyhawk. The pilot, Lt Ricardo Lucero, ejected and the white dot above the ship at left of centre is his parachute descending into the sea. He was rescued by a Royal Marines raiding craft. (*Malcolm Duck*)

10. Hit by four bombs and several cannon shells HMS *Plymouth* wrestles with a fire started when one of her own depth charges was set off by a bomb. The bombs did not explode and *Plymouth* survived. (*Trustees of the Royal Marines Museum*)

11. The cargo ship *Atlantic Conveyor* was a cornucopia of precious stores and an *ad hoc* aircraft carrier transporting Harriers and helicopters. The Harrier pilot here is using her mast as a reference point as he lands on her foredeck. A heavy lift Chinook helicopter is on the quarter deck under wraps. This photograph was taken while *Conveyor* was at Ascension Island. (*Graham Adcock*)

12. *Atlantic Conveyor* was due to unload her helicopters on the night of 25 May. That evening two Exocet missiles hit her, the second going through the hole made by the first. She burned for several days, then sank. The Harriers had already flown, but three of four Chinook heavy lift helicopters went down, as did six Wessex. This loss affected the tempo of the war and resulted in the 'tab' of the Parachute Regiment and the 'yomp' of the Royal Marines. (*Trustees of the Royal Marines Museum*)

13. The derelict meat processing plant at Ajax Bay was 45 Commando's objective on the initial landings. It became the logistic focal point because it was the only place with hard standing. The close proximity of so many warlike stores meant that the Field Dressing Station in the building on the right could not display a red cross. (*Chris Baxter*)

14. When the derelict meat factory was bombed, one parachute retarded bomb went into the roof space and did not explode. The parachute and the hole made by the bomb are visible here. The medics continued to operate until the end of the war with the bomb lurking above their heads. (*Malcolm Duck*)

15. The mortar and anti-tank ammunition of 45 Commando burning after being bombed – five men were killed and fourteen wounded. (*Malcolm Duck*)

16. The Sea King and Wessex helicopters were the workhorses of the war and had to carry the artillery ammunition that should have been lifted by the Chinooks lost in *Atlantic Conveyor*. (*Trustees of the Royal Marines Museum*)

17. Key members of 45 Commando Group about to receive CO's orders on 26 May for the 'yomp'. *L to R.* Lt Col A.F. Whitehead (CO), Capt M.P. Hitchcock, Maj R.J. Davis, Maj G.R. Akhurst, Capt D. Dalrymple, Capt D.M. Gillson, Capt I.R. Gardiner, Lt J. Haycock, Capt A.G.H. Cameron, Capt I. Ballantyne, Lt M. Evans, Capt M.A.F. Cole, Capt M.R.G.H. Irwin, RSM P.R. Chapman, Sgt H. Higgins, Maj R.C. van der Horst, Lt R.O.W. Passmore, Lt M.Y. Cooke, CSgt J.M. Ross, Cpl B.C. Thompson, Lt D.J. Rudd, Surg Lt D.J. Griffiths, Lt R.J. Byford, Lt M.K. Taylor. *(Charles Laurence)*

18. Landing craft being loaded with 600 men of 45 Commando, to be sailed across San Carlos Water to start the Yomp on 27 May. Landing craft were a core movement asset. (*Chris Baxter*)

19. X Ray Company being entertained by their Company Commander as they cross San Carlos Water. Corporal Frank Melia on the left and Corporal Tom Spence on the right seem unimpressed . . (*Trustees of the Royal Marines Museum*)

10. Corporal Mick Tagg at the start of the Yomp as we leave Port San Carlos. Each man is carrying upwards of 120lbs (55kg). (*James Kelly*)

11. Yomping. (*Wynne Jones*)

22. Brigade Headquarters striking camp. But the ground and the weather was typical for us all. (*Trustees of the Royal Marines Museum*)

23. Regimental Sergeant Major Pat Chapman setting off from Teal Inlet. (*Trustees of the Royal Marines Museum*)

4. *L to R standing.* Lt Dominic Rudd, L/Bdr Gary Ecclestone, Bdr Roger Chapman, Maj Gerry Akhurst, Mne Clive Pattle, Lt Col Andrew Whitehead, Sgt Nutty Edwards, Capt Mike Hitchcock, Mne Mick Hoad, Unidentified *kneeling* Unidentified, Mne Keith Brown, L/Cpl Crowe Crosby, Mne Neil Gribby. (*Trustees of the Royal Marines Museum*)

5. *Left to right.* The Author, Major Gerry Akhurst RA, Captain Derek Dalrymple RA, Captain Alasdair Cameron RA. (*Alasdair Cameron*)

26. Lieutenant David Stewart RM.
(*Wynne Jones*)

27. Lieutenant Malcolm Duck and
Corporal Doddy Kendal.
(*Trustees of the Royal Marines Museum*)

28. *L to R.* Sergeant George MacMillan and Lieutenant James Kelly. (*James Kelly*)

29. *L to R.* Sergeant George Matthews and Lieutenant Chris Caröe. (*James Kelly*)

30. *L to R.* Lieutenant Clive Dytor and Sergeant Yorkie Malone. Dytor is wearing a reversible arctic/temperate waterproof. (*Malcolm Duck*)

31. Lieutenant Paul Mansell RM. (*James Kelly*)   32. The Reverend Wynne Jones RN. (*James Kelly*)

33. A typical stone run. These rivers of stone were major obstacles to men carrying heavy loads, especially at night. (*Malcolm Duck*)

£5,000 more than it should have done. This presented me with an interesting problem. In war, it is the easiest thing in the world to write things off to enemy action. But there was no legal accounting device that I knew of to explain how we had made such a huge gain out of the violence of the enemy. We finally decided that this was the money from the sale of the pallet load of cigarettes that had arrived as manna from heaven. I can't remember by what sophistry we explained how we had come by the cigarettes, but no doubt the original owner was able to write them off to enemy action – which in a sense was true enough!

In spite of the good offices of David Pendleton, cash remained in short supply in parts of the Fleet. For some officers whose duties required them to visit several ships, the simplest way of settling mess bills was to leave a cheque. One Royal Artillery officer, having enjoyed the hospitality of the wardrooms of *Ardent*, *Antelope* and *Coventry* duly left cheques in each ship in settlement. As each of these ships was sunk in turn, his friends began to wonder whether he was jinxed or if he had somehow hit upon some fiendish way of getting free booze.

The air attacks continued over the following days but as time went on, it seemed that the climax had passed. The Argentine Air Force remained a threat right through to the end of the war. They attacked the Brigade logistic base successfully on 27 May and enjoyed a number of notable successes elsewhere. They sank HMS *Coventry* on 25 May and towards the end of the war they destroyed *Sir Galahad,* and damaged *Sir Tristram,* killing 50 men: soldiers of the Welsh Guards, Royal Engineers, Royal Army Medical Corps, Royal Fleet Auxiliary officers, and Hong Kong Chinese crew. And somehow, in spite of many attempts to catch them, Argentine C130 Hercules transport planes flew regular nightly sorties in and out of Stanley airfield, right up until the last night of the war.

But the loss which had the greatest effect on the land campaign, and which most directly affected 45 Commando, was in a sense inflicted by accident. This was the sinking of *Atlantic Conveyor*. We had got to know her at Ascension and on the trip south. Men from 45 Commando had provided her with working parties, rearranging stores within her capacious bulk. They had always come back from these chores well fed and cheerful, speaking very highly about the way they had been looked after. Clearly she was a happy, well run ship. On 25 May, she was with the Carrier Group and was due to run in to San Carlos Water that night to discharge her cargo, including six Wessex and four Chinook helicopters. Her cargo of Harriers had already left her. The Chinooks in particular would be welcome because they could each carry about 60 men, or ten tons of stores. Provision of sufficient artillery ammunition to the guns is usually the greatest problem the logisticians have to solve before and during a battle. This was an especial problem here because there were no roads to share the transport burden. Men can walk if necessary, but they can't carry artillery ammunition very far. These helicopters were ideal – they would nearly double the lift capacity available and would allow the Brigade simultaneously to complete the logistic offload and develop assault operations. Late that night we heard *Atlantic Conveyor* had been destroyed by Exocet missile. One solitary Chinook had been airborne and was saved.

Two Exocet missiles had been fired by Super Étendard aircraft at the Carrier Group. They headed towards the first target they saw, HMS *Ambuscade* which, seeing them coming, fired chaff which successfully decoyed them. Emerging from the chaff cloud, they headed to the next most obvious target, *Atlantic Conveyor*. She had no means of firing chaff and the missiles piled into her, the second missile following through the hole made by the first, and setting her unquenchably alight. She sank two days later. Any thought that we might be flown round the battlefield in helicopters evaporated for ever. We would walk and anything we couldn't carry would be left behind.

The destruction of *Atlantic Conveyor*, her burning, and the rescue of survivors was watched by Lieutenant Bill McRae, the assistant quarter-master of 45 Commando, who was with part of our logistic echelon on *Sir Percivale* nearby. He saw a number of brave rescues carried out, with the crewmen of helicopters hanging off the end of winch cables while being battered by large waves. Years later I met the chief officer of *Atlantic Conveyor*, John Brocklehurst. He, together with the ship's captain, Captain Ian North, and the attached Royal Naval officer, Captain Mike Layard, were the last to leave the ship. This wasn't the first time that Ian North had had to abandon ship, as he had been sunk twice during the Second World War. They were about to lower themselves in a lifeboat, when they saw that the lifeboat would be in danger of sitting down on a life raft that was already in the water beneath them. So they climbed down a rope hanging from the lifeboat and entered the water near the stern. A considerable swell was running, and the overhanging stern was rising and dropping. Brocklehurst felt himself being pulled in to the side of the ship and had to swim hard, fighting to get away. The same forces pulled Captain North and Captain Layard in under the stern. Layard managed to pull the older man out towards a life raft, but they were sucked in and sat on again by the ship. Struggling to the surface, Layard found that North had not surfaced. Mike Layard, even in his semi-drowned state, dived to try and find him, but North was never seen again. Ten others were also lost. The loss of Captain Ian North, his ship and a substantial portion of his crew, was a personal as well as a professional one to many marines. It also drew our attention to the significance of the Merchant Navy's contribution to the success of our endeavours. Quite patently the war could not have been conducted without the capacity provided by the merchant ships like *Conveyor* which had been 'taken up from trade'. Their crews were civilians, and nowhere in their employment contracts did it say that they had a liability for war service. Yet, virtually to a man and woman, they allowed themselves to be press-ganged at no notice without demur and delivered their services with efficiency, gallantry and a smile, and some, like those in *Conveyor*, delivered their lives. This was the sort of service the Merchant Marine had provided in both the First and Second World Wars and it is a wonderful testimony to the quality and character of their people that the country was able to assume that they would, without hesitation, do so again.

On 26 May, we received our orders for the breakout east from the beach-head the following day. 2 Para were ordered to march south and capture Darwin and Goose Green. This had originally been a 45 Commando raiding task and our commanding officer had been briefed as such, but 2 Para were holding the most southerly of the defensive positions and therefore were closest to Darwin and Goose Green, so it became their objective. 3 Para were to come east with us and march to Teal Inlet. 45 Commando was to be ferried by landing craft to Port San Carlos on the other side of the water, to march from there. Our first objective was to be Douglas Settlement. No helicopters were available. We were to carry everything we possessed.

Our five days ashore had been helpful in a number of ways. The Ajax Bay Air Show had impressed upon us the gravity and the implications of what we were doing. We really were at war. While waiting for the logistics to come ashore, we had patrolled the area extensively. We were looking for Argentine observation posts. A pair of eyes and a radio reporting on ship and unit movements would have been of considerable value to the Argentines and one such observer was eventually discovered by a British gunner, who had left his own observation post to go for a crap. From these patrols we learned that the ground was rougher than Scotland and walking with heavy loads would be especially difficult. The patrols ironed out many kinks and the need for every man to think for himself and to be prepared to remain alert, in spite of the difficult ground and awful weather, was reinforced in a way that simply cannot be achieved in peacetime. The weather was cold and it rained a lot; although our trenches afforded some shelter, it was impossible to get properly dry. It always takes a day or two to get into the way of things when one lives in the field. After five days ashore we were now acclimatised both physically and professionally. We had got into our routines and were now in good order. After three days, I was offered the opportunity to take the Company down to the beachhead and board a ship for a wash and a hot meal. This was a thoughtful, well meant offer and I was tempted. I consulted Sergeant Major Bell. We both felt that even a short visit to a ship would mean another period getting used to the cold and wet. We agreed to decline the offer. I didn't tell the men. If I had done so they might have lynched me there and then, but perhaps on reflection they would have understood – or perhaps not! We had by now refined the kit list and some non-essential items were discarded. For instance, spare clothing, other than socks, was a waste of time. One simply ends up carrying two sets of wet clothing. We had waited long enough. Nobody knows what is going to happen next in war, and nobody knows how long it is going to last. But the sooner we got going, the sooner it would be finished.

At first light the following day, we moved out down to the jetty. As we filed past our logistic echelon, we were issued with rations. Our pockets bulged. We boarded the landing craft and sailed out into San Carlos Water, past the spot where *Antelope* went down. Yet again, the Argentine air force missed their chance to destroy the Commando in landing craft in daylight. I decided it was time for some music. Scottish regiments are lucky. This would be the very moment when the regimental piper would stand on the freeboard of the landing craft and give us an uplifting blow. We had no piper but I had my mouth organ which, unlike the pipes, can be carried in a pocket. I got it out and started to play a couple of tunes. One or two men started singing. Marine Iain Leiper was familiar with all the good Irish rebel songs and sea shanties. Whatever I played, he seemed to know the words and soon we had a real sing-song going. It wasn't very beautiful but it was good, operational music.

We passed close by the side of HMS *Arrow*, a sister ship of *Antelope*. Some good-natured jibes passed between the marines and the sailors lining the guardrail, each watching the other with curiosity. With her rusty sides, *Arrow* was showing signs of having been at sea for several weeks, but she looked good. She had taken part in the rescue of sailors from *Sheffield* and *Ardent* and she herself had been damaged by 30mm fire, from air attack on 1 May. Her sailors seemed confident and cheerful. One could sense their high morale, even from a passing landing craft. Marine Dave O'Connor decided this was too good a chance to miss. He climbed up on the freeboard of our landing craft, dropped his trousers and bared his backside to the sailors on *Arrow*. This was reciprocated by at least one sailor. Having dipped ensigns and exchanged salutes thus, we progressed down the loch.

So, singing sea shanties and Irish rebel songs, and baring our arses, we proceeded on our way to battle. Surely Churchill would have approved.

Chapter 6

Yomping

He gave her a home built of gold and steel,
A diamond car with the platinum wheels.

Forty minutes later, we disembarked at Port San Carlos and started walking towards Newhouse of Glamis. This was when the fun stopped. As 45 Commando set off in one extended snake on the long 600 ft high ascent out of Port San Carlos, the reality of this new game began to impress itself upon us. Each man was now carrying something like 120lbs and some were carrying as much as 150lbs – between two-thirds and three-quarters of their own body weight. Some men found it difficult to lift the rucksacks on to their backs without help. They devised a means whereby they 'climbed' into their load while lying on the ground, rolled over and then got their mates to heave them to a position from which they could get to their feet. Very few men had carried such a weight before and certainly not when faced with the prospect of doing so indefinitely. To begin with, we were walking parallel to the soldiers of 3 Para, who were heading directly for Teal Inlet. Our paths slowly diverged until we parted altogether. A couple of their soldiers unwittingly followed us for a while, until someone pointed out the error of their ways. Somehow, the Paras seemed to be carrying less than us. Then we saw why. One of the Islanders had made himself available and was following up the back of their snake with his tractor and trailer loaded up with kit. What a sensible idea. We envied them. But they were following some semblance of track. No tractor or trailer could traverse the ground we had to follow.

The 22 kilometre march to Newhouse turned out to be one of the worst of my life. The weather was not too bad, but the ground was very boggy. The weight we carried meant that at every step we went in up to our shins and sometimes our knees, or even further. The boggy bits were interspersed with robust, tufty, grass-covered hummocks which, however one stood on them, conspired to turn one's ankle. There also seemed to be many streams. Under normal circumstances, some would have been small enough to jump over, but no one jumps very far with loads like these. We tried taking rucksacks off and throwing them over, two men heaving each rucksack. But in the end, all streams were simply waded. The ground was pretty steep in places, but worst of all was this cursed weight. I suspected that we didn't need to carry so much kit and that made it worse. I allowed my irritation to burn up some of my energy.

But the marines were magnificent. Five small, tracked over-snow vehicles carrying the non-manpackable secure voice radios, the mortars and their ammunition and other essential headquarters equipment brought up the rear, but the whole Commando walked, including the commanding officer and most of the men in his headquarters. We lost the first man not long after we left Port San Carlos. He wasn't very well and perhaps we shouldn't even have let him start. Over the course of the day, another six fell out from X Ray Company – fifteen altogether from the Commando – all with twisted ankles and other associated injuries. Some recovered and joined us later, but those who fell out were clearly very upset and they were a sad sight, sitting disconsolately at the side of the line of march as we stripped them of their radio batteries, machine gun ammunition, grenades and 66mm launchers. Most were picked up by the over-snow vehicles. However, later on in the yomp, Marine Rick Turney from Yankee Company, who ripped an Achilles tendon, waited two days before he persuaded a passing Sea King helicopter to pick him up. He was eventually evacuated to *Sir Galahad* and arrived shortly before she was bombed. He, and several others similarly evacuated, survived unscathed. Marine Kevin Woodford from Zulu Company, who went down with bad blistering and was also evacuated to *Sir Galahad* was less lucky. He lost a leg. His mates back in Zulu were mercilessly unsentimental: 'Well, at least he won't have to worry about his blisters.'

The rest went on with the greatest of stoicism and good grace all day and through to 0200 hours the following morning. I was immensely proud of them. Night-time marching is a different order of unpleasantness. An inescapable feature of walking at night in a long line is a great deal of stopping and starting. The man in front pauses to find a way across a stream or similar obstacle. The man behind him stops and waits. The man behind him bumps into him, waits, and so on. A way is found across the obstacle, men start to move, they run to catch up, then get separated in the dark. How often did this concertina sequence repeat itself! The effect gets magnified the further down the line, and for those near the tail-end of a queue of 600 men bumping, stumbling, standing and running through the black, boggy night, life was hell. Moreover, for the person at the front of the line, marching on a bearing and choosing the route, the responsibility is a heavy one. A mistake with the bearing, or an unfortunate choice of route which might demand a retracing of steps, would have serious repercussions for so many very heavily loaded, tired men. This duty fell to Lieutenant Paul Mansell for part of the journey. Fresh out of training, he was extremely conscious of this additional burden, which focuses the mind mightily. Lieutenant Paul Denning noted with apprehension that we would soon be arriving at a point on the ground where three maps met. It would be just our luck to be hit then ...

I was heavily preoccupied trying to keep people together, and finding groups when they got separated, but by the time we leaguered up after fifteen hours marching, I was near my wits' end. We encountered a number of wire fences along and across our path. These added to the obstacles, but if they were running parallel to our march they were a useful aid to navigation. When we stopped and waited, men would race each other in a sideways shuffle to be the first to get to a post and rest the bottom of their rucksack on it. Those who couldn't get a post would resort to the top strand of wire, which of course sagged, but even crouching with some of the weight being taken by the wire was better than nothing. Eventually the wire could take no more and broke, leaving a long line of men lying on their backs like upturned turtles, unable to get up without help. Our good humour was sorely tested on that march. But it survived. I fell in with our unit provost sergeant, Colour Sergeant Bill Eades. Never at a loss for words, he mused, 'I wonder who's going to play my part in the film?'

Earlier that evening, when we stopped to cook our meal before the light faded, Marine George Wiseman of Zulu Company celebrated his eighteenth birthday. His section commander, Corporal David Smith, duly presented him with a mug of hot chocolate and a service issue 'fly cemetery' Garibaldi biscuit, crowned by a candle more commonly used in snow holes in the Arctic. It was not a birthday he would ever be likely to forget.

As Marine Wiseman was celebrating his coming of age, we heard the explosion of bombs in the area whence we had come. Cookers were doused and the rest of our meal was eaten cold. The air attacks were plainly continuing in our absence. We saw the loom of fires on the horizon. Either a ship or a land installation was burning. We feared for our people. For much of the early part of that night, the sky was lit with flashes from secondary explosions as ammunition exploded and fires burned. The Argentine Air Force had made a concerted attempt to destroy the thousands of tons of stores and ammunition at Ajax Bay. Our quartermaster, Captain Alex Watson, told me afterwards what had happened. The only warning they had came from a man who had seen a pair of aircraft bombing the other side of the bay. This was enough for many people to get to their trenches and put on their helmets. Two more Skyhawk aircraft dropped two bombs each on the meat factory complex. They were French 400 kg bombs with retarding parachutes. One struck below the gable end next to our motor transport officer, Lieutenant Brian Bellas. It destroyed all of 45 Commando's Milan anti-tank missiles and many mortar bombs, leaving Brian alive but very deaf. Another one came through the roof but did not explode. Instead, it buried itself in the meat refrigeration machinery in the wall next to Alex. The noise was earth shattering and men could not hear what they were saying to each other for hours afterwards. The confusion in the approaching darkness was dreadful, with men scrabbling with their bare hands to free the dead and injured. The fires threw light and shadow into stark contrast and stopped people developing their night vision. But there was no panic and, with Brian Bellas to the fore, everyone set to the job in hand with resolute ferocity, ignoring the burning, cooking-off ordnance and firecracker reports of exploding small calibre rounds. They knew there were unexploded bombs around, but they kept on working to get casualties out.

It wasn't until the following morning that they had a clear idea of who had survived. The sergeant major's 'bible' containing comprehensive details of all personnel under command had been blown skyhigh, so identifying exactly who remained after the dead and wounded had been accounted for was not at all straightforward. It was made even more difficult by losing the sergeant major, Warrant Officer Mike Gibson, and the company quartermaster sergeant, Colour Sergeant Jim Stallebrass, who were both among the wounded. Sergeant Roger Enefer, Corporal Kenneth Evans, Lance Corporal Peter McKay and Marine David Wilson were all killed. Marine Paul Callan died of his wounds later. There were 14 others wounded. Once the sun was up, having had enough of buildings with leaking roofs which attracted bombs, Alex moved his men up to the hillside trenches vacated by us the day before.

Flight Lieutenant Alan Swan of the Royal Air Force was the bomb disposal man who found himself dealing with the unexploded ordnance. Some time later he described his experiences to me and to others. He himself had narrowly escaped being killed in the raid, having been in the vicinity of the exploding ammunition only seconds earlier. He knew that one bomb had exploded and knew about the bomb in Alex's fridge. A third bomb had travelled through the whole length of the roof void of the meat factory, over the operating theatre, through the gable end and had then bounced several hundred metres up the hill, passing between two marines on sentry. Swan was guided to it and eventually blew it up in the dark. Alex's bomb was dealt with by shoring up with sandbags the intervening walls between the bomb and the operating theatre.

Having thus accounted for three bombs, Swan was anxious to ascertain the whereabouts of the fourth, presumably lurking somewhere unexploded. Responding to reports of a second bomb hitting the roof, Swan started exploring with his torch. Soon he found a parachute hanging out of a bomb-shaped hole in the wall twenty feet above his head. Climbing up a ladder with his torch and squeezing through the hole, he found the bomb in the roof void directly above the operating theatre. He considered the options. It was the same type as the one he had just blown, but he couldn't blow this one. It was not a type he was familiar with and might also have an anti-removal device on the fuse. It was also possible that the Argentines had mixed time-delay-fused bombs with impact-fused bombs, though he felt on balance that if they had it would probably have gone off by now.

Swan discussed the situation with the senior medic, Surgeon Commander Rick Jolly, and recommended that they evacuate the building. From Swan's point of view this was undoubtedly the correct advice to give. However, Jolly was very reluctant to abandon the building and to try to set up an equivalent facility on the blasted heath. His patients would be in almost as much danger from the delay and the elements as they would be from the bomb. Besides, experienced doctor and naval officer that he was, Rick Jolly drew upon his knowledge of human nature. He reasoned that the Argentine pilots would know that a number of their bombs had not exploded in the previous raids – after all, we had told them as much with our press releases. He felt that, rather than encouraging their armourers to indulge in fancy tricks with time-delay fuses, they would be grabbing them by the scruff of the neck and telling them to make sure the damned things exploded. Some bombs had indeed exploded in this raid, both here and on the other side of San Carlos Water where 40 Commando had been hit. These unexploded ones, therefore, were almost certainly misfires. On reflection, Swan agreed with him so they decided that the best thing to do was to leave the bomb where it was; and in order to reassure everyone else, Alan Swan and his team set up their camp beds underneath it.

Meanwhile, under the inspired leadership of Rick Jolly, the medical staff in the field dressing station below the bomb carried on operating on casualties without pause. Rick was eventually decorated by both the British and the Argentines for the work he and his team did on saving wounded men, regardless of nationality. He thus became one of the few men in history – perhaps the only man in history – who has been decorated in war for the same act by both sides. Among his patients was Ricardo Lucero, the Argentine pilot who had been rescued after ejecting into San Carlos Water. Having lived to tell the tale and to survive being bombed by his squadron comrades, Lucero was to die in an air accident 28 years later.

Even in the chaotic hell of this air raid, men were able to find humour. The Brigade ordnance officer, Captain Martin Tracey, subsequently described how shortly before the raid he had passed a ribald remark to a marine who had chosen a quiet moment to have a wash, and was standing stark naked in a basin of water, completely covered in soap. The marine was shielded from the blast by a building. After hurriedly taking cover, Martin looked round to find that the marine was standing exactly as he had been before the attack, but now wearing his steel helmet.

Once it became quite clear that there was no time delay on the unexploded bombs, they became something of a tourist attraction. The resident marines of the Commando Logistic Regiment would invite their visiting mates in to see the sinister beast lurking in the fridge space and, at a suitable moment, would scare the pants off them by taking a flash photograph.

And at his farewell party from the sergeants' mess some months later, Sergeant Major Gibson, now recovered from his wounds, was charged with leaving the scene of an accident and presented with a bill for the loss of 45 Commando's reserve ammunition.

As mentioned, we carried on marching through that night until 0200 hours. We had by then arrived in the vicinity of the isolated farmstead of Newhouse of Glamis. There was no one there. The order came to bed down and to be ready to march off again at first light.

We had no tents. However, our bivouac shelters or 'bivvies', were very straightforward and very effective. A bivvie is simply a waterproof poncho supported by a stick and rubber bungee at each end, pegged into the ground at the sides and at each corner. Two men can clip their ponchos together and make a double shelter. It takes practice and self discipline to live in a two-man bivvie. There is no room to spread things out. Everything must remain packed unless it's being used. You must also be able to find things in the dark – you can't rummage around looking for bits and pieces – so each item has its precise allotted place in the pack, or in your pockets, where you know you will find it. Nothing must be left behind, so even sweetie wrappers are preserved as if they are ten pound notes. You have to be ready to move at very short notice, so you don't undress. You take your boots off if you can and you put them inside your sleeping bag so they don't freeze. Your socks are wet of course, but if you have a dry pair in your pack you might put them on to sleep with. Meanwhile, your wet ones are tucked inside your shirt, in the hope of making them less wet. Sooner rather than later, all your socks will be wet, so you had better get used to it. Your rifle lies beside you so you can use it, or grab it and run *in extremis*. Only one person can move around at a time, so careful coordination is essential. Life has to go on and you have to cook, to get in and out to go on sentry duty, or to perform the normal bodily functions. So you get to know your bivvie partner – your 'oppo' – better than most married couples. Only the most careful consideration for each other is acceptable. All this has to be learnt. We had all practised it on Dartmoor, in North Norway, on Rannoch Moor, in the Cairngorms and other similar places. Men who were slow to learn were known as 'tent rhinos'. They either got punched in the nose, or found that no one would share a bivvie with them. No one stays a tent rhino for very long. A bivvie isn't exactly five-star accommodation, but it reduced the wind to an acceptable draught and kept one tolerably dry. With a dry sleeping bag, a plastic roll mat, a hot drink, a trusty companion, and a cigarette: truly one lacked for nothing.

In these circumstances, it is a central tenet of life that you look after each other. From a military point of view, this of course makes sense. Only through good teamwork are you ever going to succeed and everyone is a key member of the team. Everyone therefore has a responsibility to ensure every other team member is in good order. In the Royal Marines, this is ingrained in training. Only one of the four timed Commando tests is done as an individual. In all the others, it is the speed of the slowest man that counts, so the stronger men are bound to help those who need it. They gain nothing by rushing off on their own. Individuality and personal success is welcomed and encouraged, but it must be directed for the benefit of the team.

This ethos is reinforced by training in the Arctic, perhaps the most unforgiving environment on earth. There, a mistake or cut corner can immediately plunge one into an emergency situation. As well as attending assiduously to one's own administration, everyone is constantly looking out for each other – checking for white spots on a companion's face that might indicate frostbite, noticing a change in behaviour that might presage hypothermia, and so on.

This culture was a salient feature of life in the Falklands, but of course it didn't always work out quite as planned. Dave O'Connor and his oppo, Taff Spears, had a routine for drying each other's sleeping bags. When one of them went on sentry, the other would turn his sleeping bag inside out and try to dry it over the solid fuel cooker. It was surprisingly effective provided the bag wasn't absolutely sopping. One day the inevitable happened and O'Connor managed to burn a big hole inside Spears' bag. Taff Spears was a Corps heavyweight boxer and a man to be feared. With some trepidation, O'Connor turned the damaged bag the right way round and laid it out on the roll mat and went to sleep. At 'stand-to' the following morning, in the gathering daylight, Spears was found looking like a half-plucked duck, with feathers in his hair, his moustache and all over his clothes. Natural justice prevailed and they swapped bags. Soon Dave O'Connor's new bag was so thin that he had to share with another marine.

The personal characteristics required by a soldier are far more complex and subtle than simply aggression and physical strength. These attributes may be required from time to time, but far more commonly in demand are patience, sufferance, self-discipline, a sense of humour, a delight in the ridiculous, unselfishness and consideration for others. Over-assertiveness, or anything else that runs counter to the well-being and the success of the team, is most unwelcome.

The leadership quality of the junior commanders is every bit as important under these circumstances as it is in the heat of battle. The troop officers and troop sergeants must routinely and firstly attend to the health and well-being of their men, regardless of how wet, hungry and uncomfortable they may be themselves. The section corporals, who have all the responsibilities of rank and few of its privileges, are intimately acquainted with every blister, every cut, every mood change, every wrinkle in each man's socks. They are constantly on hand to make sure that corners are not cut in the cold or in the dark which might prejudice a man's fitness for his duties and his part in the team. The corporals of X Ray Company ranged widely in personality and experience. Among the leading characters were large, gentle, giving, Mick Tagg, a member of Greenpeace and a rock upon which his section leant; Bob Colville, uncompromisingly professional; Frank Melia who celebrated his twenty-first birthday at Ascension Island and who would soon be selected for the SBS; the Irish Tom Spence, a fantastic motivator with a wicked sense of humour; Steve Borwell, self-assured, witty, laid back but strong and tough; Phil McGlynn, charmingly old fashioned, straight, courteous and wise; Pat O'Hara, steady, dependable, durable; Hugh Knott, an experienced and proficient trainer of men; 'Roscoe' Tanner who had taken over command at short notice and was soft spoken, determined and reliable. These men and many others like them, whatever their experience or ability, or their strengths and weaknesses, were those upon whom we depended to be key leaders in the structure and composition of this and every other company, and whose professional performance would define defeat or victory.

It had been a dry night during our march to Newhouse. We would be marching again in a few short hours. It didn't seem worth the effort of putting bivvies up in the dark. As an alternative, we also had plastic bags in which we could stretch our sleeping bags and, in theory, keep them dry. We could sleep inside those for a few hours. I gave the order to bed down without erecting bivvies. This was a mistake. It rained during the early morning and the plastic bags were useless and did not keep the rain out. Our sleeping bags were soaked.

The last bastion of a man's morale is his sleeping bag. The comfort and resource it offers is prodigious. When one was being shelled, or heard bombing close by, it was an instinctive reaction to wriggle deeper into one's 'green slug'. When all else failed and the world crumbled around us, even if our sleeping bags had failed to turn up in the evening, one was always vaguely comforted by the prospect of climbing into a dry bag eventually. So when my citadel was drenched by rain, my morale was at its lowest. I awoke about five that morning after a fitful sleep to find my bag and I were soaked through. After mentally weeping for an hour or so, I perceived the rain was becoming less persistent. Aha, I thought, if it stops, I could get up and stamp around in the wind and start getting things dry. As the rain faded away, so I began to gather my depleted spirits. The rain stopped. I waited ten minutes, just enjoying not getting any wetter. The rain started again. I pulled the wretched sodden bag over my head and smoked a cigarette. It was the last barrier between me and despair.

My morale was never again so low as it was then. I was subsequently to spend more uncomfortable, more bitter, wetter, colder nights and it was not the last time my citadel was breached. But one hardened. One got used to it.

As part of our briefings, we had been told the true story of a sailor from the Belgian barque *Leopold* which had run aground on the Falklands in the winter of 1858. As a crew member, he had been perched on the outer end of the ship's jib boom when she ran on to a steeply shelving rocky beach. The man was deposited gently into the tussock grass well above the high water mark. The ship then slid back into the fog and sank with all hands. The sailor was discovered three years later, physically fit but 'in a rather deranged state'. But he had survived. We too would survive.

For the first and only time in my life, I was to experience a strange interaction between mind and body, born out of the fact that we had no idea how long this was going to go on for. When one goes on exercise, one usually knows when it will end. Even the longest exercise rarely exceeds seven days in the wilds. The body adjusts to this timescale. But when we started our famous 'yomp' the timescale was open-ended.

We had no idea how long it might last and the body adjusted to what the mind knew. We refined our methods of living in this inhospitable place to such a degree that by the end, we had become almost like wild animals, or like the Belgian sailor: in complete harmony with our surroundings. We neither knew nor cared whether it was raining, snowing or blazing sunshine, all of which one got in any half-hour period. We had gone feral. We envied nobody their ship, vehicle or tent: we preferred it out of doors. No doubt there was a correlation between our morale and our progress eastwards. But never let it be said that we had come to the end of our endurance by the time we reached Stanley. We could certainly have continued as long as necessary. We felt we could have gone on forever.

All the men who survived that first march stuck it right through to the end. Yes, we would have to fight the Argentines sooner or later, but meanwhile our battle was with the weather. We had to survive to fight. There was no contemplating victory if we couldn't beat the weather. The Duke of Wellington is said to have remarked that the battle of Waterloo was won on the playing fields of Eton. Wellington was a very sensible man and I doubt if he would ever have said anything quite so daft. Whatever the truth of that may be, the Falklands War was won on Dartmoor, the Norwegian snowfields, and on the sub-Arctic plateau of the Cairngorm Mountains.

At first light we struck camp and set off once more, but now it was broad daylight and we were beyond the air defence umbrella of the ships and missiles in San Carlos Water. We were not defenceless against aircraft, however, as we had a detachment of Blowpipe shoulder-launched anti-aircraft missiles with us. And with each company packing 19 machine guns, we were a prickly hedgehog in our own right. There was an increasing likelihood that we would encounter the enemy, so now we advanced in tactical formation. This meant that instead of a long snake, we spread out into arrowhead formation by companies, poised to go straight into action on contact with the enemy. X Ray Company went in front. We also left our rucksacks behind. Each man carried only what he would need to fight. Rucksacks were to be brought forward by helicopter at last light when we reached Douglas Settlement. It was 12 kilometres to Douglas Settlement and compared to the day and night before it was an easy march.

We entered the settlement late in the afternoon. I was immediately struck with the smell of the peat fires, so familiar to me from the Highlands of Scotland. The Argentines had treated the people of Douglas roughly and eaten much of their food. They had all been locked in the schoolhouse for several days and their property had been ransacked. When we got there, the Argentines had gone and the people in Douglas were very pleased indeed to see us. Their joy and gratitude at our arrival was very touching and if anyone had wanted any evidence to justify why we had come all this way, it was here. For many marines this was a pivotal moment. Hitherto, the underlying reasons for our deployment had been largely academic, but this contact with these good folk dispelled any residual notion that they were not really British. We were proud that we had been able to liberate them. Phil Witcombe, who had served in the Royal Marines detachment on the Islands some years before, was able to meet old friends, but this was my first meeting with the islanders. Having been brought up on a farm in Ayrshire, I was struck by how similar they were to the people of my childhood. It was almost as if I had come home. Their accent had a gentle antipodean timbre to it, but their attitudes and outlook were distinctly rural Scottish. Even the names were familiar, and I remain in touch with Bill and Clara Mackay to this day.

We dug a defensive perimeter around the settlement in case of attack, sent out a number of patrols to check the surrounding area, and took stock. We were depending upon helicopters to bring up our rations and our rucksacks, but they failed to materialise. Having advanced in fighting order, we did not have even a wet sleeping bag to climb into. We were tired and soaked and I feared this night would be even worse than the last, but it was not to be so. There was a large sheep shearing shed and we made best use of it. We were able to let about two thirds of the unit sleep in the shed at any one time and rotate them through the trenches outside. This gave most people a break from the biting wind, but it was draughty and still very cold in the shed. I put my gloves and my Green Beret on my feet to try and stop them dropping off altogether.

However, this was luxury compared to the previous night and to what the men outside in trenches were enduring. Having dug their trenches it wasn't long before they were 'spooning' like newlyweds to try and retain some warmth. This applied particularly to Major Richard Davis and all of Yankee Company. They had been deployed to clear an enemy observation position beyond the settlement. They waded across Douglas Creek up to their waists, then having found and cleared the abandoned Argentine positions, they dug in and spent a very cold, uncomfortable, hungry night in their trenches. The dawn 'stand-to' could not come soon enough for men wet from wading the creek, huddled together in their holes in the ground with nothing more than a plastic fertiliser bag to protect them from the elements.

We had eaten our last rations at breakfast that morning and we were hungry. The people of Douglas were open-handed with such food that they had. Sheep meat was a staple for them. Indeed, they ate so much of it that they called it 'three-six-five'. They gave some of us a bite of mutton, but they too were in straitened circumstances. The Argentines had left some ration packs behind and these were shared out. These packs were good, especially since they each contained a miniature of whisky and ten cigarettes. But for the first time in my life, I discovered what it is like not to have any food to eat when I needed and expected it. I felt quite giddy and inclined to smoke more cigarettes than usual. Cigarettes are a prop to one's nerves, an aid to concentration, and there is no physical circumstance, however dangerous or uncomfortable, that can't be improved by finding a cigarette you haven't sat on and broken, a match still dry enough to light, and getting a burn going. They also help to suppress hunger pangs. It was not the last time that we appreciated the famous smoker's three-course breakfast: a cigarette, a cup of coffee, and a cough. We were lucky to have the coffee.

Light smokers became heavy smokers, non-smokers took it up and I, a hitherto intermittent social smoker of other people's cigarettes, became a twenty-a-day man. The only problem was that one couldn't normally smoke cigarettes at night and that was usually when the need was greatest, although I confess I managed to smoke quite a few at night too. One gets quite good at hiding the light and with the constant wind that attended all our doings, the danger of the enemy smelling us was hardly a consideration. While I would never encourage smoking, the fact is that for us, and for others like us, cigarettes were a priceless boon. And if, as a commander in war, you can keep your men alive long enough for them to die of lung cancer, you've done pretty well.

In fact, apart from the risk of violent and terminal interruption by the enemy, the life we led was a pretty healthy one. Water, although it seemed to be everywhere, was not always where we wanted it, and had to be sterilised. One or two men suffered from upset stomachs, but usually because they cut corners. All the coughs, sniffles and colds usually associated with living on board an air-conditioned ship disappeared in the wind. Many of us developed cold sores on our hands: deep painful clefts in the flesh by the nails and elsewhere – clefts which would not heal while we were exposed to the elements, but which disappeared as soon as we arrived in Stanley.

Because our feet were wet virtually all the time, many men suffered from non-freezing cold injuries – the first stages of trench foot. This took the form of numbness and a prickly, tingling sensation. At night, if you were able to warm your feet up, they could be very painful and starting up in the morning could hurt like hell. The feet had often swollen during the night and it was not always easy to dragoon them back into the prison of one's boots. However, once marching, one's feet got wet again almost immediately and returned to their normal numb, tingling state. We were in fact inflicting permanent damage on our feet, but this was hardly a consideration for men who, more than anything, wanted to remain in the line of march with their comrades. Apart from lifelong dicky feet, the only other perceptible after-effect on my health was that soon after we returned home I was laid low with the worst flu I have ever had in my life, before or since. I was not alone.

After the war, much hot air was expended on the subject of boots. Why didn't we have decent footwear? We in 45 Commando did have decent boots. Most of the Unit wore the Hawkins Cairngorm mountain boot, which was comfortable, strong and serviceable, but there was then no boot in service anywhere which would have withstood the watery assault that ours had to cope with. The Cairngorm boot held the water in and was impossible to dry once wet. It was also a heavy boot. Even now, there is no boot in the world which keeps the water out once you've waded ashore from a landing craft, or plunged up to your thighs through your first river of the day. The education of the man wearing it is in many ways more important than the boot, for provided you know how to look after yourself – boots off when you can; powder your feet; treat the blisters; try to wear dry socks when you sleep; dry out your wet socks under your armpits or in your groin while you're marching – then your feet will continue to give acceptable service, and stop your legs from fraying at the ends.

But there were not enough Cairngorm boots to go round, and the standard issue DMS boot was still being worn by many men in the Commando. This boot was in general use throughout the British forces: a single-skinned, leather, lightweight boot with a moulded rubber sole. The bulk of the boot-wearing British forces were vehicle-based in Germany and the DMS reflected this. Since the Korean War, there had been no great pressure to invest in a boot that was suitable for prolonged use in foul conditions and those units which needed such gear had had to resort to commercial sources. The men who wore the DMS boot were undoubtedly handicapped and no matter how careful they and their NCOs were, many feet became a painful, soggy, bleeding, blistered mess.

Ever since warrior-man has had to use his brain at the same time as his feet, the military problems which face him have had to compete for his attention with the discomfort – often pain – emanating from his wet and cold feet. Other men may be different, but I always found that the condition of my feet had a heavy bearing on my frame of mind, on how clever and bullish I felt. In war, your opponent is always trying to stop you achieving your aim. For the commander trying to out-think the other side, it is an intensely cerebral activity, which he usually has to conduct in the face of a thousand distractions. Napoleon is some-times said to have lost Waterloo because he was suffering from an acute attack of piles. I can well believe it. It is difficult enough at the best of times trying to devise a cunning, devastating plan with which to out-manoeuvre the enemy, and it is made no easier when one's mind is distracted by a nagging physical distress such as piles – or the freezing, sodden lumps of meat inside one's boots.

Some years after the war, boots with a one-way porous membrane came into service which allowed sweat out without letting water in. Only then were we to discover the pleasure of dry feet in the field. When it first happened to me, it was almost like an out-of-body experience and to be ranked in my view alongside the invention of gunpowder or the wheel. But in the Falklands, in this respect at least we were no different from soldiers in Haig's British Expeditionary Force, Raglan's army before Sevastopol, Lee's Army of Northern Virginia, Wellington's Peninsular Army, or a numberless multitude of soldiers of a thousand armies in wars since time immemorial: namely, unless you are campaigning in the desert, sooner rather than later you get cold, wet feet.

We were, in the main, adequately equipped for our foray into this demanding environment, but only because our mountain and Arctic role had driven the development and acquisition of good weatherproof clothing. Our excellent windproof jackets and trousers, Cairngorm boots, Arctic socks, duvet boots and rations were all products of our specialised role. Had we relied upon what the British Army had provided for itself in Germany, Northern Ireland and on Salisbury Plain, we would have been in dire straits. Even so, many men had supplemented their equip-ment with private purchases of gloves, bungees, gaiters, sleeping bags and Barbour jackets. The stamp of a peace time vehicle-borne army was evident in other ways and there was no lightweight folding or telescopic stretcher of any kind. Furthermore, the standard helmet was a most unpopular item, in spite of its potential for saving life. It was heavy, uncomfortable and the straps were cumbersome for frozen hands. It was a damned nuisance when fighting among the rocks and most men chose to wear their Green Beret instead, as indeed did I. Body armour was a thing of the future, although one marine in X Ray Company wore a 'bullet proof vest' bought by and worn at the insistence of his mother. He was ribbed mercilessly, although perhaps his mother wasn't so daft: merely a little ahead of her time.

The rucksacks with our spare rations were flown in at first light so we were not very hungry for very long. However, from now on, men started building up little stockpiles of food against a repetition of the failure of the rations to materialise. We had absolute faith that we would not be allowed to starve, but we knew our logistics system was under severe strain. Moreover, carrying heavy loads in this cold, wet environment we must have been burning up calories in prolific quantities. It is questionable whether the standard ration packs, which were nutritious enough in normal circumstances, would have been sufficient even if we had received our regular issue. Fortunately, again, we were able to draw on our Arctic kit, and the Arctic rations were more appetising and had more calories. Furthermore, with the addition of Tabasco sauce, curry powder and garlic salt, great heights of culinary excellence could be scaled.

Even so, food became an all pervading preoccupation. Brigadier Bernard Fergusson, who commanded a Chindit column in the Burma campaign in World War Two, wrote in his book *The Wild Green Earth*; 'Without hesitation, the lack of food is the biggest single assault on morale ... one is in the dismal condition of having nothing to look forward to. Man is still an animal, and consciously or unconsciously looks forward to the next meal.' We could certainly testify to the truth of that. As well as feeling giddy and impelled to chain smoke, I found myself becoming jumpy and irritable. It became very difficult to concentrate. In fact I found it difficult to think of anything but my empty belly. Sleep, never easy at the best of times, was not made any easier when the rumblings and grumblings of one's innards became an incessant clamour for satisfaction. Some men were constantly hungry. It seemed that the fitter the man, the hungrier he was. Marine Leo McDermott, a member of the English national karate team and an international athlete, suffered more than most. Even the cardboard boxes in which the rations didn't arrive looked tempting to him. The slightly older man, with perhaps half an inch of spare around him, was under no great disadvantage for not having honed his body to too fine an edge.

After the end of the fighting, we discovered that the *Stromness* had sent enough steak ashore for the whole Commando, thoughtfully cut up into strips so we could cook it in our mess tins. Bread, fruit and even whisky had also been supplied. It also transpired that the good folk of Arbroath and elsewhere in the UK had dispatched all sorts of comforts to us. We never saw any of it, of course. Even if it hadn't suffered depredations from every thieving hand in the communication link from the UK to the Falklands, it is highly questionable if the logistic chain would have been robust enough to get it the final 40 miles to us for whom it was intended. One commodity that made it through was a Fortnum and Mason hamper ordered by James Kelly while we were at Ascension Island, but it didn't arrive until after we got to Stanley, just when it was needed least.

Our supply of rations was to be interrupted again, but mostly we were able to cover the shortfall with food liberated from the enemy. In truth, relatively speaking, we were not seriously hungry, and not for very long, but we got a flavour of how it might feel to be *really* hungry. What it must be like to be chronically short of food with no prospect of relief, one can only imagine. Suffice to say I have never felt inclined to leave any food on my plate, or occasionally even a startled neighbour's plate, ever since.

At the end of the war, seeing myself in a mirror for the first time in a month, I found I could count my ribs because they were sticking out of my chest, and I had legs like a ballet dancer's.

While at Douglas, we heard of the battle for Darwin and Goose Green. It was quite clear that 2 Para had fought a difficult battle extremely well. The death of the commanding officer, Lieutenant Colonel Herbert Jones, was something of a jolt. This battle has been the subject of much detailed study since, and even today the relevance of the battle and the part H. Jones played, remains controversial. I for one shudder at the notion that any of my actions might ever be subjected to the grinding scrutiny that Herbert Jones's have been. It is the ultimate duty of the officer in command in battle, if he sees things going badly wrong, to intervene personally in order to retrieve the situation. Perhaps that is what H. Jones was doing, and it is difficult for one who has never been in such a position to fault him for it. What is certain is that it was his battalion that fought and won and, rather like Nelson who was shot early during the battle at Trafalgar, his contribution was to prepare the instrument of victory. It may not have been his self-sacrifice on Darwin Hill that turned the course of the battle, but all his work, his leadership, and his moral courage in the weeks and days before created a battalion with the fighting qualities which tipped the balance.

In the wider context of the military situation in the Falklands, the battle for Darwin and Goose Green was unnecessary and was a distraction from the main thrust which 45 Commando and 3 Para were developing towards Stanley. Brigadier Julian Thompson had originally envisaged raiding the settlement as a way of fulfilling the task given to him by Major General Jeremy Moore, the land force commander, in order to establish moral and physical domination over the enemy. The raid was cancelled because bad weather on the night of 25 May had prevented helicopters from flying in the necessary artillery and ammunition to support the raid, in time for the operation on the night of 26 May. On 26 May, Brigadier Thompson was ordered by the operational commander, Admiral Fieldhouse at Northwood, to turn the operation on again and to get on with advancing out of the beachhead. But this time it was not simply to be a raid: instead the settlement was to be captured – a different undertaking altogether. By giving orders directly to Thompson, Fieldhouse was, strictly speaking, bypassing the land force commander General Moore, who was still at sea in *QE2* without secure communications. Secure communications had been fitted in *QE2* at considerable expense, but they had broken down irreparably within a day of leaving Ascension Island. In view of the naval losses, the need for a demonstrable success at that moment was pressing, and Fieldhouse was concerned that the vital political support might collapse unless he could give the politicians some good news. Moreover, pressure for a cease-fire was continuing from the UN and it was important that, if one were to be negotiated, the British were left with something more than merely a small corner of the Island far away from Stanley. The difficulty was that neither the military chain of command nor the government appreciated the extraordinary logistic pressures they were placing on 3 Commando Brigade by demanding so much concurrent activity and Brigadier Thompson was not made aware of the political nuances in the UK which had overtaken his original orders. Had there been an operational commander in-theatre, this dissonance might have been avoided.

So the battle for Goose Green and Darwin was fought for purely political reasons – which is not to say, however, that it should not have been fought. All wars are political and sometimes politics can extend its reach a long way down the chain of command. Herbert Jones and 2 Para gave Admiral Fieldhouse, the government and the country the required victory; and we in the Falklands got a boost which set the tone for the rest of the war. We had scored the first goal.

The battle also served two other important purposes. As it was taking place, Argentine reserves – perhaps 200 or so – were flown into Goose Green. They played no active part in the battle and arrived only in time to be captured. But they had been drawn from the Stanley and Mount Kent area and therefore would not now be able to play any part in that conflict either. Secondly, the capture of Darwin and Goose Green also opened up the possibility of a southern approach route to our final objective, Stanley. It is always a good idea to work out what course the enemy is most likely to expect you to take. Having done that, as a rule, it is also a good idea not to take it, but at the same time to encourage him to think that you are taking it. It is a very human tendency to have preconceptions and if you can reinforce the preconceived notions of your enemy while actually doing something else, you are on the first step towards deceiving him. Taking into account everything we knew about the Argentines' training and culture, Brigade Headquarters worked out that the Argentines would expect us to land near Stanley and attack from the south. As it happens, this unwanted battle of Darwin and Goose Green turned out to be the first stage in that deception, allowing 3 Commando Brigade to approach largely uninterrupted from the north .west. It now appears that the Argentines, virtually to the end, believed that our real attack would eventually materialise from the south, while

101

they regarded any moves that they detected from the north west as the deception.

Company Sergeant Major Bell had his own views about H. Jones's actions on Darwin Hill. Some days later, as we prepared to go into battle on the Two Sisters, he turned to me and said:

'Here, sir, I hope you're not going to do anything stupid?'

'What do you mean, Sergeant Major?'

'Well, when you think about it, most men in this company can run as fast or faster, shoot straighter, bayonet better, crawl further than you. What you bring to the party is your knowledge, leadership, your planning and your organising ability. And all that is in your head. And your head is no bloody use with a hole in it.'

'Thank you, Sergeant Major. I shall try to remember that.'

The position of the sergeant major in a company, or regimental sergeant major in a commando or battalion, is of the utmost importance. He is there to support and advise the commander in many ways. He is the guardian of discipline and standards and is the means whereby his commander gets to know much of what is happening at various levels inside his organisation, but he must also be free to tell his boss when he thinks he is wrong. He is rather like the slave in Caesar's chariot. He reminds Caesar that he is only mortal. He offers loyal dissent when it is required, whether it is asked for or not. This is a most valuable service in any organisation, and many have come to grief for lack of it. I was most fortunate in this regard with Sergeant Major Bell.

Many of the Argentine prisoners from Darwin and Goose Green arrived in *Sir Percivale* under the care of Lieutenant Bill McRae, our assistant quartermaster. His liaison officer was a Pucara pilot who spoke excellent English. When the prisoners left to be transported back to Argentina, this officer insisted on saluting and shaking Bill warmly by the hand. Bill was pleased and touched by this appreciation of the way the prisoners had been treated, even though he became the butt of much ribbing by his fellows for being an 'Argie lover'.

Some of the details of the battle for Goose Green reached us. I heard that Dick Nunn, an acquaintance of mine, had been killed. I had last seen him at Ascension Island. He was a helicopter pilot and had been flying ammunition forward to 2 Para, and picking up casualties on the way back. Dick had been trying to pick up the wounded Herbert Jones when he was shot down. His crewman was badly injured but survived. Dick's brother Chris was a rifle company commander in 42 Commando and had taken part in the recapture of South Georgia and his brother-in-law, David Constance, was a Royal Marine serving at Goose Green with 2 Para. Both were friends of mine. I felt for them.

One of the worst things about war is the uncertainty. How long would this go on for? Even when one went on a six-month tour in, say, Northern Ireland, or a ten-month tour in Dhofar, there was an end date which one consciously or subconsciously focused on. For the first time, we had no idea when this would end. I now began to think of my many other friends who were committed in this war. I wondered how many would survive, and if I would see them again. Doubts about one's own survival were never very far from the surface. For most of the time, one was in high spirits, but one could never be completely happy until it was all over. The uncertainty saw to that. However cheerful one might be, there was always the underlying knowledge that the worst battle would be the final one and that was yet to come.

We also heard tales, subsequently confirmed, that the Argentines had shot at downed helicopter pilots, while they were trying to swim ashore in San Carlos Water on D Day. Compassion for your enemy during a battle is fatal, yet compassion for your enemy after you have defeated him is a mark of your humanity. The point where one crosses the line can be one of the most dangerous moments in war. Moreover, an uncharacteristic savagery can invade a man at this point – a kind of momentum which stems from having been placed in great danger and then, almost to one's surprise, one has survived. Some men feel the urge to kill the man who a moment ago would have killed them; an urge that can be difficult to resist. Many young men, frightened, confused, with adrenalin coursing through every vein, have committed acts at such a moment of battle, which they may have regretted for the rest of their lives. With the benefit of hindsight, one presumes that this was one of those moments. The Argentines were not an inhumane enemy, but this act did arouse indignation and revulsion.

We left Douglas at first light on 30 May, completely restored. We were dry, we had rations, our blisters had been patched and it was a beautiful day. We were now heading to Teal Inlet. 3 Para had gone straight there while we went to Newhouse and then Douglas. It was a long hard march of 20 kilometres. We started by having to march about 3 kilometres south west, upstream along the side of the deep tidal Douglas Creek before crossing it, and then a couple of kilometres back on the other side before we struck what passed for a track to Teal. We could see those at the head of the Commando column, who had set off an hour before us, a mere thirty yards away across the creek, marching in the other direction. Naturally they shouted 'encouraging' remarks at us across the deep tidal ditch and we responded in kind, but I can't say we felt encouraged. Our feet got wet as soon as we set off in any case and it snowed before we arrived at Teal some 15 hours later, well after dark. We now carried our roll mats and sleeping bags strapped to our fighting order, ready to drop if we came into contact with the enemy, but also ready to doss anywhere that circumstances demanded. Rucksacks with spare clothes and rations, and other items remained at Douglas to be flown up in due course.

Information and news, although not essential for our operations, was a problem throughout the war. We were rarely able to hear the BBC World Service and news about other formations and units was always sketchy and incomplete. We always knew what we needed to know to play our part in operations, but we were all naturally curious about what was happening to other units and in the wider world. At one point during this march, a great whoop went up: 'Galtieri's dead – the Argies have surrendered!' General Galtieri was of course the leader of the Argentine Junta, and the buzz whipped by word of mouth from one end of the Commando snake, about 3 miles away to the other. Colonel Andrew Whitehead apparently thought it had originated from X Ray Company and enquired rather irritably of me on the radio where we had got it from. I denied all knowledge – 'Not me, Boss' – but I strongly suspected it was nonsense. But it was a titbit of sufficient gravity to get to the bottom of it now. If it was true, all well and good. If not, then it needed to be stamped on. We stopped and Colonel Whitehead ordered the battery commander, Major Gerry Akhurst, to open up his HF radio and try and get through to Brigade Headquarters. Communications were bad and it took him some time to get any sense out the poor baffled operator at the other end. Sadly it was indeed nonsense, but it was nice while it lasted. Throughout the rest of the march, which was not a pleasant one, my heart was still hoping that there could be some foundation to the rumour. There were others, though, who were rather glad that it was spurious, and that they would not be denied their chance of some real soldiering and of having a proper crack at the Argentines. I confess I was not so sanguine and I was not alone. There were plenty who quietly thought: wouldn't it be nice to get home in time to watch the World Cup?

It would appear that an 'Air Raid Warning RED' had been heard on the radio and shouted on up the line. Some wag somewhere, hearing this, corrupted it to 'Galtieri's dead'– a 3-mile-long Chinese whisper. When this became more widely understood, it was possible to raise a smile on even the most lugubrious face thereafter by saying; 'Air raid warning RED – Galtieri's in bed' or 'Galtieri's bought a shed' or 'I'll have a Garibaldi instead', a reference to the choice of biscuits available in our ration packs – and so on. A minor industry started, developing gloriously absurd variations on the theme. The possibilities for the whimsical, mischievous mind were endless and were a harmless, amusing diversion on a hard, unpleasant yomp. I even heard 'air raid warning YELLOW – Garibaldi plays the cello!'

Rumour and nonsense will always attend war. In at least one post-war publication, one of our officers was alleged to have used a cut-down samurai sword in the battle for Two Sisters. The reality is that Captain Dennis Gillson found a long jungle knife at Teal Inlet, presumably dropped by some soldier. Thinking it would be handy to clear the weeds and brambles in his back garden, he picked it up and eventually took it home with him, where it performs useful service in that capacity to this day.

There were other memorable diversions on this march. We stopped from time to time to eat and brew up. At one of these halts, I heard a shriek behind me and turned just in time to see a sizeable fish describe a parabola in the air. Bombardier Barry Ingleson, a real countryman, had spotted the beast in a stream – a mere ditch I had stepped across a moment before. He had 'guddled' it: gently and patiently he worked his hands underneath it, and then wheeched it out. It was a five-pound brown trout. We could hardly believe our eyes. He slung the monster on his back and we poached it when we got to Teal. It was quite the most delicious fish I have ever tasted.

Brewing up, or 'making a wet' was a most important activity. Even the shortest break in the march was an opportunity to get a wet on and men became highly adept doing it at speed. Some marines would even brag about how quickly they could do it. However, Sergeant George Matthews silenced all opposition by substituting a small wad of plastic explosives for the standard solid fuel hexamine block. Although it has a cutting and shattering effect when initiated with a detonator, plastic explosive can safely be burned in small quantities, producing an intensely hot flame which can boil a metal mug of water extremely quickly. Unfortunately, it tends to wreck the mug.

On the march, we could see the settlement at Teal for hours but we never seemed to get any closer. This was because there is no pollution in the Falklands, and the air is very, very clear. Everything tends to look closer than it really is. Thus our estimation of the Falklands kilometre was about 3,000 metres. We eventually arrived at Teal in the dark and there was snow on the ground. It had been a difficult, unpleasant march, and there were many who felt they were so tired that if the Argentines attacked at this moment, they would not have the energy to do anything about it. However, there were lots of other units protecting the place.

We spent the rest of the night in a stinking, filthy, tick-ridden, beautiful sheep pen. Absolute bliss!

The following day was a joy. Our rucksacks arrived in the small hours of the morning after a Herculean effort by Brian Bellas. Having no faith that he could depend on helicopters, with our over-snow vehicles and borrowed tractors and trailers, he brought forward the stragglers and our kit, threading his way around stone runs, avoiding cliffs, bogs and many other obstacles. It should have been an impossible journey with vehicles overland at night, but, with the help of a local guide, he made it.

After attending to some routine duties, I had very little to do except treat myself nicely. Teal is an attractive little place, quite Hebridean in appearance and it was looking very well in the snow. Teal was being established as a forward logistic base for the Brigade. This would shorten our lines of communication and assist hugely the supply for future assault operations. We could see *Sir Percivale*, commanded by Captain Tony Pitt, anchored in Port Salvador by Teal Inlet where she had arrived shortly before. She was the first ship to do so. She would in due course be the first ship into Stanley harbour. Many of *Percivale*'s crew were sent ashore at Teal during daylight hours for their greater safety, and the sight of these doughty Chinamen in this unlikely place became something of a curiosity.

Brigade Headquarters had also moved forward to here. I had a happy little wander around the place, meeting friends and picking up rumour and gossip from the number of units that had turned up. I spent several hours nibbling biscuits and drinking hot coffee in my sleeping bag.

If you look carefully at the wooden floors of certain houses in Berlin, you will see burn marks from the small stoves that Russian soldiers used to cook their food, when they occupied that city at the end of the Second World War. Should the curiosity of any future visitor to the sheep shearing shed at Douglas, or the sheep pens at Teal, be aroused by the many small burn marks on the floors there, then the answer is at hand. They too came from our solid fuel hexamine cookers.

Brigadier Thompson visited us at Teal. He leaned over the side of my sheep pen puffing on his pipe, looking for all the world like a farmer inspecting his stock, and said, 'Hello.' Since I was in a sheep pen, it seemed the only natural thing to do was to bleat back. This was taken up by other 'sheep' in adjacent pens and soon the entire 'farm' was bleating, braying, mooing and clucking, eventually breaking down into much riotous human laughter. We all faced much discomfort, danger and uncertainty, and the burden Brigadier Thompson carried was immense, but everybody was cheered and heartened by this absurd encounter. We knew that he knew what we were enduring and he knew that we were ready to laugh at it.

Marines in Yankee Company were also finding opportunities for fun. During the night, Lieutenant Andy Shaw commanding 5 Troop was woken up by a sentry. The sentry was worried. A frogman had emerged from the beach in front of him, handed him a package and told him to give it to the Brigadier. Shaw was immediately awake as the sentry put the suspicious package in his hand and he asked him where the frogman was now. Back in the water apparently – no doubt swimming in the direction of the mainland. With three tours in Northern Ireland, improvised explosive devices and booby traps were not unfamiliar to Shaw. His first cogent thought was that this was a practical joke. But how could the lads have pulled this one off? And besides, the sentry looked genuinely concerned. He examined the package carefully. It was bound in black masking tape. Surely the Argies didn't rely on this stuff as well?

Curiosity gradually overcame suspicion as he peeled the layers back and felt only a soft inner; no batteries, no wires, no smell of almonds. He became bolder. But what if it really was intended for the Brigadier? Eventually he reached the centre, now committed, and fully prepared to deny everything. To his unbelievable joy he found a packet of Chilean pipe tobacco. This threw up a completely new set of dilemmas. Shaw smoked a pipe. So did Richard Davis, the company commander, and the Sergeant Major. And so did the Brigadier.

Of course, it could be poisoned. That at least was the flimsy excuse he invented to explain his first pipeful, but as the days went by and the tobacco dwindled, his imagination ran out of plausible ideas. Twenty years later he confessed his crime to Brigadier Julian Thompson and gave him a packet of similar tobacco to make amends. The Brigadier was kind enough to say that the tobacco had probably been of more use to Andy than it would have been to him. Shaw has yet to confess his selfishness to his company commander. Whether he will ever find the courage to tell the Sergeant Major is highly doubtful. It is also doubtful if we will ever know whether the contents of the package really did originate in Chile, or from the more readily available organic matter to be found lying around Teal Inlet.

That night, a concern arose about the security of Teal itself. Brigade Headquarters was by now established there and it was becoming a major supply base. With 42 Commando well forward on Mount Kent and 3 Para having preceded us on the march now at Estancia House, Teal was by now some way behind the front line. However, it was felt that if the Argentines wanted to counter-attack, or to pull off a propaganda-winning special forces patrol, here was the target for them. Furthermore, ever since the bombing of the Brigade maintenance area and the meat factory at Ajax Bay, there was a general uneasiness about sleeping in isolated buildings, however tempting they were. The Argentines did have a limited night bombing capability with their Canberra bombers. At Douglas we heard bombs going off in the night somewhere not far away. Nothing came of it. The Argentines would have been unlikely to know we were in the sheds at Douglas. But Teal was now an important logistics centre and headquarters, and this would certainly be known to them. They could hardly fail to know this since, much to our dismay, it had been announced on the BBC World Service. So, a move out of the sheep pens, however bleak the alternative, was not entirely unwelcome.

Late that night, Colonel Whitehead issued orders for a general deployment into firm defensive positions around Teal. Every man was digging a trench by first light. I had never sited a defensive position in the dark before. There are great dangers in doing this and in a number of instances in British history we got it badly wrong. In particular, during the South African War, in January 1900, a British force climbed up a 1,500 ft hill called Spion Kop during a dark misty night to capture it from the Boers. They reached what they thought was the top, routed a Boer picket, and started digging trenches. At dawn, the mist persisted and they continued digging. When the mist cleared, they found to their horror that they were overlooked by several positions nearby on three sides. The Boers quickly recovered and started pouring fire into their trenches. Spion Kop was eventually abandoned after much slaughter: all because the commander couldn't see the position in daylight. Mindful of this, I did as wide-ranging a reconnaissance as practicable and was ready to move to new positions at dawn. In fact, we were well sited. But as a practice, I don't recommend it.

The Commando quickly settled down into their trenches, which mostly filled with water after a few feet down. So we built up parapets where we could and set up our bivvies next to the trench. The prospect of jumping into a trench with water up to one's armpits was not an attractive one, but no doubt preferable to being blown to bits.

Ever since that day at Ascension Island, when the confusion surrounding the Argentine freighter had been all too obvious, I had been teaching my Company that nothing goes to plan. I had said to them that the minute they stepped over the guardrails of the *Stromness*, the plan would change. The fact that I had been wrong, because the plan hadn't even survived that long, only served to reinforce the message. The result was 120 men who expected nothing, but were ready for anything. The other companies had learnt the same lessons from their own experiences and this attitude permeated the entire Commando. Every man now knew that nothing ever goes to plan. This should not discourage one from making a plan – you must make plans – but you must also be ready for circumstances to force you to change it at any time.

I daresay we would have preferred to have stayed indoors, but we very quickly adjusted to our abrupt removal from our nice, comfortable, filthy sheep pen to a less than hospitable hole in the ground. After a fortnight of living in the field in this foul weather, and humping our kit over fouler ground, the Commando had begun to revel in its readiness to accept whatever was thrown at it. The attitude was, 'We can do it – what is it?'

While we were at Teal, a patrol of Argentine special forces approached 45 Commando positions and managed to surrender without being shot. A similar group surrendered to 3 Para near Lower Malo House. They had decided to surrender after having watched the action at Top Malo House where their comrades had been observed, attacked and destroyed by the Mountain and Arctic Warfare Cadre. The Cadre consisted of a group of instructors who, in peacetime, oversaw the training in mountain and Arctic warfare skills of the Brigade and they trained instructors in this most demanding of specialisations. There were about 20 NCOs and a couple of officers led by Captain Rod Boswell, a widely liked and most professional operator. During the war, the Cadre was used as a Brigade reconnaissance troop. Indeed, the war was in effect the final exercise for the mountain leader students for that year. They were highly skilled and experienced men, special forces in all but name. The Cadre had been deployed in patrols to try to identify Argentine observation posts along our routes of advance. They had found Argentine special forces using Top Malo House and, in a remarkable operation arranged at very short notice, they had mounted a devastatingly successful assault. They killed five, wounded seven and took the remaining five prisoner. Three of the Cadre were wounded. The patrols that surrendered to us and 3 Para did not want similar treatment. These were the first Argentines we had seen. They looked just like our men. We had always been conscious that we might be spotted by observation posts during our yomp. It was good to know that at least these eyes and ears of the enemy, in front of us and on our flanks, were now out of action.

Another special forces soldier who visited 45 Commando was Corporal Tom Melia of the Special Boat Service. He had heard a rumour that a Corporal Melia had been killed and was desperate to find out if it was his brother, Corporal Frank Melia of X Ray Company. Happily they were able to meet and reassure each other that they were both still alive, although for their parents with two Corporal Melias in action, the anxiety never fully subsided until both got home. The dead man was in fact Corporal Mick Melia, no relation, a Sapper who was killed at the battle of Darwin and Goose Green.

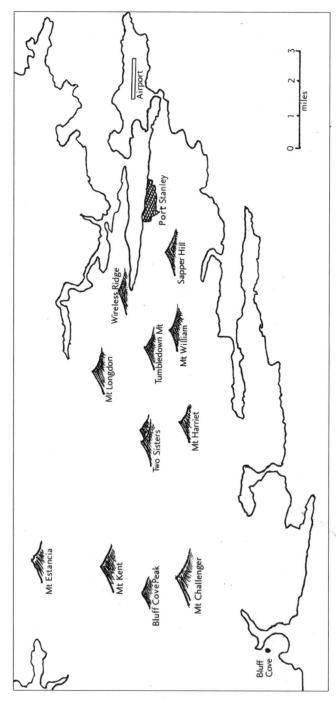

Map 3. The Approach to Port Stanley – all these mountains would need to be neutralised or taken before the war was won.

There were other brothers serving in the Task Force. Marine Geoff Russ of 3 Troop X Ray Company had a brother, Dave, serving in the logistic complex at Ajax Bay. Neither was nominated as the other's next-of-kin and so each would have to rely on informal means of communication if anything happened to the other. While Geoff knew his brother was exposed daily to Argentine air raids, Dave knew Geoff was at the point of the spear with X Ray. Not until the Argentine surrender was announced, did Dave feel able to walk the 300 yards to the logistic headquarters to see if his brother's name was on the list of casualties posted there. They were eventually to meet on Stanley jetty.

The following day, 2 June, the Commando expected to fly by helicopter to a patrol base at Bluff Cove Peak, nearly 30 km to the south east, in the shadow of Mount Kent. This was to be our base for mounting attacks on the hills to the west of Stanley. The weather closed in and flying was not possible. We waited a further day and night in our trenches and the weather cleared. No helicopters were available. So we yomped to Bluff Cove Peak. It took us two days.

We arrived at our patrol base in a valley to the west of Bluff Cove Peak just before dark on 4 June, as the wind stiffened and it started to rain yet again. It had been a long hard march with an overnight stop in bivvies near Lower Malo House. The tussock grass hummocks had been especially trying to walk over and boulders and screes had seemed to fill every space where there was no tussock. We were again wet and tired, but we no longer cared. We were now a mere 17 km from Stanley. We were completely attuned to our environment and there was certainly no going back. We were entirely convinced of the justness of our cause and that we would win. We knew we were going to take casualties, possibly in quite considerable numbers. But while we would all have whooped in relief if the Argentines had surrendered without a fight – as we did when 'Galtieri was dead' – no man who was with the Commando would have wanted to be anywhere else. We were with our friends. We had yomped every inch here and we were proud of it. If they had produced helicopters now, we wouldn't have wanted them. We were damned if we weren't going to yomp the whole way.

While at Bluff Cove Peak we were issued with – oh, joy of joys – a new, clean pair of socks! Most men wrapped this new treasure in a plastic bag to be saved for a dry night inside a dry sleeping bag. That glorious moment was not to arrive until we got to Stanley two weeks later, but it was nice to know they were there. The exception was Marine Mackenzie of Zulu Company, who had been a Highland shepherd before joining the Royal Marines. He had never worn socks and wasn't going to start now. Socks were for wimps. His issue of socks were gratefully snapped up by the 'wimps' in his company.

We also got our first mail since 10 May, a month earlier. I received letters from my parents and my wife, Louise, which cheered me greatly, and many others had similarly welcome letters from home. Other cheering missives were the many photographs from young women, some in very interesting positions and most with very few clothes on, who had been persuaded by the tabloid newspapers to send these as tangible evidence of their support for us in the South Atlantic. As a rule, most men regarded the jingoistic attitude of newspapers like the *Sun* with deep suspicion and contempt. War hath no fury like a non-combatant. But pictures of naked women expressing their undying support for the boys ... now, that was something else!

Other letters were less welcome. Paul Mansell of Zulu Company received a summons for careless driving, demanding his attendance at Newcastle Crown Court by 2 July. The three large volumes of *How the West was Won* which Marine Jeoff Maughan received as his first instalment of free books, after joining a bookclub were greeted with much laughter but remained unread. No doubt they will still be there, under the turf where he buried them at the base of Mount Kent, together with the two pairs of extra large tights that Corporal Bob Colville's mother had thoughtfully sent him. She had been encouraged by the *Sun* to believe that they would help to keep her boy warm. But they were so large that he could only keep them up by hitching them on his equipment. The thought of being captured while trying to wrestle ammunition through his tights was enough to deter him from testing their thermal properties. But the very idea of it did wonders for his section's morale.

We anticipated staying here until the attacks went in on the hills around Stanley. This would be the base from which we would now patrol and from which we would mount our attacks. We dug trenches – or swimming pools – and found dips in the ground to erect our bivvies. Nothing was out of the wind. Our patrol base was a grubby, bleak, boggy place and the position was split up by a number of stone runs. These were extraordinary features, presumably glacial in origin, which I had never seen before. They were huge rivers of boulders, some of the stones being the size of a small car. They were covered with a lichen-type moss which was slippery when wet, which it always was except when the stones were covered in ice, when it froze. The stones often moved when one stepped on them. Crossing them by day was difficult enough. Crossing them by night was hell. I myself fell several times and was lucky not to break something.

When in static or defensive positions, one always posts sentries by day and night. It is a long accepted reality that two of the more likely moments for an enemy to attack are at dawn or dusk. Thus it is normal procedure to supplement the sentries with a 'stand-to' at those times in the day. 'Stand-to' – an abbreviation of 'stand to arms' – is when everybody puts his equipment on and with his weapon – you are never without your weapon – he mans the trench or position from which he would fight if attacked. It is customary then, for troop and company commanders to visit their men in sentry and stand-to positions, the purpose being not only to check that all is well, but also to support and encourage the men. What can look like something of a chore is in fact a wonderful opportunity to hear what the men are thinking. I carried a bottle of whisky during the campaign. A third of it was in a Schweppes tonic bottle in my rucksack, there was a second tonic bottle full in my sleeping bag and in my pocket I carried a hip flask, which I kept topped up from the other two. A tot of whisky from the flask into a section mug of coffee at stand-to was always appreciated and helped to bring a smile. But, having gone to 'cheer up the chaps', I found that it was I who drew support, encouragement and strength from these moments. The gentle ribbing, the crack, a shared cigarette or a coffee: all brought a disproportionate pleasure to me. Above all, the good humour and steadiness that my marines unfailingly displayed in these inhospitable conditions I found uplifting and humbling. Those wry smiles and murmured conversations at stand-to remain among my most treasured and abiding memories of the war.

We had by now been warned that our likely objective would be the hills known as the Two Sisters. During the next few days, we conducted a variety of patrols, both to protect our position and to find out more about our eventual target. Mount Kent was the pivotal feature nearby. Argentine forces had been seen in its vicinity and a British special forces patrol had been inserted on to it two weeks before. It had been planned to fly 42 Commando to take over from them on the night of 29 May but, after a hair-raising flight in a blizzard, in which helicopters were forced to land and take refuge with engines and rotors still turning on the ground, the attempt had been aborted. Another attempt was mounted on the night of 30 May and was successful, in spite of a fire-fight between British and Argentine special forces near the landing site. 42 Commando had held the feature in its entirety but were now going to leave to prepare for their own attack on Mount Harriet. It was imperative that Argentine forces were not allowed to put an observation post on the vacated position. The Surveillance Troop of 45 Commando, commanded by Lieutenant Andy Smith, would therefore set up their own observation posts to continue building up our knowledge of what lay in front of us, while X Ray Company would send a troop to hold and defend the top. On 5 June, I sent Chris Caröe up with 2 Troop, together with Alasdair Cameron. They were met at the top by an officer from 42 Commando who, with the parting words, 'It's a real dump: are you taking over with just one troop? Wow! I couldn't hand this place over to a nicer guy,' promptly left. They got up there and set up home on the top in half-decent weather. The following day, Brigade Headquarters deemed that one troop was not enough so Colonel Whitehead told me to take the remainder of the Company to join Caröe.

At first light on 6 June, the weather was fine. I heard the sound of a light helicopter arriving near Commando Headquarters. It was a Gazelle from 3 Commando Brigade Air Squadron. I sprinted across and somehow communicated with the pilot. He was Captain Nick Pounds, the commander of our own Montforterbeek Flight, whom I knew well. Would it be possible to do a reconnaissance flight of the top of the hill and find out precisely where Caröe was? If so, I would be able to ensure that we took the easiest route and not waste time and effort. Ever obliging, Nick agreed. I climbed in and sat down inside his draught-free cockpit. All the air from inside my clothes suddenly wafted up through the opening in my jacket past my nose and for the only time during the war, I was reminded that I hadn't washed since leaving the ship. The recce flight was successfully completed and I shortly rejoined the Company.

The march started well enough and after a little while we came across a gunner observation post, manned to my surprise and delight by Mike Goodfellow, a Royal Artillery officer with whom I had served in the Dhofar War eight years before.

Then the weather changed. In clement weather, the march up Mount Kent would have been a pleasant walk; an ascent of about 1,000 ft, over 4 kilometres, with a view of Stanley and the rest of the known world from the top. Instead, we had a dreadful scramble in quite the most ghastly weather I have experienced outside the Arctic. To say it rained heavily hardly does it justice. It was more like a combination of a wind tunnel and the inside of a car wash, all at around zero degrees centigrade. It blew like hell all day and the torrential freezing rain sliced through our useless waterproofs. Mount Kent is 1,500 ft (457 m) high and, apart from South Georgia, is the highest piece of land between the South American mainland and the Antarctic. When it is nice it is very nice, but when it is bad, it is horrid. This day it was vile. It took two hours to get to the top and I, and a number of other heavily laden men, were occasionally lifted up by the wind, removed several yards and deposited on our backsides. It was impossible to see more than 20 yards, and I couldn't have got any wetter or colder if I had been for a swim in the Barents Sea. The already resident 2 Troop were fine, having established themselves while the weather had been dry and the wind less violent, and were tucked into cracks and crevices.

With 1 and 3 Troops we found shelter as best as we could. We tried to put up bivvies and cook food and prepare hot drinks. Men were finding it very difficult to erect bivvies in the wind and without shelter we would soon be in difficulties. Again, the marines were magnificent – so patient, so resilient, so positive. But after sending out a couple of clearance patrols, it was quite clear that we weren't achieving anything that wasn't being achieved by 2 Troop on their own – except exhausting two troops. I decided to seek the Commanding Officer's permission to come down again. I could not get through on my radio, so I used Chris Caröe's signaller, Marine Mike Chadwick, to help. As he lay inside his bivvie, I lay in the freezing bog outside with my head poking in, using his radio trying to get through to headquarters. It was still pouring with rain. We were now in survival conditions. If we couldn't find shelter or get down soon, we would have hypothermia casualties – and I might be among the first! Marine Chadwick earned my deep gratitude by feeding the distracted face in his bivvie with lit cigarettes and mugs of hot coffee. Eventually I got through. Colonel Whitehead readily agreed that we should come down. However, I was now unable to get in touch with David Stewart and 3 Troop. We left the message with 2 Troop that 3 Troop should come down the hill. It was now getting dark and we stumbled down the hill to comparative safety and comfort.

It was pitch black when we arrived back at the patrol base and everything was sopping wet through and through, including our sleeping bags. We were able to cook a meal in the Regimental Aid Post and I was most grateful to our doctor, Surgeon Lieutenant David Griffiths, who gave me a slug of medicinal whisky. The rain subsided soon afterwards and we prepared for the night. I waited and waited for news that David Stewart and 3 Troop had come down, but eventually heard that 2 Troop had been able to look after them and they had stayed up the mountain. In fact, this was not the case – they had not found 2 Troop. Instead they spent a most uncomfortable night and very nearly had hypothermia casualties.

This was the only time the weather beat us, although it didn't beat 2 Troop, or Surveillance Troop, or the Radio Rebroadcast Team who, like 42 Commando before them, stayed on top of Mount Kent for many days. The weather and general conditions for them were appalling. To begin with they were in simple survival mode. The wind and rain ripped apart their shelter tops and scattered any unsecured kit across the landscape. They had to find hollows amongst the rocky outcrops where they could get out of the driving wind and rain and erect a temporary shelter. Corporal Frank Melia's section huddled up together, soaked to the skin like a bunch of drowned rats, making hot 'wets', while one man remained outside on sentry, changing over every 30 minutes. As they slowly warmed up, their spirits rose and they even made up the lyrics to a song, which they performed as the 'Falklands Veterans' Choir' at the sods' opera on board *Stromness* on the way home. Sung to the tune of Cliff Richard's *Summer Holiday*, it started, 'We're all going on a pusser's holiday . . .' The Pusser, a corruption of 'purser', is the term widely used to refer to the Royal Navy.

A bivvie no longer sufficed and in any case they were almost impossible to erect. Instead, men built survival shelters, cutting slabs of peat to build walls around crags and overhangs. They took pride in making these as strong and as comfortable as possible, and some were structures that might easily have survived to the present day. Occasionally the weather was so ferocious that, rather than expose themselves to the elements to relieve themselves, they used their mugs and emptied the contents out the door.

They were shelled from time to time, and on one occasion made the mistake of burning some rubbish, which attracted a barrage. The wind was so strong that men on sentry duty were in danger of being blown clean off the top of the mountain. One man got what can be best described as 'trench hands' and had to wear socks on them. On the other hand, when it stopped raining, clothes and sleeping bags exposed to this blast could be dried in about 15 minutes. And every now and then, the clouds would clear, the sun would shine and they would be rewarded with a stunning view of Stanley and virtually the whole of East Falkland.

For the second and last time, my citadel was breached: but a wet sleeping bag is better than no sleeping bag, if you can keep out of the wind. It was now approaching mid-winter, and each night lasted around 15 hours. That night, I slept for two hours and smoked twenty cigarettes for the rest. Messrs Benson and Hedges, and the suppliers of all those Argentine fags we liberated, I thank you! As luck so often had it, the next day was a beautiful one and we were able to spread out our clothes and dry ourselves.

In spite of the unpleasant conditions on top of Mount Kent, 2 Troop made themselves useful and seemed to thrive in the lousy conditions. Several times they found themselves relaying radio messages which otherwise would not have got through. They also found opportunities to hit the enemy on Two Sisters. They observed that the Argentine soldiers on Two Sisters were being fed centrally and lined up twice a day for a hot meal. This ceased abruptly after Alasdair Cameron shelled the breakfast queue on 8 June.

One day they were tasked to locate and retrieve documents from a Landrover, on the exposed forward slope of the mountain. This was the result of a map reading error and the Landrover should have been placed somewhere else altogether. More helicopters were finally arriving. These were naval anti-submarine helicopters, which Admiral Woodward had ordered to be stripped of their anti-submarine gear and redeployed to support the land force. Many of the pilots were inexperienced in land warfare and the business of flying men and equipment around a battle-field was very different from their normal task of hunting submarines in the North Atlantic. Perhaps for pilots used to flying over featureless expanses of water, one mountain or hill looks very much the same as the next. But the decision to re-allocate these anti-submarine assets was a brave one and that the aircrew were able to switch roles so successfully, with so little preparation, was a wonderful testament to their flexibility and courage. They made a most valuable contribution just where and when it was needed most – notwithstanding their unpredictable map reading!

The errant Landrover was a Brigade Air Squadron vehicle that had inadvertently been planted on the forward slopes of Mount Kent, in full view of the Argentine positions in Stanley. The Argentines were very quick to react, bringing an immediate artillery barrage down on the vehicle, although the helicopter got away unscathed. The Landrover was eventually found by 2 Troop and the code books and radios recovered and duly returned to their owners. The rations and the booze that they also found were not. The Landrover was peppered with shrapnel and there were around 10 shell holes in the surrounding area, and it was clearly still under observation because the patrol came under accurate artillery fire as they withdrew. A Landrover parked near the top of Mount Kent looked as out of place as a ghost at noon.

While we were stumbling around Mount Kent on 6 June, the Commando Reconnaissance Troop commanded by Lieutenant Chris Fox was hitting the enemy on Two Sisters. From time to time, through the rain, wind and mist, I had glimpsed Two Sisters and had seen the occasional shell burst on its forward features. I knew that Chris Caröe and Marine Chadwick had been doing invaluable work relaying artillery fire missions. Chris Fox's patrol, together with four sappers from Condor Troop, had inserted themselves deep into the enemy position in the dark and the mist during the night, and discovered much needed information. However, when the mist cleared during the day, they had to fight their way out, and in so doing they killed five Argentine soldiers. Their only casualty was a hole in Chris's finger. Chris's luck held right through to the end, even when, after the surrender, in the course of examining one of the abandoned Pucara aircraft sitting on the apron at Stanley airfield, he climbed into the cockpit and sat in the seat. Having satisfied his curiosity, he climbed out again. About a minute later, the ejection cartridge went off firing the empty seat high in the air. He was fortunate to avoid the fate of one Argentine soldier who, when gathered with many other prisoners at the airfield after the war, took shelter from the elements in an aircraft cockpit. Once again the ejection cartridge fired spontaneously and the seat was blasted up in the air, but with him in it. He was not strapped in and was killed.

We continued to build up our knowledge of the ground and the enemy on Two Sisters, and that night, 6 June, two patrols from Zulu Company explored the area to the west of the northern Sister. On their way out, they were nearly hit by speculative Argentine artillery firing on possible approach routes. They identified machine gun positions and artillery defensive fire grids and added to our accumulating store of knowledge.

Yankee Company also patrolled actively and they achieved a notable success on 7 June. Lieutenant Andy Shaw and 5 Troop found an abandoned Argentine position north of Mount Kent. This had been the base for the troops who had flown from Mount Kent to reinforce Goose Green. They had surrendered there with the remainder of the garrison. Shaw's troop searched the camp thoroughly and, sure enough, Corporal Willie Hannah found, in a Landrover trailer taken from the Royal Marines garrison at Moody Brook, a map, a map overlay and an operation order. When passed up to the Brigade Intelligence Officer, Captain Viv Rowe, this revealed much useful information about the disposition of Argentine forces in the region of Stanley, including the fact that the unit concerned had been part of the strategic reserve. It was most helpful to know that these reserves were now out of the equation and although the papers were not up to date they helped to confirm some things which had hitherto been estimate and conjecture.

On 8 June, X Ray Company was ordered to send a fighting patrol into the objective the following night, to harass the enemy and to inflict casualties. This was a very different proposition to the patrols of the previous night. It is most important to give a patrol a clear mission. A fighting patrol requires a very different approach to a reconnaissance patrol and no patrol should ever be required to do both. The latter ideally should not be seen or heard. It is usually smaller and, if it engages the enemy at all, it is either by indirect artillery or mortar fire, or *in extremis* to get itself out of trouble. A fighting patrol has a brief to get stuck in and start a fight, and is configured appropriately. I gave David Stewart and 3 Troop this job. He and his troop sergeant, Pete Jolly, prepared well. During the day on 9 June, he took all his NCOs to a vantage point where he was able to observe Two Sisters from a distance and talk the ground and the patrol through with them. He had been briefed by all the key officers in Commando Headquarters including the commanding officer, and had been given all the information gathered by the previous patrols, and a team from Chris Fox's recce patrol went with him, led by Corporal Wilkie. I gave him an artillery observer, Bombardier Ingleson, and some assault engineers led by Corporal Thompson in case he encountered mines or other obstacles. He also took the best radio I had, together with Marine Iain Leiper, one of my excellent signallers. David Stewart and Pete Jolly thought the whole thing through and I discussed it with David at length. It was tempting to get involved in the planning myself, but that was not my job. It was clear that David knew what he was doing and that he was getting the right information from all the relevant agencies. I gave such directions as I thought essential and then kept myself right out of it, but available to help if asked.

After giving his orders, David conducted rehearsals and I never saw a patrol so well founded; I had high hopes for their success. My chief fear was the lack of cover in the bright moonlight. There would be a full moon for much of the night, and although the weather would undoubtedly interrupt the moon, this would be unpredictable and could not be relied upon. As I bade them farewell at 2100 hrs local time, I had a last minute attack of the horrors. I could see them with the naked eye for 300 metres and after that, with binoculars, for over half a kilometre. However, the Argentines didn't spot the patrol until they were upon them. The patrol moved to the southernmost of the Two Sisters, a hill which was to be X Company's objective during the attacks two nights later. There were black holes and hummocks in the peat bog. Instead of spreading out, the men huddled together in blobs and moved slowly across the open ground, the idea being that a casual observer would see a blob rather like a peat hummock. Thus they inserted themselves across the Murrel River, over open moonlit ground into the bottom of the position. The lead section commanded by Corporal Bob Colville, covered by a fire section under Corporal Hugh Knott, found two men asleep behind a machine gun. An NCO was apparently about to check on them when Colville's section killed all three at very close range. This awoke the other defenders. A flanking movement was seen by Corporal Knott's section. Knott hit the first man in the chest with a 66mm and Lance Corporal Hind shot the next man with his LMG. In the subsequent fire-fight, they were then engaged by three machine guns and, getting low on ammunition, now had to fight their way out. This was the most dangerous part of the patrol. There would be no disguising themselves as peat hummocks this time as they re-crossed the Murrel River and the

1,000 yards of moonlit open ground between them and the rocks which offered cover to the west.

David Stewart ordered Bombardier Ingleson to bring down artillery fire on the eastern end of the southern Sister, from where a heavy weight of fire was streaming down on to the ground across which they would need to run. There was also a machine gun out to the south, somewhere towards Goat Ridge, that was much closer and firing directly across their escape route. This gun had to be silenced if they were to stand any chance of getting out unscathed. By its very nature, artillery always takes longer to arrive on the ground than the people who call for it, want it. This was no exception. They couldn't wait for it to arrive and to be adjusted to the target. David Stewart sent Marine Gary Marshall with his LMG and Sergeant Pete Jolly, with his binoculars and his cool head, up to a position where they would be able to silence this machine gun. The only suitable place was in full view of the enemy further up in the rocks. Under fire from the enemy on the ridge, they put down well-aimed shots and silenced the machine gun to the south. Marshall also coolly gave fire control orders for others to engage the enemy at the same time. Stewart now gave the order for the Troop to withdraw back down over the open ground to the rear, one section at a time with covering fire from the remainder of the Troop. From positions further down the slope, they could better identify the closer enemy positions and made use of the 66mm to attempt further to neutralise the enemy – Marine Fletcher proving to be a dab hand at this. Still no friendly artillery fire appeared, so they had only their own weight of fire to cover their withdrawal down the open slope. David Stewart watched his marines zigzagging down the hill with tracer flashing over their heads. His turn was next. As he ran down the hill from one peat hummock to the next, he saw in front of him Pete Jolly and Corporal Thompson running five yards apart separated by a burst of tracer. He could hear the crack of the rounds as they went past and occasionally saw a green flash as rounds struck the rocks at his feet.

All sense of time was lost and, with bullets ripping up the bog around them, they skirmished backwards, running like hell in the bright moonlight to get to the nearest decent cover. Marine Geoff Russ, the GPMG gunner for Corporal Colville's section, gave covering fire until he was virtually out of ammunition and, in the long sprint backwards, got separated from his section. The time for stealth had long since passed and all notion of using passwords was forgotten. Shouting 'Royal, Royal' he was able to find and rejoin his comrades. They eventually reached the Murrel River and, as they did, the enemy fire tailed off and they could slow the pace. They reached the rocks on the west side of the river, but enemy artillery fire now started to fall too close behind them for comfort. So, with Marine Roberts shouting, 'Last one to the top's a sissy!' again they upped and ran as fast as they could, on up into the next rock formation until they were well out of range. At last they were able to take stock and gather themselves for the journey home. No one had been hit.

Marine Iain Leiper, the signaller whom I had detached from my headquarters, and who had been in the thick of it, reached for his handset to send an initial report. It had been shattered by a bullet.

A number of Hugh Knott's men had eaten almost all their rations before this patrol, on the basis that if they were going to get killed, they might as well do so on a full stomach. They now felt a bit daft facing the next 24 hours with nothing but a Mars Bar and some rolled oats. We managed to club together and saw that they didn't go hungry.

By any standards, this was a successful patrol, and had a considerable bearing on our subsequent operations. They had clearly been very lucky, but the execution had been as skilled as the preparation had been meticulous. It is said that fortune favours the bold and the brave. It favours neither. Fortune favours the professional.

But not all was success. Andy Shaw with 5 Troop Yankee Company was tasked the following night, 10 June, to go round the eastern end of Two Sisters and find out what was there. A section of two mortars was detached from the Mortar Troop to move themselves forward to a position from where they could support the patrol with indirect fire. Shaw had taken such precautions as he could to avoid meeting his own mortar section. However, map reading in bad visibility at night in the Falklands was always extremely difficult (as I was to discover myself with my entire company less than 24 hours later) and the two groups met at a place where the mortars should not have been. 5 Troop saw the mortar section first. From the direction of travel, it seemed likely that they were an enemy patrol heading towards our positions. However, Andy Shaw checked on the radio with headquarters that there were no other patrols out. He even checked with the neighbouring unit, 3 Para, that they had nobody out in that area. He finally spoke to the mortar section on the radio. He asked them where they were. They said they were on high ground close to their final position. Moreover, before the 5 Troop patrol had started, while waiting for last light before setting off, a Gazelle helicopter had flown to Shaw's position and he had been handed a written memo from the Commando operations officer. It read: 'Beware counter-attack from 601 Commando. Carry on with task.' This had served to accentuate the risk in Shaw's mind of encountering 601 Commando Company of the Argentines' special forces. Shaw was now looking down at this group 200 yards away. Could this be part of a counter-attack on 45 Commando? There was no way they could be the same people he had been talking to on the radio because his patrol was nowhere near the mortars' objective. Soon, they were less than 100 yards away. Shaw could see no identifiable weapons or headdress. He opened fire. After about a minute, he shouted an order and one of the mortar-men must have heard him because a shout in English came across: 'We are call sign 52!' They stopped firing. Eventually, proper identification was made, but by then Sergeant Bob Leeming, Corporal Peter Fitton, Corporal Andy Uren and Marine Keith Phillips of the mortar section had all been killed.

I listened to the latter part of this incident on the radio, and to the evacuation of the casualties, with Chadwick and Caröe again acting as radio relay. We were due to attack the Two Sisters the following night. It struck me that the shock this would have on the unit might seriously affect morale. I wondered if the remainder of the Mortar Troop could now be relied upon. My fears were groundless and Mortar Troop, under the command of Lieutenant Dominic Rudd, delivered a sterling perform-ance on the night. The commanding officer described the sequence of events at the beginning of his orders for the attack the following day. He said that however regrettable it was, the time for mourning our dead was not now. The rest of the Commando followed his excellent lead: we put the whole dreadful matter behind us and cracked on. The incident had no effect whatever on X Ray Company so far as I could discern.

Incidents where you shoot at, or are shot at by, your own side in war – 'blue-on-blues' or 'friendly fire' or 'own goals' – are all too common. Most soldiers with any war experience have been involved in a blue-on-blue. X Ray Company had already been shot at by the Commando Logistic Regiment in Ajax Bay. In the Falklands War, HMS *Cardiff* was later to shoot down a British Army helicopter, and a Special Boat Service sergeant would be killed by the Special Air Service. Three civilian women were killed by British naval gunfire on one of the last days of the war. I knowingly gave my own grid reference when calling for mortars on Two Sisters. On the northern Sister, it was sometimes difficult to tell which was Argentine artillery and which was ours. That is the inevitable consequence of using artillery and mortars in a close quarter battle. There were other instances in the Falklands of blue-on-blue and there were certainly lots of near misses. God alone knows how many the Argentines had. In Oman, in a hasty frightened moment while under fire, I mixed up east with west on the radio and misdirected an air strike on to myself. No one was hurt on that occasion, but I had earlier mortared myself by mistake and wounded one of my own soldiers. I once took part in a discussion on the subject of blue-on-blues with a group of Second World War veterans. One of them said that he had landed on the Normandy beaches on D Day and fought for nine months all the way to the River Elbe and he had been bombed by every air force except the Luftwaffe.

Given that war is usually conducted by tired, confused, frightened young men under intense pressure, while handling equipment designed for the specific purpose of killing, and that decisions almost always have to be taken with incomplete, imperfect and sometimes wrong information, blue-on-blues are an inescapable concomitant to operations. It is deeply painful to inflict casualties on one's own side, but while always doing everything we sensibly can to avoid them, we must accept them as the mistakes made in good faith that they always are. Those men killed in such incidents are killed in action, just as surely as if they had been shot by the enemy.

The Argentine Air Force remained a concern as always. The longer we stayed in this open bleak place, the more likely we would be attacked. It finally happened one night shortly before we left. An Argentine Canberra bomber dropped its load near Commando Headquarters and Zulu Company, who heard and felt the ground vibrate but remained undamaged. No one got out of his sleeping bag. Our neighbouring unit to the north, 3 Para, in the area of Estancia House, was hit by Pucaras one day. This was observed by marines in 5 Troop. The loud bang was followed by what looked uncannily like a mushroom cloud. Thoughts of weapons of mass destruction occurred to some men and they began to regret having ditched their respirators early on in the yomp. Andy Shaw found one marine who, although he had ditched his respirator, had retained the renewable canister that screws on the front. Shaw could not contain his laughter when he saw the marine in his green slug sleeping bag, pinching his nose, eyes tight shut, inhaling through the black canister stuck in his mouth.

We had been ready to attack towards Stanley for several days and were keen to get on. However, it was judged that 3 Commando Brigade should wait until a second brigade, 5 Infantry Brigade, had been brought up into a position whereby they could take the next sequence of hills after our attack. In this way we would be able to maintain momentum if Stanley proved to be a tougher nut than we expected. With five battalion-sized manoeuvre units, 3 Commando Brigade could almost certainly have finished the business on its own, but it was undoubtedly prudent to have a second brigade. We were about to step into range of the full force of the Argentine artillery and any loss of momentum while within this envelope would have been highly problematical, to say the least. I, for one, was perfectly happy to share the fighting with another brigade.

This brigade, 5 Infantry Brigade, was the British Army's lip service to the 'rest of the world' and 'out of area'. They were supposed to be prepared for intervention operations around the world, but they were structured, trained and equipped for nothing more violent than the lowest levels of insurgency. This was the result of the Army's narrow focus on Germany. They had surrendered any serious capability of projecting expeditionary military power beyond Central Europe, in spite of Britain's many residual commitments outside that area. Forces earmarked for 'out of area' or 'rest of the world' operations came not only after Germany, but after Northern Ireland in the priority order. This may be understandable, but little thought had been given, and even less resources had been devoted, to the notion that such a force might have to fight anything more lethal than unruly tribesmen.

By chance, X Ray Company had acted as the enemy for 5 Infantry Brigade on an exercise in England two months earlier, so I had seen the brigade commander, Brigadier Tony Wilson, perform on exercise, and had got to know his key staff officers quite well. Even as a visiting player, I was not filled with confidence. While the staff were conscientious and professional, their commander appeared to be overly concerned about how he and his brigade might appear to others, including me. The headquarters did not feel like a happy place. Nevertheless, before the Falklands War, the brigadier and his staff had been well aware of the shortcomings of their brigade and had tried to remedy them. They had had to suck hard on the hind tit of supply to get decent modern kit and had not always been successful. For instance, I was surprised to find that they did not have the not-very-new range of Clansman radios. While I worked with them, the standing joke in their headquarters was a variation of the Japanese-soldier-found-in-the-jungle-long-after-the-war-has-finished joke. The Japanese soldier emerges from the bush and asks two questions. First question: 'Who won the war?' He is told that the Japanese lost. 'Ah, so,' he says, then asks, 'And has 5 Infantry Brigade been issued with Clansman radios?' They were issued with Clansman radios for the Falklands War, but they still had to struggle to get the Army to agree to exchange their UK clothing and personal equipment for something more appropriate to the South Atlantic.

In the Falklands they were in an unenviable position. Whereas 3 Commando Brigade had its own artillery and logistic regiments, its own helicopter squadron, and its own engineers, all of whom had worked together for years on Arctic, amphibious and all-arms, joint, conventional exercises, 5 Infantry Brigade's equivalents had been plucked off the shelf and thrown together with them for one exercise in summer weather in Wales, just before they sailed. 3 Commando Brigade was equipped with modern over-snow vehicles, the only motorised transport that could reliably cross the Falklands terrain. There weren't enough of them to provide bulk movement, but at least the headquarters of the Brigade, and those of the commando units, were mobile. Apart from a few small first-generation over-snow vehicles, 5 Infantry Brigade only had wheeled transport, which was substantially useless. Their logistics comprised one ordnance company with some medical and other specialists attached, with stocks and wheeled distribution equipment and vehicles enough for fighting a few dissidents with small arms – just the sort of enemy X Ray Company had been asked to simulate two months before. So logistically, they would be largely dependent upon the resources of the Commando Logistic Regiment, itself already under strain from supplying an enlarged 3 Commando Brigade. Moreover, 5 Infantry Brigade's two most battle-ready units, 2 and 3 Para, had been taken from them and given to 3 Commando Brigade. As replacements, they were given the Welsh and Scots Guards. Fine regiments they are, but both battalions had recently been committed to London ceremonial duties, and neither was equipped or trained for the sort of environment or operations on which we were now engaged. The Brigade Headquarters certainly wasn't. The headquarters at neither battalion nor brigade level had been exercised in any meaningful way in recent memory. Not least of the shortcomings was the lack of experience of joint warfare or an understanding of the need to coordinate and communicate all actions with other interested parties. The third battalion was a unit of Gurkhas. They too are excellent troops but, seen from an unsentimental non-British perspective, we were sending Asian mercenaries to fight a white man's war, so they came with some constraining political baggage.

Initially, 5 Infantry Brigade were briefed that they would garrison the Islands after we had recaptured them. Then they were told they would fight. It took years of expensive, assiduous, rigorous preparation to make 3 Commando Brigade ready for just this sort of operation, in precisely these arduous conditions. Indeed, many Royal Marines had to pinch themselves as a reminder that this was not simply another exercise. Not so for 5 Infantry Brigade, and to pitch the men of this semi-trained, improvisatory, ill-supported, unready formation into an amphibious, high intensity, joint, conventional conflict, at no notice was, to say the least, to ask a very great deal of all the people in it.

Eventually, 5 Infantry Brigade advanced along the southern approach to Stanley, opened up by 2 Para's victory at Darwin and Goose Green. This was not an approach route that the amphibious planners would have chosen under any circumstances. For one thing, it had been assessed that the Argentines expected us to use this route and it is rarely advisable to do what your enemy is expecting. It was also fraught with difficulties and had been dismissed by the amphibious planners as being too far, too dangerous, too difficult to support by sea and not much better by helicopter. So it was to prove. Use of this approach by 5 Infantry Brigade was to have the benefit that it distracted the Argentines from 3 Commando Brigade advancing from the north west; but at a cost.

The methods applied were controversial. It started with 2 Para discovering by telephone that there were no Argentines in either Fitzroy or Bluff Cove. Now back under command of 5 Infantry Brigade, and with the agreement of their brigade commander, Brigadier Wilson, 2 Para hijacked the precious single Chinook on 2 June and, packing men in as if on a London tube, they flew 50 km forward and took possession of Fitzroy and Bluff Cove. They were now sitting on ground of great potential value, but were also very isolated and vulnerable. They needed to be reinforced very quickly indeed. But an inherent problem was that the brigade was hobbled with poor communications and no usable transport of their own. They had no means to back this move up and had not consulted those upon whom they would have to depend to do so. When he heard about it by accident, this bold but unilateral initiative placed the commander of the Land Forces, Major General Moore, in a very difficult position. He either had to tell 5 Infantry Brigade to undo it, or immediately back them up. A withdrawal would have been humiliating for Wilson and the Paras and would have been difficult to explain to Northwood, forever looking for good news to give to politicians. And yet to back them up would put even more strain on a fragile logistic chain which was already struggling to sustain 3 Commando Brigade in the north. Moore chose to back them up. The advance along the southern route finished with the capture of Sapper Hill, twelve days later. In between these events, the Chinook and its strap-hanging Paras were very nearly destroyed by British artillery; 600 Scots Guardsmen were almost sunk at sea by British warships; four British soldiers were killed by HMS *Cardiff* which shot down their helicopter; a landing craft from *Fearless* was bombed in Choiseul Sound killing six men; and 50 men, mostly Welsh Guards, died when the Argentine Air Force damaged *Sir Tristram* and destroyed *Sir Galahad*. Many more were injured. These disasters and near disasters were individually the results of many and various factors, but they were all part of the struggle to balance 5 Infantry Brigade after its initial, precipitate, ill-thought-out move.

Commentators have criticised 5 Infantry Brigade then and since, but it seems to me that if there is blame to be laid, it should lie further up the chain, where decisions were made about the equipment, structure, training, deployment and command of British Army formations. One is not privy to the process whereby 5 Infantry Brigade changed in the minds of its masters from a garrison force to a fighting brigade, but it is not difficult to see how an urge not to let 3 Commando Brigade hog all the action might have played a part. What is certain is that what this brigade faced in this war was nothing like what it had prepared for in peace. Under the circumstances, the individual officers and soldiers in 5 Infantry Brigade performed remarkably well. They, and the many

Army personnel serving in 3 Commando Brigade without which it could not have functioned, did all that was asked of them and more. But the reputations of the Army chiefs were salvaged from a mess of Crimean proportions only by the innate spirit of their soldiers and junior officers, the battleworthiness of the Parachute Regiment and the dogged gallantry of the Scots Guards on Tumbledown Mountain.

Dug in as we were on the rear slopes of Bluff Cove Peak, we could not see the disaster at Fitzroy, where the Argentine Air Force reminded us again that they could bite and bombed *Sir Galahad* and *Sir Tristram*. However, if one walked a short distance to the top of the ridge, one could see the smoke rising from the burning ships. The detailed chain of events which led to those ships being bombed in an enemy air attack has been trawled over by many others, most authoritatively and comprehensively by Michael Clapp and Ewen Southby-Tailyour in their book, *Amphibious Assault Falklands*. But in reality, it was a disaster which could have happened at almost any time and could have been a great deal worse. The presence of a TV film crew seems to have inflated the significance of this incident as it almost always does. The course of the war was not materially affected. War is a constant balancing of risks and decisions have to be taken based on incomplete, uncertain and even wrong information. It is inevitable, therefore, that the dice does not always roll in your favour. But we felt for the Welsh Guards. There, but for the grace of God, could have been us or any one of a number of units before we landed. After this, the Chinese crews of some of the surviving logistic ships at Teal Inlet would come ashore during the day whenever they could.

By 11 June, all was ready and in the morning we were called to receive our orders for our attack that night. The Brigade plan was to attack the outer ring of three hills on the approach to Stanley. In the north, 3 Para would attack Mount Longdon. In the middle, 45 Commando would take the Two Sisters, and in the south 42 Commando would capture Mount Harriet. Each unit would be ready to exploit forward to the next range of hills if the opportunity presented itself. 2 Para would be in reserve, ready to reinforce or exploit as required.

With the aid of a model of the ground, improvised with stones, string, rifle slings and other sundry bits and pieces that came to hand, Colonel Whitehead gave his orders for the attack on Two Sisters. The hills themselves are two parallel dragon's back-like features on an east–west axis. The northern Sister is divided into two features, of which the west is the higher. The southern Sister on the other hand got progressively higher

127

as one went eastwards, finishing in a rocky, precipitous 1,000 ft peak. This was therefore the highest of all the hills that were fought for during the war. It is also the more westerly of the Sisters and was therefore nearer to our line of approach. The saddle between the Two Sisters is about 1,000 m across.

Like all good military plans, that for the attack on Two Sisters was simple. In fact, the ground gave us little alternative. The feature offered three fairly clear company objectives. From the information we had received from Brigade intelligence, and from what we had gleaned from our patrols and observation posts, it appeared that the two hills were held by a reinforced company. There would probably be two platoons on the northern feature and one on the southern. It was suggested that there might even be only a strong standing patrol on the southern feature at night, but I could see no good reason for that notion. We had already encountered and killed a force greater than a standing patrol there. In similar circumstances, I would have reinforced it, not reduced it. We could expect the Argentines to be supported by artillery and mortars, machine guns and anti-tank weapons. We had seen some of the machine-gun positions and it wasn't difficult to work out where the others might be. One would normally expect barbed wire to be in abundance in such a defensive position, but none had been found. The Geneva Convention requires that when one lays minefields, one marks them with wire and signs. One minefield was reportedly in the vicinity of the northern Sister. We had looked for, but not found any minefields. That did not mean that there weren't any. It would be prudent to assume that there were. We were also told of the possibility of some kind of wire-fired underground mine on the saddle between the two main features, that had been observed by a Mountain and Arctic Warfare Cadre observation post on Goat Ridge. There was, in addition, a separate company from a different regiment on the north-east shoulder of the north Sister. It had been there before the other company occupied the Two Sisters and apparently covered the Murrel valley towards Mount Longdon. We did not know if it had been integrated into the defensive plans for Two Sisters, but we had to assume that it might be able to influence the battle.

X Ray Company was given the southernmost Sister as its objective. Zulu Company, commanded by Mike Cole, was to capture the nearer western part of the northern Sister, and Yankee Company, commanded by Richard Davis, would take the further eastern part. Because the southern Sister was detached and closer, a three-phase operation suggested itself. Moreover, once the southern Sister was in X Ray's hands, it would be possible to attack the northern Sister without interference from the south. The approaches fell into place nicely. X Ray would come direct from the west, and start the attack at 0100 hrs GMT – 9.00 pm local time. Meanwhile, Zulu and Yankee would march off to the north and approach from that direction with Commando Tactical Headquarters. Zulu Company would attack the western end of the north Sister at 0300 hrs GMT – 11.00 pm local time. That would give X Ray Company two hours to capture the southern Sister. Even if that had not been achieved, the enemy on the southern Sister should be too preoccupied with X Ray to be able to provide significant support to the northern Sister. Once Zulu had done their stuff, Yankee Company would follow through to capture the eastern end.

Enemy fields of view and fire throughout the Falklands were long and clear, and long before we arrived in the South Atlantic, it was assumed that all battles of choice would be fought at night. The supply of artillery ammunition would be a top priority, but still there would never be enough to support a long approach and a battle, so we expected our battles to start silently, with the artillery and mortars on call for when the shooting started. So it was with Two Sisters. A fire-plan was prepared, ready to implement on call. Incidentally, it was given the nickname of 'Iron Lady' in honour of Prime Minister Margaret Thatcher – Derek Dalrymple sent a copy to the Iron Lady herself after the war and got a personal reply.

By dividing the battle into three consecutive phases, each attack would be able to benefit from the concentration of all the artillery, rather than spreading it out between concurrent attacks. In addition to our six Royal Artillery 105mm guns, we would have HMS *Glamorgan* supporting us with her two 4.5 inch weapons. Her guns would be directed by the naval gunfire observation team led by Captain Chris Brown, another artillery officer whom we had got to know well, and who had a busy and gallant war going from one battle to another performing this important task. The support of *Glamorgan*'s guns – the equivalent of an additional battery – was a powerful and most welcome addition to our firepower. The commanding officer of *Glamorgan* was Captain Mike Barrow and I knew him well. He had been the captain of HMS *Diomede* when I had served in her and it was very good to know that my old boss and his ship would be out there supporting us. That was the good news. The bad news was that she would have to leave the gun line in order to be out of range of land-based aircraft by daylight. This meant she would have to stop firing at around 2.45 am local time – 0645 hrs GMT – about four hours before first light. Moreover, we knew that the Argentines had a land-based Exocet missile on a flatbed trailer on the airport road, waiting to hit targets like *Glamorgan*. *Glamorgan* would be firing from a position south and west of Stanley, but so long as she kept the strip of land at Seal Point between her and the missile, she should be shielded from this danger. So there was all the more reason to finish our battles as quickly as possible. Time would be of the essence.

In addition, X Ray Company was to have the Anti-tank Troop of 40 Commando, equipped with Milan missiles and commanded by Lieutenant Steve Hughes, attached to us for the battle. Our own Milan missiles had been destroyed in the bombing at Ajax Bay and 40 Commando was not involved in any of the battles that night, so this was an excellent task for them. The Milan missile was a wire-guided device with a maximum range of 2,000 metres. We were not expecting tanks but the Milan could be a very powerful bunker-buster. It had no night sight, but with some creative use of torches and by observing the tracer from our machine guns, Steve Hughes and his men would make a most important contribution to the battle. I was also given a section of Royal Engineers led by Lance Corporal 'Floyd' Paterson, in case I encountered barbed wire or a minefield.

Regimental Sergeant Major Pat Chapman ensured that we had all the ammunition we required and the necessary arrangements for casualty evacuation and ammunition resupply were dealt with. Then Colonel Whitehead discussed all the likely possibilities with us. What would we do if X Ray got stuck? What would we do if Zulu or Yankee got stuck? We brainstormed it. It was his intention that, if all went well, we would maintain the momentum of the attack and carry on to attack Tumbledown Mountain that night too. He invited us into his head and, by the end of this discussion, we had the clearest possible impression of what he and the Brigade commander wanted of us, and why. We understood the priorities and the constraints that we were all working under, such as limited time and limited artillery ammunition. In this way, we felt confident that we would know what to do whatever eventually presented itself, including the demise of the commanding officer. In his book, *The Rules of the Game*, Andrew Gordon says that Horatio Nelson's 'greatest gift of leadership was to raise his juniors above the need of supervision.' No one can supervise anybody effectively during a battle in the dark and the first thing that breaks down during a battle is communications. Everything depends on trust. However, Andrew Whitehead made quite sure that we were equipped to take decisions which would match his and the Brigade commander's intentions, whatever unforeseen circumstances might arise. Nobody would not know what to do.

By attacking in darkness, we might also give ourselves the benefit of surprise. Man is not naturally a nocturnal animal and the normal place for a man during the dark is in his bed. A man who is not in bed at one o'clock in the morning has usually been got out of it and is looking forward to getting back into it. Because he can't see very well in the dark, he is more easily frightened. Coordination and movement are much more difficult; confusion, chaos and failure lurk within arm's length on night operations. All night operations are incipient CMFUs. But with experience and training, men can learn to make darkness their friend. The attacker in any operation normally has the initiative. In a night attack, if he knows what he's doing, his initiative is all the greater. But it does require highly trained troops working to a simple, flexible plan. The Duke of Wellington was fond of comparing his plans with those of the French. French plans, he said, were like a harness. They were elegant and elaborate, but when they broke it was difficult to improvise. His plans on the other hand were more like a piece of old rope. When that broke, he simply tied another knot in it.

Colonel Andrew Whitehead's plan was simple and robust. My two concerns were: first, that I thought our intelligence had underestimated the strength of the enemy on the position. I turned out to be right, but there was nothing we could do about it and it made no difference. Second, I was also concerned about the moon. A half moon would rise just before the time when we were due to attack. We might find ourselves crossing the open stretch of ground between our start point and the bottom of the objective in moonlight. If we were seen before we hit the objective, we could start taking heavy casualties from the Argentine Browning .50 machine guns before we could get enough artillery down on the ground to make a difference. However, as mentioned above, Colonel Whitehead had given me 40 Commando's Milan missiles to shoot us in. I would site them at our start line to cover our advance across the 1,000 metres of open ground. Under my direct control, they could provide instantaneous support. In a shoot-out between a Milan and a Browning, I'd back the Milan, provided the firer could see the target. If we could just get a toe-hold in the rocks at the bottom western end of the Sister, the Argentines would never get us out.

Taking all this in, I made my plans and prepared my orders. I brainstormed some ideas with Sergeant Major Bell. He suggested that we put a fire team out on our left flank as we approached and as we moved up the mountain. If we were discovered before we got into the rocks, having the ability to shoot from the flank could help get us out of trouble. And if we got stuck working up the narrow dragon's back, it might help to unlock the battle. An excellent idea, I thought, and who better to command the flank fire team than the Sergeant Major himself.

I gave each troop its own particular portion of the Company objective. James Kelly and 1 Troop had the lower end. They were to lead the assault. James had also scouted out the route for me and would navigate us from our patrol base to our start line, about 1,000 metres short of the objective. With the responsibility of leading across the open ground and breaking in, 1 Troop would potentially have the most dangerous and difficult job of all. Once they were in, I would send 3 Troop with David Stewart through them to take the middle section, then Chris Caröe with 2 Troop to take the top. The Sergeant Major, with his heavy weapons section of six machine guns, all three of our 84mm Carl Gustav anti-tank weapons and a slack handful of bunker-busting 66mm, would move parallel and 200 metres to the north of the lead troop, and support all three troops in turn.

With all the attachments, the company was now 150 strong. My headquarters was in danger of becoming unwieldy, so I cut it down to my artillery and mortar controllers, two signallers and a couple of others. Phil Witcombe would look after the rest. I and my streamlined head-quarters would follow behind the lead troop at each stage. I would carry the company command net radio and Marine Chadwick or Corporal Morrison would carry the unit command net.

If we hit mines, we would simply have to press on. Casualties would be left behind. Captain Dennis Gillson, commanding Headquarters Company, also came with X Ray Company with a team of his men. His designated task was to establish the nucleus of Commando Head-quarters if we advanced on to Tumbledown. In the event, he would not be required for this task, but just having him there with his men was an excellent insurance against the unexpected. It was good to know that Dennis and his team would follow up behind the leading troops and attend to casualties if necessary, and during the battle they earned their keep handsomely by acting as a radio relay station when communica-tions broke down between the key elements of the Commando. Before the day was out, Dennis would also find himself clearing mines and burying the Argentine dead.

Much thought had also gone into ensuring that we would not have to wait long for ammunition resupply and casualty evacuation. Major Rupert van der Horst, the Commando second-in-command, and Regimental Sergeant Major Pat Chapman, would bring three over-snow vehicles right forward behind the companies, ready to replenish us immediately on demand after the battle.

The Commando chaplain, the Reverend Wynne Jones, was going to join us. Afterwards, he told me that he had chosen to come with X Ray Company because he thought we would take the most casualties. Had he told me this at the time, I might have agreed with him; although I might not have thanked him for the encouragement. Royal Naval chaplains are unusual in that, in a hierarchical military organisation, they carry no rank. They are simply chaplains. Charged with being 'a friend and advisor to all on board' they share the rank of whoever they are speaking to. The accessibility this gives them is unique. Personalities remain important of course, but the good ones use this precious gift

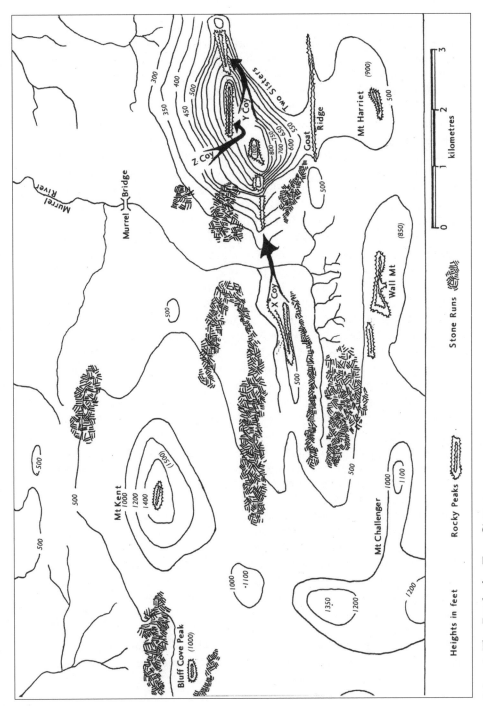

Map 4. The Battle for Two Sisters

to great advantage. All chaplains serving with the Commandos have to pass the Commando Course and win their Green Beret, and there is a tendency for some remarkable characters to gravitate to the Royal Marines. Wynne Jones was one of these. His presence had a curious effect. X Ray Company was as impious a group of young men as one might meet anywhere and there were few who would have confessed allegiance to any formal religion. And yet it is only 'religion' which addresses the question of what happens to you after you die. It has been said, 'there are no atheists in the trenches'. This is an over-simplistic way to describe the many and various ways in which men cope with the possibility of death on the battlefield, but certainly, the notion that death might not be the end is an appealing one when the possibility becomes real. So, to have this man of God in our midst was a wonderful source of comfort. Some chaplains believe their job is to evangelise among their flock, or to be ready to comfort the wounded. The wounded and the dead are certainly their concern, but in fact their primary function is the same as everyone else's who is in support, or in the chain of the command: to help marines to do their jobs. The chaplain's real job is to offer spiritual support to men facing death in battle, thereby helping them to fight. This can only be done *before* they are shot. Wynne was famous for saying, 'I'm interested in the living, not the dead.' How much of it was Wynne's personality, and how much was the idea that his presence somehow lent an air of legitimacy and respectability to our endeavours is difficult to say. But for sure, his presence was highly beneficial and we thought the world of him. We were very proud that our chaplain had come into battle with us, unarmed, but carrying a rucksack full of useful things, like first field dressings, saline drips and cigarettes. All chaplains or ministers should be present where and whenever their flock needs them most and that is precisely where Wynne was.

Like the commanding officer, I used an improvised model of the ground to deliver my orders. I explained the plan in detail to my troop commanders and to their section commanders. I wanted to make as sure as I could that every single man knew what I knew. Success would depend upon each man knowing what our mission was, and playing his part in support of that mission, without necessarily referring to his boss. They were each going to have to make many decisions that night in my name. The better informed they were, the better equipped they would be. Moreover, commanders get killed in battle. Everyone must be prepared to take over from their boss, if the boss goes down. This might mean not just one level, but even two levels up. There are plenty of instances in history where NCOs ended up commanding companies, or junior officers commanding battalions.

After I had delivered my orders, everyone went off to conduct his own planning and orders process. On completion, I found a piece of ground roughly comparable to the hill we were going to attack and we conducted rehearsals. Not everyone has the time or opportunity to do this, but if one can, one should. Like a circus ringmaster or a dancing instructor, I got them on the ground and shouted everyone through the various phases of the operation. I threw a number of 'what ifs' at them.

'1 Troop, you are approaching your objective and there is no one there. What are you going to do?'

'Anti-tank Troop; the mist has come down and you can't see the tracer or torches. How are you going to direct your missiles?'

'Corporal So-and-so, your troop commander is dead, you are now troop commander, your troop is stuck; how are you going to call for artillery? Now do it.'

And so on. A grand conversation started between groups and individuals. There was no joviality now. Every thought and word was concentrated on the job in hand, and directed at the mission. All the 'actions on', all the 'what ifs' were played out time and time again. 'What will we do if we get shot at from over there?' 'What will we do if we get stuck here?' In this way, we all got a picture into our heads of how things might pan out on the night. Nothing would go to plan, of course, but any picture is better than no picture. Each man knew where the other troops and sections would be, thus helping to avoid blue-on-blues. He would know who was at his side, who was covering his back and whose back he was watching. I would have liked to have conducted night rehearsals too, but they are much more difficult to organise and would have required the use of radios. Any transmission would, at the very least, have aroused the suspicions of the Argentines. Besides, we didn't have time.

The distance to our start line was about 6 kilometres. We had done a reconnaissance of the route. I judged that the journey could be done in two hours, possibly three. I allowed four hours. So we would leave at 2100 hrs GMT – 5.00 pm local – about an hour after last light.

Now we were on our own. Earlier in the afternoon, Yankee and Zulu Companies, together with Commando Headquarters, had left the patrol base to march to a position where they would be able to approach the Two Sisters from the north in the dark. Before they left, Marine Howie Watson and Marine Dave O'Connor had seen Regimental Sergeant Major Pat Chapman nearby. Both Watson and O'Connor were the sort of warriors whom Kipling undoubtedly had in mind, when he said that single men in barracks don't grow into plaster saints. Both had serious disciplinary cases pending before we left Scotland. Technically, I should have left them behind, but both were machine gunners and I was loathe to dispense with their abilities and enthusiasm in the field. Watson caught the Regimental Sergeant Major's attention and respectfully asked him if there was any news of their case. Pat Chapman replied calmly, 'If you two fuckers are still alive tomorrow, you are both going to prison.'

We finished our evening meal as the light faded. In that short hour, after our preparations were complete and before we marched off, I had time to reflect upon what we were about to face. It is not easy to describe one's feelings before one is committed to battle. Fear certainly plays a part, but it is not fear of death itself. It is more a sadness about the grief among one's family that would follow one's death. As the Company Commander responsible for the lives of some 150 men, I felt unutterably lonely, in spite of being surrounded by many wonderful people. This is the so called 'loneliness of command' and I had experienced it before, but not to this intensity. I found that I didn't want anyone to speak to me. But every individual felt lonely in his own way, each in his own little bubble, wanting only himself for company. I spent my hour smoking a cigar and preparing myself to accept whatever the night might bring.

In Northern Ireland or Oman, going out on operations, you were never sure if you were going to encounter the enemy or not. One hoped it would happen, and that it would be on one's own terms, but in reality contact was comparatively rare. The frame of mind as one left base was therefore that of a fisherman – will we catch anything tonight? How very different is the train of thought of the man committed to a set-piece battle, where he knows that ferocious and lethal contact with the enemy is an imminent certainty. A man about to go into battle is prey to many thoughts. He may be concerned about being killed or wounded. Has he seen his last daylight? How many of his friends will not live till morning? If he is wounded, how much will it hurt? Will he be crippled? What will happen to his family in either case? What happens if he is taken prisoner? If he is killed, what happens to him after death? But most important of all, will he find the courage to give a good account of himself, or will he bottle out and become an object of scorn for his fellows, the men whose respect he values most? As for the commander, he can in addition be assailed by worries about the soundness of the plan and the heavy responsibility for the lives that depend upon his ability and, above all, his strength of will. Will it be a CMFU or will you get away with something less?

All these thoughts and more, coursed uninvited through my head as I smoked my cigar during that final hour before we set off on our approach march to our start line. I found myself not only thinking of my wife and my family whom I hoped I would see again, preferably in this world, but if not then perhaps in the next; but also of friends who had already been killed or died whom I might also see again. This extended even to those like my father-in-law and my grandparents, whom I had never met. There was nothing morbid about this; on the contrary, these were comforting thoughts. Not being overly religious myself, the wish in my case was doubtless father to the thought, but I could see, not for the first time, what strength and comfort could be afforded by a strong religious belief. 'Pray for me,' wrote Sir Thomas More to his daughter Margaret Roper shortly before he was executed, 'and I will pray for you, and for all your friends, that we may merrily meet in Heaven.' What a glorious idea: and so in my time of need, I rather surreptitiously stapled myself to Thomas More's coat tails, batted all my worries and fears out of sight, and set off cheerfully at the head of my beloved X Ray Company, resolved to kill the Queen's enemies, or die myself in the attempt.

Chapter 7

Fighting

He gave her his townhouse and his racing horses,
Each meal she ate was a dozen courses.

The march to the forming up position from which we were to start our assault was a near nightmare. It was relatively easy ground and we knew the way. I had estimated it might take us three hours and had allowed an hour spare. It took us six hours. In the first place, I had not appreciated how much the Milan missiles would slow us down. Each man carried his own weapon and equipment – on average about 80 lbs. But we also carried 40 Milan missiles and they weighed about 30 lbs each. A piece of rock or a small stream which a man in normal fighting order would barely have noticed became a major obstacle. Soon after we started, a thick mist descended. This would have been a godsend if it had come later when we were crossing open ground, but now while trying to find our way it was a curse. My navigation team and I became confused and did not take the planned route. Instead, we found our-selves on the wrong side of a stone run. This was a major obstacle and it took ages to cross it safely. We eventually got to our start line by cutting the Gordian knot and taking the most direct route, but not before we had stumbled and cursed our way over rocks, cliffs and bogs for half the night. The Company was constantly being split up. I managed to lose half the Company on two occasions and wasted further time and energy going back to look for them. One of my key signallers became violently ill soon after we left base. He was crapping and vomiting at the same time. There was no point in him carrying on. We left him near an artillery battery. He would have to make his way to it himself when he could. Once the battery started firing, he would find it easily enough. Another man, Marine Jones, was knocked unconscious by his equipment when

138

he fell over a bluff. Phil Witcombe managed to resuscitate him and he bravely carried on. It had been intended that radio silence would be imposed until the assault. I broke this, judging that the risk of Argentine interception was less than the risk of not getting there at all. Had I not, we might still have been there today, little groups of men bumbling around East Falkland, still trying to find each other. However, I delayed telling the commanding officer of our difficulties until the last safe moment. We had no secure radios at company level. My messages to my company trying to find the missing bits were, I hoped, interpretable as yet another patrol. Any message to Commando Tactical Headquarters explaining our difficulties could only have one meaning.

We arrived at the forming up point for our attack two hours late, about the same time that Zulu and Yankee Companies were due to start their attacks. As I have pointed out before, no plan survives first contact with the enemy and once again mine hadn't even survived that far. We were now 150 very fed up, tired men and the real work of the night had yet to begin. But it is miraculous where reserves of energy can come from. I called Andrew Whitehead on the radio and told him briefly what had happened. I would not have been surprised if he had given me a very frosty reply. Instead, he was completely calm and patient and said something to the effect of, 'OK. Sort yourselves out. Tell me when you are ready. I will do nothing until I hear from you, then we will go together.' He then gave orders for Zulu and Yankee to go to ground and await further orders. He also rearranged the artillery fire-plan with Gerry Akhurst, as it would no longer be possible to concentrate our artillery assets on three consecutive battles. This simple act demonstrating patience, trust and understanding was enough to soothe my raddled nerves. I was able to turn quietly round to my own people and say, 'Put the last six hours behind you. Sort yourselves out, tell me when you are ready, and we'll crack on.' Ten minutes later, 150 knackered marines were as good as new.

I wondered whether I should give the order to fix bayonets. I decided against it thinking that wriggling around and through the rocks in the dark, the bayonet would get in the way. However, the troop commanders were much more sensible. James Kelly, anticipating a close-quarters fight in the rocks, whispered the order to 1 Troop to fix bayonets and they all quietly did so. This supremely functional act was, of course, not without its symbolism. The final seal upon our preparations, it linked us with numberless soldiers of previous generations in a thousand battles, who conducted a similar final act before committing themselves to the manifold unknowns that lay before them. David and Chris also ordered 'fix bayonets' before engaging their respective positions.

I gave the order to go, and James Kelly set off with 1 Troop on their dangerous journey towards the Murrel River, across the 1,000 metres that separated us from the bottom of the objective. Sergeant Major Bell and his fire team took a parallel course 200 yards to his left. The Anti-tank Troop was ready to put instant fire down and the mortars and artillery were primed to fire smoke shells. Nevertheless, I watched them through my binoculars with my heart in my mouth and my stomach in knots. Visibility was now good – far too good. The moon had risen making the journey even more hazardous still. They reached the stream halfway and then I lost them. I committed Lieutenant David Stewart with 3 Troop off on their journey across the open ground and followed them with my headquarters. I was sufficiently apprehensive to whisper to Wynne Jones: 'Pray for our souls, Vicar. Pray for our souls.'

'I won't need to,' he said. 'I won't need to.'

The sound of a crump of artillery came from over to our left. This was not aimed at us. In fact, it didn't seem to be aimed at anybody: it was speculative Argentine firing that very nearly hit the jackpot. It landed in front of Zulu, Yankee and Commando Tactical Headquarters, just where they would have been if they had not stopped to wait for X Ray. Then I saw and heard a machine gun opening up from near the top of our objective. The tracer arced across to the northern Sister. So, the battle had started. Please God, I thought, just let James Kelly and 1 Troop get into the rocks before it starts here!

The sound of that machine gun was unmistakable. I had used the .5 inch Browning in Oman. The Browning was originally designed shortly after the First World War but has been in service somewhere on land, at sea or in the air ever since. The man who designed it, John Moses Browning of Utah, was born back in 1855. In spite of that, the Browning remained, and remains still, a superb weapon, in no way obsolete. It is accurate to about 2,000 metres and can pump its half-inch calibre slug out to nearly 7,000 metres. This beast is in service today with the British forces, although we had none in service at that time. So it has been around for nearly ninety years, with the prospect of many more yet to come. Now, we were to be at the receiving end, but I did not think that, from where it seemed to be, it would be able to depress sufficiently to hit us once we were in the rocks at the bottom of the objective. No doubt the enemy would have other machine guns there, but their chance to use them to maximum effect was rapidly slipping away. James and 1 Troop were almost there. Once they were in, it would be a gutter fight in the dark which we would surely win.

With my headquarters and 3 Troop, I reached the Murrel River and started to cross. It was too wide to jump so I had to wade. It was surprisingly deep and came halfway up my thighs. It was bitterly cold.

140

James Kelly then told me what I had been hoping against hope to hear: he was secure in the rocks and had met no opposition. He consolidated his troop, on my instructions, on the bottom third of the feature. It was now only a matter of time and at what cost. I dispatched 3 Troop through 1 Troop and followed through with my headquarters. David Stewart and his men worked their way up the dragon's back and soon he told me that his objective, the second third of the hill, was clear. He asked permission to exploit forward to the top. This I readily gave. Time was of the essence, and anything that sped things up was all to the good. Time seems to pass very quickly during a battle. It felt like only a few minutes since we had left the start line but was probably more like an hour.

3 Troop was halfway up the 1,500-metre-long objective when they ran into our first opposition. They had been seen by two machine guns near the top of the ridge. Any attempt to close with them drew rifle fire from the right-hand side. They tried to move up the left side but came under fire from the northern Sister, where Yankee and Zulu were engaged in a major battle. In fact it was probably from a Browning on the saddle between the Two Sisters. I thought of masking off the northern Sister with smoke, but mortar smoke shells throw out burning white phosphorus. This is very nasty if you are near it, and I was not entirely sure where the Sergeant Major was. I decided to pull 3 Troop back and wallop the top with artillery and mortars, then send Lieutenant Chris Caröe in with 2 Troop. While 2 Troop was moving up, I decided to see what we could do with the Milan missiles and invited them to have a go. It would mean firing at near maximum range over our heads but it would help to fill the gap before the artillery arrived. Steve Hughes and his men estimated where we were from the tracer of our machine guns, and from the Argentine tracer they could guess where the enemy machine guns probably were. The first round was fired. It's a strange thing having an anti-tank missile fired over your head at night. We could see it coming towards us, quite slowly it seemed, a bright light, making a curious spluttering, farting noise very unlike what I expected. It took about a quarter of a minute to arrive and it sounded almost friendly. It looked as if it was going to hit us and we all ducked involuntarily as it passed about 30 feet over our heads and produced the most satisfactory bang on impact.

Soon 2 Troop were ready. I had asked Captain Alasdair Cameron to bring an artillery fire mission on to the top of the hill and Corporal Andrew Foster to bring down a mortar stonk immediately in front of us. In the dark, halfway up the hill, one could never be sure precisely where one was and I was disinclined to spend too much time with a torch looking at the map. But the enemy we were trying to suppress was between 100 and 300 yards further up the hill. Corporal Foster and I agreed a grid reference – our own grid reference plus 100 yards. However, given the degree of accuracy and the beaten zone of the 81mm mortar, we were in effect about to mortar ourselves. I shouted to anyone who could hear, that eight mortar rounds were coming in – to get down, count the rounds, and after eight, get up and go.

By now it had begun to snow. As I lay there waiting for mortars and artillery, smoking yet another cigarette in a hole, it occurred to me how depressingly familiar our grandfathers, and their grandfathers, would have found this battle. Young men under fire, scrambling up a rocky hill in a snowstorm in the dark, bayonets fixed, trying to find other young men and kill them: a scene which has repeated itself hundreds of times in the Second and First World Wars, the Boer War, the Crimea and in a thousand imperial skirmishes. All that technology has done over the years has been to extend the range at which some people can engage the other side. Nevertheless, there always remains the imperative for someone to close with the enemy and bayonet him if necessary. When it comes down to it, war is a nasty, vicious gutter fight where you try to exploit any advantage to gouge the other side's eyes out. In spite of the onset of technology, men still fight each other with clubs and pointed sticks.

The mortar shells soon came crashing down, mostly where we wanted them. Corporal Foster had done a good job and none of our people were hit. But Alasdair was having trouble getting artillery. Artillery is allocated according to priorities. The original plan gave X Ray priority for our attack on the southern Sister. This would then switch to Zulu and Yankee when they started their attack. Since the shooting had actually started first on Zulu's attack, the priority had switched to the northern Sister before we had fired a shot. Because we had been late arriving on the objective, the batteries were now all engaged on the other Sister. It was nobody's fault, although Alasdair was feeling pretty frustrated. It was just another change in plan. I asked Corporal Foster to repeat the mortar stonk. But then the mortars struck problems as, with the recoil, their baseplates disappeared into the bog. The nature of the topography had dictated the siting of the mortars and they were firing at the limit of their range and on maximum charge. The ground consisted of peaty, soft soil mixed with boulders. In spite of extensive preparation of the baseplates, the mortars ended up bending two bipods and buckling three or four baseplates due to the forces involved.

Meanwhile, the mortar troop was able to support us with one solitary mortar instead of six, while they dug out the baseplates. In retrospect, I should have tried harder to wrestle some artillery support from Commando Tactical Headquarters. Over a thousand rounds of artillery were eventually fired during the Two Sisters battle by 29 Commando and *Glamorgan,* not one of which was fired in support of X Ray. At this moment, Caröe's men could have done with something to keep the Argentines' heads down as they closed with them up the hill. But hindsight is the only exact science. The Sergeant Major's heavy weapons group out to the left might have been able to support a fight on the lower reaches of the hill, but up here it was too steep for them to be able to help. I ordered another fusillade of Milan anti-tank missiles, and two or three came in as before, smack on target. Several more missiles came crashing in at the extremity of their range during the course of the battle. Being a wire-guided missile, there was a risk that if we fired it beyond the range of the wires they would snap and the missile could go rogue amongst ourselves. But since this, and one solitary mortar, was all the support we were going to get, it was a risk I was willing to take. I told Caröe to get up there and kill the enemy and he and his men went up the hill to the echo.

It was an impressive performance. Not only were the enemy using an anti-tank weapon, they now brought artillery down on our hill. Some shells landed among the rocks and exploded stone fragments as well as shrapnel. Others landed on the few bits of bog between the rocks. It was one of the latter which blew over Marine Howie Watson and Lance Corporal Montgomery. It picked them up and threw them several yards but miraculously they lived. Watson was deaf and stunned, with blood pouring from a shrapnel wound in his nose, but otherwise unharmed. Montgomery had dislocated his shoulder, but the skin was unbroken. In the course of trying to find a wound, Sergeant George Matthews cut through his shirt, a non-service issue Norwegian arctic garment which Monty had paid for himself. Later, he complained about the destruction of the shirt.

Caröe's men picked and clambered their way round, up and over the rocks. It was like fighting in a built up area, or in a bombed city: two men cover; one jumps round or over; leapfrogging all the way. They stumbled across a number of bodies and bits of bodies. Our Milan missile strikes and our mortar fire had been on target. The Troop soon encountered two machine guns, near the top of the hill at the far side of a relatively open piece of ground. They were crossing a ridge line when the machine guns opened up from 200 yards away. The Browning on the saddle to their left opened up too. However, it is not unusual for inexperienced troops to fire high at night, especially when they are shooting downhill. This saved the lead section led by Corporal Frank Melia, the .5 inch bullets crashing over their heads, but into the area of my headquarters further down the hill, spattering Chaplain Wynne Jones with debris. The Troop was now pinned down and under artillery fire, which was also landing among my headquarters. When taking cover, some men found they had dived so hard into clefts in the rocks that they were wedged in and couldn't get out again without removing their equipment. Bullet ricochets, shell splinters and fragments of rocks flew everywhere around my headquarters, so it felt as if we were in the thick of the battle too.

Moreover, Zulu and Yankee seemed to be stuck on the other Sister and were being hit by one of the .5 inch Brownings on the saddle near the top of our hill. We all seemed to be losing momentum. However, Corporal Melia noted with pride that his men were going through the correct contact drills, as his section automatically began to locate the enemy and deliver accurate target indication. As they continued to suppress the enemy and win the fire-fight, he considered his options for mounting an assault. He decided to crawl forward up a gully to his left to check his angle of approach. He had covered no more than 30 metres, when he heard Chris Caröe frantically calling him back. He quickly retraced his steps and discovered that Caröe was about to direct mortar fire on to the enemy position.

Chris Caröe, in an attempt to get things moving, took three men up another gully, including his radio operator Marine Graham Adcock who was correcting the fall of the mortar as he went, but they came back down again pretty quickly, pursued by bursts of tracer. Caröe then fired his tracer rounds at a target to show Marine Dave O'Connor, the GPMG gunner, an enemy gun location. After firing eight rounds no one had spotted the fall of shot. It was only the next morning, when he paced it out, he realised it had only been 90 metres to the target. Tracer starts burning at 110 metres.

The enemy machine gunners were clearly supported by a number of riflemen. The weapon the Argentine riflemen used was the Belgian Fabrique Nationale 7.62mm rifle, very similar to our own Self Loading Rifle. Theirs was a version which could fire on automatic. A burst of 20 rounds from a FN was not very accurate, but at such close range it didn't have to be. The stalemate was eventually broken by Marine O'Connor and Marine Alex Gibb. A moment earlier Gibb had been ordered forward with his LMG by Sergeant George Matthews, to join the lead section. He had run forward in the face of machine gun bullets splattering the rocks around him. O'Connor, an experienced and skilled machine gunner, took his GPMG to an exposed position and, with Gibb, duelled it out with the Argentine machine gunner. O'Connor won. At the same time, Marine Nick Taylor took advantage of the distraction to fire a 66mm, hand-held anti-tank weapon at the machine-gun position. It went straight over the top followed by a sardonic cheer from the troop. Taylor threw away the empty and shouted for another, which was

4. This bivouac or 'bivvie' would be accommodation for one or two men. A deluxe version can be seen left rear. (*James Kelly*)

5. The Two Sisters from the south west. The nearest Sister was X Ray Company's objective. (*Author*)

36. A 155mm shell hole. The bog absorbed much of the impact, but when they landed in the rocks, shrapnel and rock fragments flew everywhere. (*Author*)

37. Argentine prisoners captured by Yankee and Zulu Companies on the northern Sister. (*Malcolm Duck*)

8. This was the ground that 45 Commando fought through in a snow storm in the dark. (*Malcolm Duck*)

9. The Author after the Two Sisters battle. (*James Kelly*)

40. *L to R.* The Author, Lt Phil Witcombe. On the morning of 14 June, preliminary orders to attack Sapper Hill have just been received. Final rapid preparations are being completed before an 11km sprint to battle. Confirmatory orders would be received and distributed by radio on the move. (*Wynne Jones*)

41. The sprint to Sapper Hill from Two Sisters on 14 June. Wireless Ridge stretches from left to right, Port Stanley and the harbour are in the centre. Tumbledown on the right is still smoking after the Scots Guards' night battle. Note the snow on the ground. Sapper Hill was in the event taken by the time we got there. (*Malcolm Duck*)

2. The arrival of 45 Commando in Stanley. (*Trustees of the Royal Marines Museum*)

3. X Ray Company arrives in Stanley. *L to R* Cpl Tom Morrison, Capt Alasdair Cameron, Author, CSM Charles Bell, L/Bdr Barry Ingleson. (*Trustees of the Royal Marines Museum*)

44. Stanley was a mess. Argentine soldiers seemed to be everywhere ... (*Trustees of the Royal Marines Museum*)

45. ... and so was their equipment. (*Trustees of the Royal Marines Museum*)

46. It being not immediately clear that the Argentine Air Force had accepted the surrender, some unarmed ships were equipped with captured modern anti-aircraft guns. (*James Kelly*)

47. These Exocet missiles had been removed from an Argentine warship, and the flatbed trailer adapted into a very effective improvised land based launcher. It was this system which hit HMS *Glamorgan* after she had supported 45 Commando. (*Trustees of the Royal Marines Museum*)

48. The Commander of 3 Commando Brigade, Brigadier Julian Thompson, arriving in Stanley. As the Landing Force Commander before and during the landings, and for the first critical battles, his plans and his leadership shaped the whole land campaign. Major General Jeremy Moore dubbed him 'Man of the Match'. The journalists Patrick Bishop and Robert Fox are behind him.
(*Trustees of the Royal Marines Museum*)

49. Many Royal Marines were delighted to find that their journey ended at a pub called the Globe Hotel. (*Graham Adcock*)

tossed to him. He fired and it hit close to the target; followed by more cheers, this time of approbation. The 66mm has a danger area to the rear of the weapon, where anyone caught in the back blast is liable to injury, and the men around Taylor were well within it. Their only course of action was to bury their heads in the rocks and stick their backsides in the air, twice. Fortunately the only damage was singed trousers. The machine gun stopped long enough for men of 2 Troop to sprint across the remaining 150 yards and get in among the rocks beneath the machine gun's field of fire.

Now it was back to street fighting again. Caröe called for his 2-inch mortarman to put some rounds down. The firing pin broke after the first round. It seemed that mortars and X Company were just not meant to be. Chris Caröe then called Marine Adcock and Marine Gibb to follow him, as the rest of Corporal Frank Melia's section put down a hail of fire. All three sprinted the last 70 metres to the gun position and saw the last defenders running away down a gully to the right. Alex Gibb fired off a magazine of the LMG and Caröe followed that with a grenade. There was a scream of pain and, the following morning, a rifle covered with blood was found with a trail of blood leading across the rocks down the hill, but no body. The rest of the troop then worked their way up to join Caröe, Gibb and Adcock, clearing bunkers they found on the way. Adcock spotted a camp of tents below and to the left of the position and two grenades were thrown, after which it was left alone as the climb down was unclear and steep in the dark. Although the immediate position was cleared, the Browning on the saddle was still in action. Caröe ordered two more 66s and the firing stopped. At dawn, a severely wounded Argentine soldier was found next to his .50 Browning.

Soon those Argentines who could, withdrew, leaving hot machine guns and a number of dead and wounded. The remaining dug-in positions were cleared like rooms in a house. Typically this is done in pairs. One man throws a grenade into the bunker, another runs in firing his rifle, shouts 'clear', and on to the next one. This was a well-practised drill. Soon, in a snowstorm, some four hours after the battle had started, the men of 2 Troop cleared the peak of the Queen's enemies at the point of the bayonet.

Zulu and Yankee Company with Commando Tactical Headquarters had set off from their start line south of Murrel Bridge to the north west of the Sisters, at about the same time as X Ray Company had arrived at their forming-up position. They had taken some care to avoid a known minefield, though it would now seem that some men almost certainly did walk through it, but without stepping on a mine. When told by me of X Ray's delay, Colonel Whitehead paused the two northern companies until he knew X Ray had started their battle. While lying below the bank of the Murrel River, the second-in-command of Zulu Company, Lieutenant Andy Holt, felt that for all the world he could have been in a First World War trench. Since we had landed he had carried a Mars Bar in his top pocket as his 'end of war treat' and up until this point had resisted eating it, even when the rations hadn't arrived. While waiting for the Commando to advance, he looked over the top of the bank just in time to see an artillery barrage landing on the ground over which they had to cross. It fell approximately where they would have been if they had not paused, and was the crump I'd heard as we were crossing the open ground. This apparently had been fired as a routine precaution and not because Zulu and Yankee had been spotted. It was at this point that Andy decided he'd better eat his Mars Bar now, otherwise it might be wasted. But as time had passed, Colonel Whitehead became concerned that we might eventually run out of darkness, so he ordered Zulu and Yankee to move again just as Andy had unwrapped the Mars Bar. He had no option but to stuff the whole thing in his mouth and advance towards the Queen's enemies impersonating a warlike hamster.

Marine Clive Pattle, the signaller carrying the commanding officer's radio link to Brigade Headquarters, was accompanying the brigade liaison officer, Major Hector Gullan, during the battle up the hill. To his surprise, Gullan offered him a Spangle sweet. Pattle accepted, the Spangle was passed across still in its paper, and went straight into Pattle's mouth. Pattle's abiding memory of the battle was advancing towards the enemy while trying to unwrap the sweet with his tongue, spitting out bits of paper as he went. It was green flavoured. He hated green Spangles.

As X Ray was working its way quietly unopposed up the southern Sister, Zulu and Yankee had moved forward towards the northern Sister and were now within between 400 and 600 yards of the hill, with Zulu Company leading. Zulu's objective was the western feature of the northern Sister. Once that was taken, Yankee would hook round behind them and to their south and take the eastern feature.

As Zulu and Yankee made unexpectedly good progress towards their objective without being detected and X Ray seemed to be progressing well, Colonel Whitehead became concerned that the two forces should not converge on each other too soon. It once again seemed possible that X Ray could finish their battle first and then be in a position to support Yankee and Zulu from the southern Sister. So he yet again ordered Zulu and Yankee to go to ground.

In the moonlight, Zulu Company could see the heads of men in the rocks ahead of them. At first they thought they might have been men on the left flank of X Ray Company, until they heard them speaking in Spanish. They resisted the temptation to open fire, hoping, like

X Ray Company, to get off the open ground and as close in to the rocks as possible before the shooting started. Then a small flare was fired from the Argentine positions and the fire-fight began with a vengeance. All hell broke loose, with tracer from many different automatic weapons raining down on them from the top of the hill, every tracer round representative of four more rounds between each one. However, as with X Ray Company, much of the Argentine fire initially went over Zulu's heads. Meanwhile, Colonel Whitehead in his tactical headquarters between the two companies, ordered artillery through Gerry Akhurst to shell the positions in front of them. Gerry immediately ordered 10 rounds 'fire for effect' on the prearranged grid on the ridge. Nothing much seemed to happen. The rounds probably fell unseen beyond the ridge, so he ordered 'drop 400 metres, repeat': this was not much better. So he then took the responsibility upon himself effectively to bring the artillery down upon themselves. He also got Dominic Rudd to do the same with the mortars. Having now got the range, he increased the intensity and slowly worked it away up the hill.

To the uninitiated reader, this procedure may seem dangerous, and indeed it is. But it is even more dangerous to be faffing around with half measures at the beginning of a battle, when trying to take control of one's own artillery. This is what often has to happen in a close-quarters battle – and for artillery, 400 metres is close quarters. Unless bold, decisive moves are taken, much time can be wasted trying to identify the fall of shot and deciding which rounds are 'friendly'. I used this procedure in Oman and indeed it was what I was trying to do with our own mortars on the southern Sister. By quickly getting a handle on the artillery thus, Akhurst undoubtedly offered the best prospect of saving British lives. During this critical phase, Gerry was using Mike Goodfellow in his observation post on Mount Kent to relay directions to the gun batteries. I knew Mike from Oman and it was good to have such a cool experienced head performing this vital function. At one point, Gerry called, 'Drop 400, 10 rounds fire for –', then as shells friendly or otherwise came crashing about his ears, 'FUCK! ...' Goodfellow's response came: 'Say again, all after "FUCK", over.'

Zulu Company was now in the sort of situation that I had feared X Ray could get into if we were discovered before we had crossed the open ground. They were pinned down, but at least with men able to take cover in the dips and hollows and behind the occasional boulder, the Argentine fire was relatively ineffective. Any attempt to move forward or back, however, would more than likely be fatal. The Argentines had by now brought their mortars into play and started shelling both companies. Each company started taking casualties from mortar and machine-gun fire. It was sometimes difficult to tell which was enemy and which was friendly artillery, so intense and so close was the action. Marine Gordon MacPherson of Zulu Company died from mortar fire and two section commanders were also wounded. One of them was Corporal Ian Spencer. He was hit by mortar fire and in spite of the valiant efforts of marines of Signals Troop to keep him conscious, he died of his wounds after being evacuated. His section second-in-command, Lance Corporal Bishop, took over seamlessly during the battle, rallied the section and led them into action with great professionalism. A Royal Engineer attached to Yankee Company, Sapper Christopher Jones, was killed by shrapnel and Marine John 'Blue' Novak, also of Yankee, was shot dead. Lieutenants John Davies and Paul Denning of Yankee were both wounded. Corporal Julian Burdett of Zulu Company, although himself wounded in the arm, chest and foot, assisted other wounded to relative safety and gave fire directions to artillery.

The deadlock was finally broken after about an hour by one of those actions which happen surprisingly frequently in history, where the decisions of a relatively junior man turn the course of a battle. Captain Mike Cole, commanding Zulu Company, had given radio orders to Lieutenant Clive Dytor, commanding 8 Troop of Zulu Company, to take the right-hand shoulder of the objective. Clive was to tell Mike when he intended to go, so that Paul Mansell and 7 Troop to his left could give him covering fire. Fire would be switched away again when 8 Troop was almost on the objective, to avoid a blue-on-blue. Clive, deciding that nothing was to be achieved lying around in the dark being machine gunned and shelled, got up and ordered his men to charge forward with him. The fact that he didn't tell Mike he was going made little difference. The covering fire was put down as intended.

Not everyone was inclined to follow Clive. At least one man shouted at him, 'Get your fucking head down, you stupid bastard!' But his section commanders, Corporals Hunt, Smith and Beatty, and his troop sergeant, Sergeant Yorkie Malone, got up with him and ordered their men to move, and soon the greater part of Zulu Company, led by 8 Troop, charged 400 metres up the hill in the face of enemy fire and fought their way into the rocks in front of them. Dytor's war cry of 'Zulu, Zulu' was taken up by the charging marines. They were fortunate in the name of their company. Whether 'Yankee' or 'X Ray' lend themselves so well to a battle cry must be open to question. Dytor's feat was the more remarkable for being conducted at night. How easy it is for a man so inclined to skulk behind a rock in the dark, while the machine guns crash out overhead. It says much for the leadership of Clive Dytor and his NCOs, and the battle discipline of the marines of Zulu Company, that they did not take that option.

148

The surprise and shock caused by their action stood them in good stead and no one was hit. Dytor's charge was certainly brave, but it was neither crazy nor harebrained. The enemy position had been prepared by artillery fire and someone had to go forward sometime. It was the next thing that needed to be done. Cole could see that and had ordered it – Dytor simply chose the where and the when. Their chances were hugely enhanced by the fact that they didn't simply charge in one mass: they pepperpotted. This is a well established infantry practice whereby one group of men dashes forward zigzagging, say 20 or 30 paces, while a second group gives covering fire. The first group then drops to the ground and covers the second group, as they get up and dash forward, and so on. Thus there is always fire being put down and the targets are constantly moving and changing – fire and manoeuvre. It takes training and good teamwork to pepperpot properly and they clearly did it well. Fortune favours the professional.

As Marine Wiseman was pepperpotting up the hill with 8 Troop, his partner, an LMG gunner, had a stoppage and then broke the cocking handle from the weapon. Thus deprived of the fire covering his movement, Wiseman found his forward dashes becoming increasingly short and speedy.

After helpless inactivity, 8 Troop were glad to get stuck in and soon captured a .5 inch Browning, cock-a-hoop at seizing the instrument of death that had kept them all at bay. During the mêlée in the rocks, Corporal George Hunt, who had been outstanding in his leadership and support to Dytor by rallying the marines and taking up the 'Zulu' war cry, was hit by shrapnel from a grenade while pepperpotting at the front. The grenade had been thrown uphill by a marine and had rolled back downhill towards Hunt, where it exploded, wounding him – yet another 'blue-on-blue'.

Freed from the flanking fire of this Browning, Lieutenants Paul Mansell and Malcolm Duck were now able to take their troops, 7 Troop and 9 Troop, deep into the position. Once in the rocks, they fixed bayonets and fought their way through the rock sangars, clearing from trench to trench, sangar to sangar, each sub-section pepperpotting with grenades. They captured about 30 prisoners. They worked their way gradually along the ridge, taking the captured Browning with them, their unfamiliarity with the weapon being no obstacle to their ability to turn it on its previous owners and, after some rough fighting at close quarters, the western peak was theirs. They also found quantities of ammunition, food, clothes, cigarettes and other supplies, for which they would be very grateful before the following day was over.

Yankee Company was now ready to move behind and to the right of Zulu, up the saddle connecting the Two Sisters to each other, to attack the east feature of the northern Sister. Many men had been lying watching the battle for Mount Longdon on their left, as well as Zulu Company's fight to their front. It had looked like a Fourth of July fireworks party. When the time came to move, Lieutenant Paul Denning found to his astonishment that the man next to him had managed to go to sleep in the midst of the din. For Lieutenant Andy Shaw, first advancing in apprehensive silence in moonlight across the open ground, then lying waiting for Zulu to do their stuff in front of them, time had become flexible, then elastic, then irrelevant. He had no idea how long they had been there. The noise was incredible. Shells were landing on the slope above and up there a furious battle – an enraged hornet's nest of fire – was seething all over the ridge in front of them. Above them illuminating shells exploded in the clouds and as they descended beneath their parachutes, in Shaw's words, 'a powerful light shone down, swinging with the oscillations, as if God was playing his torch on us frantic ants below.'

On his radio, which Shaw had to tune now as it had not been possible to do radio checks beforehand due to the imposition of radio silence, he heard that the other two troop commanders in Yankee had been hit. Andy Shaw was now the only troop officer and he had no idea whether the other two were alive or dead. In fact Lieutenant John Davies had been hit in the neck by shrapnel and Lieutenant Paul Denning had been shot through the leg. Their troop sergeants, Sergeants David Gracie and Ian Davidson, took over seamlessly, reflecting great credit on them and on the way they had been trained and prepared for the realities of battle. Lieutenant Nick Iddon was brought forward from Brigade Headquarters to take over command of 6 Troop after the battle.

As already mentioned, Marine 'Blue' Novak and Sapper Jones were also down. While Yankee were hugging the ground and getting behind whatever cover they could find, waiting their turn to go, their medical attendant, Knocker White, moved fearlessly and with no thought for his own safety between the casualties, doing his best to keep them alive. His courageous efforts brought reassurance to his company at a difficult moment, particularly for 4 and 6 Troops who were now to be without their troop commanders. And they hadn't even started the battle yet. Yankee and Zulu Companies were most fortunate not to lose more men to the mortar and heavy machine-gun fire which raked the bare slopes.

Trying to communicate with his men in preparation for their advance, Lieutenant Andy Shaw had great difficulty attracting the attention of Marine Jock Shaw lying to his left. Had he been hit? There were bullets cracking all around them. He knew he had to do something and was desperately trying to think of an alternative to crawling over to Shaw. He picked up a rock and hurled it grenade-style at him. It hit him and his head came up with a jerk. Seeing Andy's frantic signals, he crawled over. As Marine Shaw's face drew close, Andy saw he had pieces of white flannelette protruding from both ears and a fag hanging from his lip. Shells were landing closer and closer and Andy shouted at the gunner observation officer, Captain Derek Dalrymple, to adjust the fire further away. 'It's not ours,' Derek told him. Derek had been with Yankee Company on their deployment to Brunei, where he had taken great pains to train every man how to use artillery. This turned out to be useful rather sooner than had been anticipated.

Corporal Harry Siddall, meanwhile, had inserted himself into a small 'cave' formed by three or four huge boulders. It wasn't long before he realised that the lower part of his body was grievously exposed and he managed to twist himself round and bring his whole body in, so that that only a direct hit would get him. When the order to move came, he found he couldn't extricate himself. His fighting order was acting as a wedge. He couldn't move his arms sufficiently to pull himself out and his legs were poking up in the air. Panic was starting to set in as he envisaged the advance continuing without him and began to imagine how he would explain himself at his court martial, when his section second-in-command, Lance Corporal Tim Donavon, hearing Siddall sobbing with the effort, came across and heaved him out, saying something to the effect of, 'Come on, Siddall, you wimp!'

Colonel Whitehead then appeared and gave Major Richard Davis and Yankee the order to move. The plan was for Yankee Company to advance, with 5 Troop commanded by Lieutenant Andy Shaw leading, with the option to leapfrog the other troops through should they meet stiff resistance. Just prior to Yankee Company moving forward, a .50 Browning machine gun at the western end continued to fire. Major Davis told one of his Carl Gustav 84mm anti-tank teams to move out to his right to improve their angle of fire and engage the .50, which they did, silencing the gun successfully.

Zulu having taken their objective, the silence was now almost unbearable. As Yankee Company's 5 Troop advanced, a sudden cold wind hit them when they reached higher ground and the silence was broken by X Ray Company's fire streaming up the other Sister beyond the saddle. Five Troop saw their first bodies. Nobody wanted to stare. Crouching, advancing slowly beyond Zulu Company, Andy Shaw and 5 Troop were now the foremost troop. The vertical spine of the northern Sister was to their left, the pockmarked saddle between the Two Sisters to their right. A machine gun opened up close by from the left flank and they dived for cover. Corporal Bell shouted to Marine Jock Shaw to deal with it. Shaw carefully put his fag down on a rock, extended his 66mm launcher and fired. The gun fell silent and they moved on. It now began to snow; they also started to come under mortar fire. The first salvos crumped in the valley between Two Sisters and Tumbledown Mountain, but the rounds very quickly started to arrive closer and closer until 5 Troop were engulfed in a barrage of hell. Visibility had closed right down and they were now crouching in the rocks. Derek Dalrymple appeared alongside Andy Shaw and together they tried to work out what to do. Between shattering salvos, they popped their heads up and scanned the ground in front of them, frantically hoping to see a muzzle flash or something to indicate where the fire was coming from. It was an impossible task and in the end, in desperation, Shaw shouted at Corporal Harry Siddall to get up after the next salvo and run forward with him. This they did and they ran like hell. The firing stopped.

The battle had broken down into close-quarters fights among the rocks, between small groups of men.

Bombardier 'Nozzer' Holt and Corporal Siddall were skirmishing, when they stuck their heads over a boulder to find six to eight enemy. Slithering back behind the boulder in surprise, they put fresh magazines on their weapons, pulled the pins out of their grenades, went back over the rocks and killed or wounded them all. They then went on and cleared the next position in similar fashion. As they advanced along the south side of the spine – a knife edge of rock 50ft above them – in an easterly direction, Corporal Siddall encountered what they assumed was the Argentine mortar fire control party. He shot the officer and threw a grenade that wounded the sergeant. The pair went on and came across the mortar position at the eastern end of the ridge. It is not certain that this had been the position that had given Yankee so much trouble, but if it was, the mortarmen had bravely stayed to the bitter end and had, in effect, mortared themselves.

Eventually, those Argentine soldiers who were still able, melted into the night. Once Yankee Company had secured the rocky outcrops at the eastern end of the northern Sister, 45 Commando had taken their objective and completed their mission. Four men of 45 Commando Group had been killed, and ten wounded.

Of the wounded, Lieutenant Paul Denning found that it had not hurt at all. It felt as if he had been tapped on the leg by a stick. His troop had been static at the time, but when the moment came to move forward, he found that his leg had seized up and that he had been shot through the right calf. Luckily the bullet had gone straight through the muscle and had missed the bone and ligaments. He reflected that in some ways he was very lucky, in others he was unlucky. An inch one way it would have missed him: an inch the other way it would have taken his leg off. So he reckoned on balance that he couldn't complain. He handed over command to his troop sergeant, Ian Davidson, and was moved to the centre line with other casualties, including Lieutenant John Davies who had been hit in the neck by shrapnel. Meanwhile, their radio operators exchanged pleasantries about the relative discomfort of their respective bosses.

Paul and John quoted Monty Python to each other while the battle for Two Sisters continued up the hill and they waited to be evacuated. John, the more seriously wounded, was moved out first. Paul soon found himself in an over-snow vehicle with Corporal George Hunt, who was being rather obstreperous towards his mates by refusing to give up his rifle and ammunition as he claimed that he had not finished with them yet. They were taken by over-snow vehicle and Army Air Corps Scout helicopter back to the Commando Regimental Aid Post. Paul noted the name on the back of the pilot's helmet. It was Sam Drennan. A year and a half later, as he went through his own helicopter pilot's training, who should one of his instructors be but a certain Major Sam Drennan.

Paul had left his webbing on the battlefield where he had been wounded. He never saw it again. The men who carried him and John out went back to collect it and found it had been destroyed by a mortar shell which had landed on the spot where he had been lying. Luck comes in many shapes and forms, not always apparent to us at the time.

Paul continued back via Wessex helicopter to Teal Inlet, where he was checked, cleaned up, then flown out to the hospital ship *Uganda*. He found it strangely reminiscent of the cruise he had been on in her sister ship the *Nevassa*, when he was a schoolboy aged 13. While he was on board *Uganda*, the Argentines surrendered and the ship sailed into Berkeley Sound just north of Stanley. Paul was told that she had sailed inadvertently through a minefield. He was operated upon, then transferred to HMS *Hydra* and taken on to Montevideo. After 24 hours, he boarded an RAF VC 10 for the journey home to the UK. Halfway down the runway, an engine exploded and they screeched to an emergency halt. Having been shot, almost blown up, almost mined and now almost crashed on take-off, Paul was wondering how many more throws of the dice there might be. His luck held however, and after six weeks in UK he was able to run again.

He always regretted that he had never finished the journey to Stanley with his friends. Twenty-five years later, he was able to make good the deficiency when, together with John Davies and Andy Shaw, he completed the yomp and they had the beer that they had originally promised each other together in the Globe Hotel.

While we in 45 Commando were all heavily engaged on our mountain, the battle for Two Sisters continued out at sea. The knock-on effect of all the delays meant that HMS *Glamorgan* was still being asked for fire missions, when she should have been sailing away from the coast before daylight to safety from aircraft. However, Captain Mike Barrow, knowing that 45 Commando were fighting for their lives on Two Sisters, decided that he should stay as long as he possibly could to support us. He could make up time if he took a slightly more direct route out to sea, briefly exposing himself to the land-based Exocet missile at the extremity of its range. Half an hour after the planned time, *Glamorgan* ceased firing and headed off. But the Exocet operator had been waiting for this very opportunity. *Glamorgan* saw the missile coming both visually and on her radar. She swung her stern round and the missile struck the ship near her helicopter hangar. The helicopter was destroyed. She lost 13 men, some being killed in the hangar, others in the ship's galley below. A fire raged for some hours but, through the superb performance of Barrow and his crew, the flames were extinguished, the damage controlled and the ship survived. *Glamorgan* was a tough old ship and it probably helped that she had been laid down in 1962 and conceived in the 50s, when the memories of what it takes to survive major damage at sea were still fresh.

Before the Falklands War, Mike Barrow and his navigating officer had faced the possibility of a court martial for damaging *Glamorgan's* propellers on an uncharted rock in the Middle East. Any notion of court martial was quietly forgotten after the war.

Glamorgan's was indeed a gold plated contribution to the victory on Two Sisters and Captain Barrow's selfless decision doubtless saved the lives of Royal Marines. It is ironic that more British servicemen were lost at sea in the battle for Two Sisters than were lost on the mountain itself. Thus Mars rolls his dice.

Back on the southern Sister, X Ray consolidated. It was still dark and the mist was interspersed with glimpses of clear sky and flurries of snow. The occasional shot rang out, as a lone rifleman who had been bypassed by 2 Troop continued to take potshots at my headquarters. The automatic instinct is to assume the shots are intended for you and I dived into cover. However, the shooting continued sporadically and eventually stopped. I wasn't in any hurry to do anything about this brave man, as we could not be sure if we had bypassed any other positions and I didn't want to clear the position in detail in the dark. Besides, we were now under a steady artillery fire from large calibre guns. We tucked ourselves down among the rocks, away from the artillery and stray shooters. Any Argentine soldier stupid enough to be around in daylight deserved what was coming to him. But we also had to be careful where we hid. Evidence of the efficacy of the Milan missiles could be found by the remains of men who had taken cover there before us. Sometimes, one would smell the evidence before one lay in it. My signaller, Marine Chadwick, made a mental note to double boil the water when he next filled his water bottle. The smell of gore had a sobering effect, notwithstanding it was the gore of our enemies. The same could not be said about the smell of excrement, which also seemed to be in every nook and cranny where a man might take cover. But we couldn't afford to be picky and we took cover with indiscriminate gratitude.

The Argentine artillery fire was pretty accurate, so the bunkers vacated by our enemies were now put to use again and protected many men from the worst of the onslaught. The noise from the explosions was all consuming as round after round crashed in, followed by the whine and tinkle of shrapnel ricocheting around the rocks. Shells were landing within a few metres of our positions and the shock waves rattled one to the core. Men were deaf for hours afterwards and for some the damage to their hearing was permanent and irreparable.

The battle on the northern Sister seemed to subside at about the same time. Corporal Morrison, my senior signaller, had been feeding situation reports to Commando Tactical Headquarters as our battle progressed. Now I personally reported to Colonel Whitehead on the radio. It was the first time we had spoken since the shooting started. Colonel Whitehead told me that we would not now attack Tumbledown Mountain. I had rather forgotten about this contingency, but confess I was glad that we were not being asked to push our luck twice in one night. The reason for the decision was simple. The artillery was down to six rounds per gun. It was only two hours to daylight. The nearest part of Tumbledown was 3km away and Tumbledown itself was nearly 3km long. A daylight approach and battle without ample artillery was out of the question. No doubt if we had been able to attack it in the dark that night, we would have risen to the occasion. In fact, it was a misty morning and we might have been able to approach unseen, but mist can never be counted upon – if it had lifted at an inopportune moment, we could have been badly exposed. It is likely that the defence on Tumbledown had been reinforced by the time it was attacked two nights later, partly by troops escaping from Two Sisters. But judging by the punch-up the Scots Guards had, Tumbledown was always going to be a tough nut. Meanwhile, we were quite happy to leave it to someone else to crack. Besides, while Tumbledown was also defended by conscripts, they were Marines, and it would have been a pity if we had had to fight men with whom, under other circumstances, we would naturally have expressed fraternal solidarity.

The shelling on all of 45 Commando's positions started more seriously now and continued for the next 36 hours. Between 50 and 60 shells landed on our ridge, and the saddle between the two mountains became heavily cratered with many more. Yankee, Zulu and Commando Tactical Headquarters on the northern Sister took their share too. One recent commentator, seeing the number of craters there to this day, has remarked upon the weight of British artillery used to capture Two Sisters. That may have been so for the northern Sister, but many of the holes on the saddle were caused by Argentine shells and none of the craters on our Sister were British. We watched the holes appear around us. And we heard them. A 155mm shell landing close by is quite the loudest noise I've ever heard. The noise penetrates every cell in your brain and it feels as if your eardrums meet inside your head. We received no casualties, but it is indeed a disagreeable business being shelled. After being shelled there and in Oman, I was left with a feeling of surprise at how many people had survived; at how little damage was done. Artillery is more often used to neutralise rather than to destroy and, although of course it does shatter men and destroys things, its chief effect is an assault upon the mind. As random, screaming, violent destruction is hurled down upon you by men unknown from many kilometres away, the noise and the horror threaten to rip your sanity out of your head.

In our case, the intermittent nature of the shelling added to the uncertainty and danger. There might be silence for half an hour or even an hour, then one, two, or three rounds would come crashing in. Two or three rounds an hour is not enough to justify staying hunkered down in one's hole, if one has other business to attend to. They were using two guns of 155mm calibre and when the shells landed in the bog the craters were like small swimming pools. The peat undoubtedly absorbed much of the impact. When they landed on the rocks, they sent shards of broken stones and shrapnel flying with equal ferocity. When there was no ambient sound, we could hear the guns firing in Stanley and we knew to expect an incomer about 20 seconds later. More often than not, however, one heard only the terminal whistle shortly before the explosion. As a rule of thumb, the longer you can hear the whistle, the further away from you the shell is going to land. If it is coming really close, you get about two seconds' warning. I suppose if it is going to land on your head, you don't hear it until after you're dead. We had an excellent opportunity to make something of a study of this as we huddled among the rocks, where only a direct hit or very near miss would be likely to get us. Not so in the open though, where one was much more exposed. Nevertheless, men who didn't want to crap in their own positions felt that a short trip to the open ground to drop their trousers was worth the risk. The marines managed to make fun even out of this. They would wait until their mate's trousers were down, and the man was well committed to the act, and then they would whistle ...

156

When a 155mm shell excavated a hole in the bog, there was something of a competition over who would get to the shell hole first and crap in it. The crater itself offered a degree of cover and the notion, however spurious, that another shell would be unlikely to land in the same hole was attractive. But most importantly, new shell holes are warm; so what better place could there be on a bitterly cold day to expose one's nether regions to the elements?

I myself took the chance of what seemed to be a quiet moment to go out and have a pee. I hadn't finished when I heard the dreaded whistle. The shell hit the ground at the same time as I. It was a 155mm. A large lump of rock landed on my back and I was splattered with wet peat. I measured the distance afterwards. It was 19 paces. The blast and the noise were all-permeating. I wondered if my eardrums had burst; but no. However, my ears rang like hell and I had difficulty hearing for some time afterwards.

Why did the Argentines use their artillery in this way? Intermittent harassing fire has its part to play in advance of an attack, but no counter-attack was imminent. We were on reverse slopes and therefore unlikely to be observed. So the fire was not directed at any specific target. One would have thought that they would have conserved their ammunition, so that they could use it to break up any further attacks by us. But no: they dissipated it, round by round, hurling it at men dug in on hills which they themselves had already lost, as if in one final, petulant, violent sulk before they accepted the inevitable and surrendered.

It is difficult to describe faithfully the chaotic nature of a night battle as seen from the point of view of the company, troop or section commander. It truly seems like a shambles. It is not helped by the tendency, more common than is readily admitted, for commanders to suffer from mental paralysis. I found, both here and in Oman, that I was temporarily stunned when something unexpected happened in battle and a decision was required, and I know I was not alone in experiencing this. There was a degree of detachment to it as well. It was as if it was an out-of-body experience. I could almost see myself sitting there, looking like a gormless idiot. Another officer in battle that night described it as 'walking in thick treacle – the thought processes would just not play ball.' It doesn't help when you yourself are under fire or being shelled. Logical reasoning and deduction are suspended. It's not a matter of trying to think straight; more a case of trying to think at all. This is why good drills are so important. If I ever managed to take a decision, it was by snatching at the first idea which came into my head, or someone else's idea as it went past. They were as much acts of instinct, or even panic, as anything else.

The dividing line between the two becomes rather indistinct. Desperation is never very far away on a battlefield.

One loses all sense of time. Communications break down. Men get deafened by noise. Shouts become shrieks. Instinct takes over from reason. The only sure way to communicate with a man is to thump him in the back and bellow in his ear, or like Andy Shaw, to throw a rock at him; and even then there is no guarantee that he will hear or understand you, or that he has not fallen asleep through chronic fatigue. The black night is slashed by tracer and bright explosions, and night vision never develops properly. Usually you can't see each other and if you can see someone, you all have blackened faces and you don't know who it is unless he speaks – and then you may not hear him. And then an illuminating shell suddenly explodes light upon everything and everyone and you wish it hadn't. Moonlight is both a boon and a curse. Men moving are easier to see in moonlight so it tends to aid the defender, who is static. On the other hand, moonlight aids control. But generally, if you are the burglar, the blacker the night the better. One's control is depleted exponentially as the enemy is engaged. I felt increasingly helpless as options closed down, and never so much as when I failed to get artillery and mortars to support 2 Troop. There seemed so little more I could do, I found a sheltered corner and smoked a cigarette, shielding it under my Green Beret. I guess if necessary, I could have withdrawn 2 Troop from the peak, begged the artillery to plaster it and then had another go; or I could have concentrated on the .50 Browning on the saddle and approached, perhaps with smoke from the flank. It wasn't necessary. However, eventually one has to rely upon the most junior people to know what needs to be done and to do it without asking you.

This comes as something of a surprise to some civilians, even today. Many are still imbued with the notion that being in the military is all about obeying orders and that the junior ranks are cannon fodder. Nothing could be further from the truth. When one of his officers cited 'obedience of orders' as an excuse for some tactical blunder, the nineteenth-century Prince Frederick Charles of Prussia tongue-lashed him: 'His Majesty made you a major because he believed you would know when *not* to obey his orders.'

The reality is that success depends on ten thousand decisions taken at the lowest-paid level, especially when the options run out. If your people know why they are there and how it all fits into the bigger picture, they can use their brains and initiative to make it work for you. The battle for Two Sisters, and all the other battles in the Falklands War, were won by the skill, determination and stout hearts of marines, privates and guardsmen, corporals, sergeants and junior officers, seeing the circumstances in front of them, knowing what we were trying to achieve and why, taking decisions, taking risks and taking responsibility; doing what they could with the resources at their disposal to contribute towards victory. I didn't fire a shot in the Falklands and neither did the other company commanders in 45 Commando. Much the same applied to 42 Commando, although one company commander using a night sight did find an opportunity to take a rifle potshot at an enemy. But in the normal course that should not be the company commander's job. My personal intervention might have been required if things had gone badly wrong, but my job and that of all the other officers and NCOs up the chain of command to the Ministry of Defence, was to play our parts in getting our people to the right place, at the right time (approximately), with the right equipment; mentally, physically, intellectually and spiritually fully prepared for battle. But ultimately it was up to them. For ever after, I have been keenly conscious that my reputation, indeed my life, rested upon the shoulders of teenaged marines, some of whom were not yet 18 years old. *They* knew their jobs and *they* did the business.

Lance Corporal Montgomery had been evacuated by helicopter before dawn, the aircraft bringing in rifle and machine gun ammunition, and taking Monty out. We had also expended many 66mm anti-tank weapons. The resupply, which had been brought forward by Rupert van der Horst and Brian Bellas picking their way round stone runs in the dark under artillery fire, in a gallant odyssey in our over-snow vehicles, was now on the northern Sister. I needed someone to collect it. Marine Dickie Birch volunteered. Marine Birch was a slightly older, quiet man who had joined the Company under a cloud. He had been a landing craft marine in the Hong Kong detachment. There, he had struck a naval petty officer and had spent some time in detention before being sent home. When he arrived with us, I said that I didn't care what had happened in the past. As long as he did his job well, he would be welcome. He became the Company Clerk and a respected and dependable member of the Company. There wasn't much clerking to be done in the Falklands so he became my self-appointed bodyguard, carrying a machine gun and preceding me in the line of march. He was heavier than me so, rather like the servant of Good King Wenceslas in the snow, more than once I was thankful for being behind him and thus able to avoid the more treacherous bits of bog in which he had sunk up to his knees.

We now watched the faithful, steady Birch head off across the saddle to get the 66mm ammunition. As the occasional shell came in, he would hit the deck or jump down into a crater, then reappear and set off once more. We feared for his safety, but had it not been a man's life in the balance we would have laughed. It was almost like watching a cartoon. In fact we probably did laugh. When he got to the other side, he flopped to ground next to a colour sergeant, who said to him, 'Did you see that idiot dodging the fire?' Dickie Birch replied, 'That idiot was me – have you got a fag?' The fag was duly dispensed. A couple of hours later he reappeared on our Sister carrying two sandbags. We congratulated him warmly and thanked him until we emptied out the bags. It was the wrong ammunition. Amid much ribbing and laughter, Birch, with a rueful smile, offered to go back and get the right stuff. By then I had decided that we were not about to be counter-attacked, but if we were, we had plenty other ammunition to withstand it. We resupplied in slow time later in the day.

With the smell of peat smoke again in my nostrils, this time from the fires started by tracer rounds buried deep in the ground, I scrambled to the top of our Sister at first light. It was encouraging to see Stanley for the first time. How long it would take us to get there would remain to be seen. When I looked back down the ridge and saw what we had done, my spine froze. Potentially, the position was impregnable. If the Argentines had held it the way we would have held it, we would never have got them out. By now the exertions of the night and the previous day, plus the realisation of our enormous good luck began to have their effect. I felt physically and mentally drained. We all did. When Colonel Whitehead joined us soon after first light, we agreed that, with 30 marines to defend this place, we could have died of old age before we would have lost it. The Commanding Officer was clearly very pleased with all that had happened and his visit lifted us. He had been with the leading company during the fight for the northern Sister throughout the battle and had personally overseen both that battle and our fight for the southern Sister.

The choice of location for the commanding officer in battle is of the greatest importance and requires fine judgement. Firstly, he needs to be in a position where he knows what is going on. He also needs to be able to communicate with his companies and his attendant artillery officer needs to be able to communicate back to the guns. It is nice if he can tell his boss, the brigadier, what is happening, but in reality this can be left to other people whose real job it is. He can pick up a lot on the radio, but he can only get a real feel for the battle by seeing it with his own eyes. And yet, if he is too far forward, he is in danger of himself being embroiled in the battle and not free to influence it when it goes wrong. He needs to be rather like a circus ring master: detached and fully in control of the performance, but ready to get in there and kick the lion's arse when it sulks in a corner. His ultimate duty is, through his personal intervention and example if necessary, to turn a CMFU into a SAMFU. This cannot be achieved sitting in a headquarters tent or vehicle several kilometres behind the forward troops. It can only be done when he is forward, in a position where he is able to take such uncommitted reserves as he can find and personally direct them to the centre of gravity, to change the course of the battle.

In the battle for Two Sisters, we knew Andrew Whitehead was there. We could hear his calm, authoritative voice on the radio and I knew he could see what was going on. I was in no doubt that if my battle had gone badly wrong, he would have brought either Zulu or Yankee across and sorted it out. Similarly, he was in a position to direct me to bring X Ray across to join him on the northern Sister and throw our weight into that battle if required. Always near the lead company, he was exposed to much the same artillery and machine-gun fire as they were, but it was undoubtedly the right place to be. You cannot be expected to lead right from the front as a commanding officer, but you do need to lead from the place where you can command most effectively. Andrew Whitehead led 45 Commando in the battle for Two Sisters, in both name and deed.

In the daylight, we found a number of thin wires running up and down our ridge. Tripwires! Booby traps! Mines! We were always on the lookout for mines. We knew there were minefields around. The other companies had skirted one minefield on their approach and Staff Sergeant Pete Thorpe of Condor Troop Royal Engineers was later to lose his foot on a mine while trying to extract a damaged vehicle with injured gunners, near Murrel Bridge. We had been expecting them and I was surprised that X Ray still hadn't encountered any. Everybody stood petrified until someone remembered that the Milan was a wire-guided missile. These were the control wires of the missiles that Steve Hughes' men had fired over our heads. We did find the mines, but they were still in boxes. The Argentines either hadn't had time, or hadn't bothered to lay them. We were glad of that. We were also glad of the boxes because they were useful to help keep out the wind.

Our attached Commando Royal Engineers from Condor Troop had prepared a number of plastic explosive charges to be used if we encountered mines during our assault. With professional relish they now set about destroying these mines and other Argentine ammunition with their unused charges. In the course of gathering up the ordnance, Sapper Mick Mullarkey dropped a rocket projectile as he took cover from an incoming artillery shell. The rocket suddenly sprouted fins and armed itself. Eventually this rocket and all the other Argentine ammo was placed in a large shell hole and was prepared for destruction with plastic explosives. It was going to be a whopper of a bang.

Just as Corporal Brian Fairburn was about to set it off, a helicopter approached and landed on the hill and out jumped a section of Gurkhas, who proceeded to take up all-round defensive positions in and around the shell hole. While Corporal Fairburn stayed his hand, Sapper Molly

161

Morrison approached and asked the officer where he thought he was. He was told, 'Goat Ridge', so Molly pointed out Goat Ridge off to the south. The Gurkhas promptly evacuated the lethal shell hole, reboarded the Wessex helicopter which had remained on the ground with its rotors turning, and flew off. Shortly afterwards the ground shook with one of the biggest explosions any of us had ever heard. We were showered with debris for almost a quarter of a minute.

We spent the day attending to our administration and burying the Argentine dead. The Commando had taken 44 prisoners, many of whom were wounded. Searching for and evacuating the wounded was not always straightforward while artillery fire was coming in. Those who could walk were gathered centrally and driven out in over-snow vehicles, or flown out. The most severely wounded were picked up where they were. This included one man found by Dennis Gillson with part of his skull missing and his brain visible inside. He was patched up with a first field dressing with as much care as possible and flown out by a Scout piloted by Captain Jeff Niblett of 3 Commando Brigade Air Squadron in between explosions, in full view of enemy positions on Tumbledown.

We found seven dead soldiers on our Sister. We buried them *in situ* and made a careful record of the positions of the graves, which we submitted to the authorities. I personally supervised the burial of what appeared to be an officer and a sergeant, although it was difficult to tell who they were, or confirm their rank. I was sombred to note how like my own marines they looked. Their identity tags were aluminium discs with typed labels sellotaped on to them. These were useless, because they disintegrated in the wet; they were indecipherable mush when we found them. We were not impressed by the failure of the Argentine army to afford their dead soldiers this elementary service. The grave we dug was too small to begin with. The marines wanted to break the legs of the corpses to make them fit the inadequate space. Shells were coming in and we didn't much want to hang around in the open. But I stopped them and, notwithstanding the sporadic artillery fire, we made the grave fit the bodies rather than the other way round. I said a few words in prayer. At least by burying them thus, they would be 'known unto God' even if not to their own perfunctory administration.

It wasn't so easy for the others, though. Sergeant George Matthews was supervising the burial of another man, who seemed to have been pointing at something when he was killed. His arm was sticking straight out and rigor mortis had set in. They had to break his arm to bury him. Corporal Frank Melia was with another burial party supervised by Phil Witcombe. He had made Phil aware of a puff of smoke from a round in the valley between the Two Sisters, but Phil was preoccupied with delivering an appropriate passage from the bible over the open grave.

The next thing they heard was the dreaded whistle of the incoming round. They all dived to the nearest cover, which for Corporal Melia, was on top of the bodies in the grave. He was lucky not to join them on a permanent basis. The shrapnel carved a neat nick out of the top of his head. Our company medic, Medical Attendant Mark Hopper, cleaned the wound with Argentine brandy and stitched him up on the spot.

Our chaplain, Wynne Jones also held a burial service for two Argentine dead which appeared to be greatly appreciated by the prisoners who attended it. He was told that one was a major and the other the son of a general.

At least we found the digging easy enough. Wynne Jones returned to Teal Inlet to bury our own dead and found himself conducting a joint service with the chaplain of 3 Para. They had lost 18 men on their attack on Mount Longdon and the grave had to be over 40 feet long. The size of the grave and the nature of the ground demanded more drastic measures than mere pick and shovel. Bill McRae had to resort to Colour Sergeant George Frith's expertise with plastic explosives to get down far enough. Just as they were about to blow, a helicopter appeared and failed to respond to their signals to clear off. Fortunately, it got away with a thorough spattering of peat.

That evening, when he was preparing his meal shortly before last light, Brian Bellas observed a single young marine appear quietly from nowhere and approach the graves. Oblivious to anyone who might have been watching him in the fading light, this man removed his head dress and, standing by the graves, took his rifle from his shoulder and placed the muzzle on his boot, taking up the position of 'resting on arms reversed': the traditional position of vigil of the warrior over the graves of his fallen comrades. There he stood for some minutes, then returning his weapon to his shoulder and replacing his Green Beret, he quietly disappeared off into the thickening night.

As well as the mines, we found prodigious quantities of ammunition, food, clothing and equipment on the position. It was just as well. Our rucksacks with the sleeping bags again failed to turn up and it froze that night, 12 June. But for the Argentine blankets and other clothing, it would have been even more uncomfortable than it was. The marines enjoyed exploring the enemy positions, and to watch them going through the camp at the top of the hill was strongly reminiscent of a family of tinkers picking over a rubbish tip. Some men decided that the boots on the Argentine dead were better than theirs and did a swap. Most were quick enough to do the exchange before the corpses were buried, but not all. One marine on the northern Sister, desperate to replace his own falling-apart boots, inquired of the burial party at which end of the newly dug mound were the feet. He then rummaged around with his hands in the soft earth until he found what he wanted. He had to explore several graves until he found the size he needed. Socks were included in the bargain.

We filled our faces with enemy rations, and the fags and whisky in each pack were much appreciated. Their rations also contained a tin of delicious stewed Argentine beef. We were less impressed by the pictures of the Virgin Mary and the saints, although the paper was useful for writing on. Some men were puzzled by the flat round tin of clear jelly they found in the packs. It didn't taste so good, but it helped the biscuits go down. Only when they saw others cooking with the tins did they realise their mistake. From this time onwards, I ate a mixture of Argentine and British rations and I ate very well. While men went around with bulging pockets and big grins, a closer look revealed red-rimmed eyes sunk in blackened, gaunt faces, deeply ingrained with fatigue. But there was no real prospect of proper rest in the near future. Adrenalin, nicotine and caffeine would have to keep them going for now.

We also found a number of second-generation night-viewing devices. Some were in boxes and did not look as if they had been used. They made our first-generation heavy and cumbersome image intensifiers look distinctly old fashioned and we were fortunate that they had not been used to good effect.

We found weapons enough for over 30 men, including two Brownings and a recoilless anti-tank weapon: some standing patrol! We tried to tidy the place up, but great care was needed when gathering up weapons. At one stage a shot rang out and we all hit the deck. Marine Gillon had picked up a rifle, which had gone off as soon as he lifted it. No one was hit.

The other companies were going through the same routine. The reported underground mine ready to be fired by wire was not found, although a booby trapped rifle was. After Yankee Company had consolidated their positions on Two Sisters, Major General Jeremy Moore, the Commander Land Forces flew in to visit the Commando and to see first-hand what lay ahead. He was met by Richard Davis, who a couple of months earlier had said farewell to General Moore at Brunei Airport. The General had been about to retire from the Royal Marines when the war started and, as well as visiting Yankee Company training deep in the jungle of Brunei, he had been revisiting the scene of an action where he had won his second Military Cross twenty years before. So when he and Richard met again on Two Sisters they could not but smile as they remembered the farewell in Brunei barely two months before, at which General Moore believed he was heading for retirement and Richard thought he was going on leave. Together they moved forward to the western end of Two

Sisters, where General Moore was able to get an unobstructed view of Tumbledown, Sapper Hill and Port Stanley, with smoke billowing in among some buildings and damage visible to one or two others.

During the course of the day, a small team of forward air controllers arrived on our Sister and asked to be taken to a good vantage point overlooking Tumbledown. Presently we watched a Harrier perform a remarkable flight pattern, tossing a bomb while turning up and away in a dramatic loop. This was a laser-guided bomb, possibly the first time such a weapon had ever been used in action.

That evening, as I was giving my instructions for the night, a figure appeared out of the darkness on our position. We were somewhat edgy, but worries evaporated when we heard Wynne Jones call out of the gloom in a strong Welsh accent: 'Hello X Ray Company, hello X Ray, it's only the Vicar, and I've forgotten the fucking password!' He had brought with him a rucksack full of rations he had 'proffed' while burying the dead.

We tried to make sense of the position we had captured and imagined what it had been like to defend it. Frank Melia was horrified to discover in the daylight that at the end of the gully he had been going up when Chris Caröe called him back was a .50 Browning machine gun mounted amongst a rocky fortress. He was not the only one to count his lucky stars.

Of subsequent British published estimates of Argentine dispositions, the one which reflects most closely what we found there is in Hugh Bicheno's *Razor's Edge*. It seems that our intelligence picture was pretty accurate and that the Two Sisters were indeed defended by a reinforced infantry company comprising three of its own platoons, plus one or two platoons from another company. There was also a support element including engineers, two 81mm mortars and three .50 Brownings – between 170 and 200 men in all. One platoon was defending the southern Sister and two platoons the northern one. The mortars were sited at the eastern end of the northern Sister and the Brownings on the saddle between the two main peaks. One of the additional platoons was on the saddle, providing close support to the Brownings. The fifth platoon seems to have been on the southern Sister until the battle started, when part of it moved off to the south to try and set up a flanking position under the mistaken impression that the attack was coming from that direction. This is possibly why X Ray met no opposition on the lower reaches of their Sister, although we found little evidence that this had been a recently occupied defensive position.

In addition, there was a separate company from a different regiment in the area to the north and east of the northern Sister, but this apparently played no real part in the battle, except perhaps to assist soldiers of the defending company to make good their escape to Tumbledown and Sapper Hill. One wonders what the coordination between the two companies had been like.

It can't have been much fun for the defenders of the hills around Stanley. For a start, there were no roads to most of them. So resupply would be by foot or by helicopter. They would have suffered the same constraints as us in that regard. However bad the weather was, perversely its very awfulness may have worked to our advantage. Digging in and defending in filthy, wet, windy conditions, and living in bunkers and holes in the rocks, manning open trenches, not knowing if, when, and from where the enemy might attack. All this would probably be more corrosive to morale for them than for us who, while we were more completely exposed to the elements, at least would be moving, advancing, attacking – doing something – and certain in the knowledge that one way or the other it was going to end before long. Their circumstances would have demanded excellent leadership, just as ours did. They, hapless men, didn't get it.

We wondered what had happened on that hill during the time between Chris Fox's Recce Troop patrol and our attack. When 3 Troop attacked, the Argentines had men defending on the lower features. This is indeed where they should have been, making it difficult for us to get into the rocks. At the battle of Magersfontein in South Africa in 1900, the Boers, as well as defending the high ground, had dug a concealed trench along the bottom of the hill. So when the British advanced out of the night to attack the hill, they were cut down in large numbers before they could get near enough to break in. This is what I was concerned that the Argentines would do, but instead they abandoned the positions at the bottom of the hill, thereby forfeiting much of the range and firepower of their Brownings. Once we were in the rocks, it must have been like a man with a swarm of hornets in his clothes. In the end, the only thing he could do was take off his jacket and run. The position was dirty and smelly and there was no evidence of any attempt at sanitation. Some of the dead we found had not been killed during our battle, but had been left unburied from the time of the fight of two nights before. All this indicates poor leadership, and perhaps a breakdown of discipline after the patrol of David Stewart and 3 Troop. The fact that a cadre of some 20 men had stayed and fought in the dark – some to the death – in these circumstances is testimony to their individual courage and steadfastness.

166

45 Commando's remarkable victory was due to a number of factors. Firstly, we were certainly lucky. The Argentines appear initially not to have placed much importance on Two Sisters as a defensive position. They thought the British would come from the south, so initially their defences were laid out with this in mind. However, when they realised that we were coming in strength from the west, they saw the Two Sisters was the key to the door to Stanley, re-orientated their defences and devoted substantial resources to Two Sisters. Even so, while they laid mines in defence of the northern Sister, they apparently didn't do so for the southern Sister. Neither did they use their radars or night vision devices to good effect. Nevertheless, a 700ft ascent up a mountain with many rocks, ridges and crevices, against a reinforced company armed with anti-tank weapons and .50 Brownings supported by mortars, 105mm and 155mm artillery, all backed up by another company from another regiment within striking distance, presented a most formidable objective in anyone's book. They did not try to counter-attack us at any stage. A more experienced enemy might have concealed themselves until we had gone past, or hidden off to a flank and then attacked us from the rear. The confusion created could have been enormous and might well have delayed us into daylight. But it didn't happen.

There can be little doubt that our active patrolling in the days leading up to the battle had helped to shape the minds of the defenders. We also had the position under observation and had brought harassing artillery fire down on it regularly in the days preceding our attack. Had the Argentines stayed on, or reinforced, the lower reaches of the southern Sister, X Ray could have had a very difficult time breaking in. But it seems that we had terrorised them to the point that they abandoned it, and indeed they left their dead there for us to find two days later. A conversation Corporal Hugh Knott had with one of the prisoners we guarded in Stanley afterwards rather confirms this view.

Our 66mm anti-tank launcher was a battle-winning weapon. It was lightweight and accurate and an excellent strongpoint buster. And when we saw what the Milan missiles had done to the bunkers, we were very glad they hadn't been firing at us. The weight of fire we had been able to put down with the Milans and our 19 machine guns per company had saved British lives. Our men did fire rifles and used their bayonets, but we were able to bring a machine gun to every fire-fight. This made us very difficult to resist. Although X Ray fought without any artillery support, the bold, skilful and copious use of artillery and naval gunfire on the northern Sister weighed heavily in our favour there. In addition, the artillery possibly played a part in preventing the adjacent company from playing any significant part in the battle. Having time and being able to conduct rehearsals also gave men confidence and helped to ensure that each man knew his part, and the part he might be expected to play when the plan ran out, which it most certainly would. Moreover, Colonel Whitehead's style of leadership was 'mission based': he told his people in detail what it was he wanted and why. He invited us into his brain so we knew exactly how he was thinking, thus equipping us to make decisions in his name with the confidence that we were doing his will. But he left the 'how' to the judgement of the on-the-spot commander. This allowed his company commanders to respond to the realities that faced them and not to be tied in a straitjacket to an over prescriptive plan. His planning, his willingness to trust his subordinates to get on with their jobs, while being ready to intervene personally on the spot at critical moments, shaped the whole battle.

Most important of all, the skill and courage of our marines at street and gutter fighting, pepperpotting – teamwork – no movement without covering fire – and night fighting, ensured that we would win one way or the other. The time and resources the Royal Marines had spent in teaching, training, encouraging, informing, practising, inspiring, training again, rehearsing and leading, all paid off. 'Train hard; fight easy', someone once said. Well; no fight is ever easy, but unless you train, train, train and train some more, your fights are likely to be long, bloody and difficult, and in absence of the necessary skills, victory is more than duly going to depend upon the gallantry and self-sacrifice of your men and their junior leaders – if indeed you win at all.

On 13 June, our second night sitting on Two Sisters, we watched the Scots Guards attack Tumbledown Mountain. It looked like a slow, hard slogging match and we felt for them, especially since we knew we would probably have to do something similar a couple of nights later. We had been warned that our next objective would be Sapper Hill on the night of 15 June. This too would be a night battle. We would not have the opportunity to do a reconnaissance and neither would we be able to soften it up the way we had the Two Sisters. The Reverend David Cooper, chaplain to 2 Para, has described what it is like for men who are about to go into battle for a second time. It is, he says, rather like a man who has had a severe electric shock being invited to stick his hands into the socket again and turn the switch on. No one asked aloud why we were now being required to fight our second battle, while other units had yet to see a shot fired, but I know some men briefly thought it; and then dismissed the thought.

If we needed any antidote against complacency, the Argentine Air Force provided it yet again on the afternoon of 13 June. Commanding officers of units had been summoned to 3 Commando Brigade Headquarters for orders. At around the scheduled time of the meeting, seven Skyhawks in two groups – a four and a three – bombed the headquarters.

The tent in which the meeting was due to be held was shredded, but no one was hurt. The meeting had been postponed. This was nearly one of the most disastrous attacks in the war: it could have killed or injured most or all of the key people in the Brigade command structure. We were very glad they were safe, although the luxury of this knowledge allowed us to enjoy a certain *schadenfreude* at the thought of our superior headquarters sharing some of the flak.

On the morning of 14 June, we were ready to receive our orders for the attack on Sapper Hill planned for the night of the 15th when, at around 9.00 am local time – 1300 hrs GMT – we suddenly received a very different set of orders. We had already been warned that we might have to move at very short notice, so meals had been eaten and everything was packed. Colonel Whitehead told us that after 2 Para's attack on Wireless Ridge, and the Scots Guards' on Tumbledown, Argentine soldiers had been seen streaming back to Stanley. There were rumours of white flags having been seen, although to this day I have not met anybody who saw one. We were to move in hot pursuit of the enemy and attack Sapper Hill as soon as possible. We were given an order of march, a time to move, and that was it. The rest would follow by radio. We needed nothing more. We were off. The Commando moved along two routes, both north of Tumbledown. Those 11 kilometres were taken at the gallop. They took us about four hours. Orders for the attack on Sapper Hill were received by radio and noted down on the march. We were given the start line, the order of attack, and the artillery fire plan, and all this was absorbed, digested and the relevant orders passed on down the line. We were a slick, worked-up, experienced fighting machine and very soon every man knew what he needed to know to play his part in the next attack.

What we didn't know was that the Welsh Guards, now with two companies of 40 Commando under command, were also about to attack Sapper Hill. Charlie Company 40 Commando, commanded by my batch-mate and friend Captain Andy Pillar, was to deploy by helicopter to the road adjacent to Mount William, to lead the advance to Sapper Hill. The leading troop, 9 Troop commanded by Second Lieutenant Carl Bushby, was lifted by two Sea King helicopters to secure the landing site. However, through yet another map-reading error by the anti-submarine pilots, they were dropped on the edge of Sapper Hill itself, which was heavily defended by the Argentines. On landing, they were subjected to a fierce fusillade of small arms fire. Both helicopters took a number of hits but miraculously remained airworthy. Nine Troop had been briefed that the ground was mined either side of the designated landing site but, even before realising that the pilots had made a mistake, they had thrown caution to the wind and dived into whatever cover they could find to return fire on Sapper Hill. A short but intense fire-fight broke out, two marines were wounded and a number of Argentines were killed or wounded.

Meanwhile, Andy Pillar had arrived at the correct landing site only to find no one there. He soon established that his leading troop was isolated a mile further on being heavily engaged by the enemy on Sapper Hill. He now moved the rest of Charlie Company at best speed on foot towards the beleaguered 9 Troop, requesting, but not getting, artillery to hit Sapper Hill. By the time Andy married up with Bushby and 9 Troop, the Argentines had broken contact, evacuated their positions and were heading out of sight down the reverse slope of Sapper Hill towards Stanley. Andy dropped off medics to treat the wounded and pressed on to Sapper Hill, now in the company of a couple of Scimitar light tanks from the Blues and Royals. Further fire missions were called to destroy the fleeing Argentines, but these too were denied as reports started coming in of white flags being raised over Stanley. By the time Charlie Company was firm on Sapper Hill, the enemy positions had been completely abandoned and all that remained were a few corpses and the detritus of the site's long occupation. Taking advantage of this inadvertent *coup de main*, the rest of the Welsh Guards moved in behind them. Charlie Company's attack on Sapper Hill was essentially the last action of the war.

As we in 45 Commando approached Sapper Hill, we saw much of this action unfolding in front of us, first with astonishment, then horror, as two blue Sea King helicopters gaily landed on what we knew was a heavily defended position. We heard the fire-fight and wondered what on earth was going on. But we eventually climbed up Sapper Hill without a shot being fired by us, to find the Welsh Guards ensconced on the top. They looked to us incongruously clean and well fed. It was good to meet Andy Pillar and share a dram with him.

Sapper Hill was a well prepared defensive position. It was near to Stanley and relatively easy to resupply and the Argentines had devoted considerable resources to it. We had almost certainly walked through a minefield during our approach. If the Argentines had decided to fight, it would have been a difficult battle for whoever assaulted it. Why two separate units attacked Sapper Hill was not clear then. It now seems that it was an ill-judged unilateral initiative by 5 Infantry Brigade. The potential for 'blue-on-blue' was awful. But on the ground, we did not feel at all cheated that it had been taken relatively easily by our fellow Royal Marines.

As we were advancing towards Sapper Hill, rumours had started to come through about a surrender. One of the last acts of the war was a Harrier strike, directed by Gerry Akhurst as part of our assault on Sapper

Hill. After dropping the first bomb, Gerry was told of the possibility of surrender. He aborted the next strike and directed the Harrier out to sea, where it dropped its second bomb. Quite apart from sparing the lives of Argentine soldiers, this possibly inadvertently avoided a most ghastly 'blue-on-blue' on the Welsh Guards. Our Commanding Officer ordered Gerry Akhurst to find out on the artillery command net what the true situation was. He had also been directing fire on the rear of Sapper Hill, but as it appeared that the Argentines were on the run he ceased firing. He now paused to set up a better radio link. There was no conclusive information and by now he was on his own, some way behind the Commando, but he was able to flag down a passing Gazelle whose pilot allowed him and his radio operator to sit on the landing skids while he flew them forward to catch us up.

We were loathe to believe the rumours of surrender, only to have our hopes dashed. We always had to be ready to fight for Stanley, a battle that would probably be fought in daylight to minimise civilian casualties, or to start all over again on West Falkland. However, the near bloodless battle for Sapper Hill rather lent weight to the possibility of surrender. Another straw in the wind took the form of a flight of Royal Navy helicopters conducting a flypast, with a flying White Ensign suspended underneath. Did they know something we didn't? All very pretty and inspiring; but now – can you please bring us our rucksacks? A few days earlier, I had seen the journalist Max Hastings apparently attract a helicopter by waving his stick at it and persuading the pilot to give him a lift. We could have done with his talent just then.

We dug in on the top and waited for news. No rucksacks appeared. The temperature throughout the war fluctuated between +5° and −5° Centigrade. In the wind, the effect of the cold is magnified very significantly, so even in a 10mph breeze −5° can easily feel like −15°. This night it was at least −5° and a brisk wind swept the hill all night. There were one or two Argentine blankets, but most men had to lie down on the peat in their trench and try and sleep in what they had marched with. Marines living under arduous circumstances will share much with each other. Food, fuel, cigarettes, clothes: all take on a common ownership. I have even shared a toothbrush with a fellow officer, and although a sleeping bag is a difficult thing to share, I have done that too. But this night we had nothing to share that would keep us warm. We had sprinted to Sapper Hill in battle order. As with the battle for Two Sisters, we had carried nothing that wasn't essential for fighting with. For the record, I have catalogued what I carried in battle at Appendix 1. It will be seen that it does not include a sleeping bag.

That night was the coldest of the war, and the most uncomfortable night of my life, before or since. For yet another night, I didn't sleep a wink. One was lucky on average to get four hours sleep in 24 in the Falklands. Even at rest in our patrol base, there were sentry duties for the marines to perform and patrols to be carried out, and many other distractions for officers and NCOs. The weather; one's aching feet; a soaked sleeping bag: all conspired against sleep at the best of times and one tended to snatch half an hour here or an hour there, as and when one could. But this was enough. Four hours sleep out of 24, even if only an aggregate of four hours, is enough for a man to continue indefinitely. However, without a sleeping bag, it was very difficult to sleep at all. My marines in the morning after the battle for Two Sisters might have had four hours sleep in the previous 48 hours. Argentine artillery and lack of sleeping bags militated against rest for the next night, then we watched the battle for Tumbledown the night after that, knowing our turn was next. So this night on Sapper Hill was the fourth or fifth with next to no sleep. Commanders who are not rested tend to make irrational decisions. Fortunately, there were very few decisions to be made by me that night.

I was very concerned that we might have people seriously suffering from hypothermia. From time to time I would lie down in my trench and try and sleep, but to no avail. I spent most of the night stamping around the position, checking on the men, chain smoking cigarettes, and cursing the taskers of helicopters who apparently had enough aircraft to conduct a flypast, but not enough to bring up our rucksacks. I needn't have worried. The marines lay huddled together like puppies sharing each other's body heat. But while I was indeed very cold, I wasn't so cold that the idea of a cuddle with either Marine Birch or the Sergeant Major appealed, so I carried on stamping, cursing and smoking.

Late that night, we heard that it was all over. We also heard that Belgium had beaten Argentina 1–0 in the World Cup. We almost felt sorry for them. One need hardly describe one's feelings. But it was only the inner warmth that victory gave me that kept me going that night.

Our sleeping bags arrived during the following day and we stayed another night on Sapper Hill. Most of us slept tolerably well and, thus rested, would have been ready again for anything. On 16 June, we marched down off the hill into Stanley. It was an emotional hour or two. We had survived in the wilds for nearly a month. We had marched further, carrying heavier loads, than anyone else. We had crossed East Falkland and we had, every man of us, yomped every inch of the way; and we had fought and won a major battle. I can think of few prouder moments of my life, marching at the head of my men carrying a full rucksack, accompanied by Sergeant Major Bell, Phil Witcombe, Alasdair Cameron, Corporal Tom Morrison and Bombardier Barry Ingleson carrying our huge, home-made company flag.

Presently, we stepped onto the hard-topped Stanley road. This was the first hard surface we had walked on since leaving the *Stromness*. My feet and knees took a little while to attune to the unaccustomed jarring. We were far from being the first unit into Stanley. Others had been there for a couple of days, but we were welcomed by a number of small groups of civilians, clearly very appreciative, who clapped and cheered as we walked passed. That was nice. We enjoyed that.

We also passed a number of Argentines, both alive and dead. The live ones smiled at us. I hope we smiled back but we may have been too astonished. There were also piles of surrendered weapons, a wrecked helicopter, and other detritus of war.

After a while we found the road was blocked by a large number of soldiers of the Parachute Regiment. They were in light order and had evidently been under cover in Stanley for a couple of days. We were carrying very full rucksacks and as well as just coming down from the high ground, some of us no doubt felt we occupied something of the moral high ground too. As we waited, nothing much seemed to be happening. They were apparently parading for a church service. Soon the badinage started from X Ray. No reaction from the Paras, who remained admirably restrained as if on parade. Then someone shouted a cruel remark, calculated to hurt and offend. I doubted if the Paras could possibly keep their restraint much longer, so with visions of the Argentines being treated to a battle between the Paras and the Royal Marines, I immediately led the Company off the main road uphill into the town and found an alternative route which bypassed the blockage.

We were to embark in the logistic ship *Sir Percivale* for the time being so we marched to the pier. As we approached the jetty, there were even more live Argentines, including the crews of Panhard armoured cars who offered Marine Chadwick some oranges. Chadders accepted and this time did smile back. There seemed to be more Argentines wandering about than there were Royal Marines, but there was no difficulty. *Percivale* was alongside but not quite ready to take us, so we sat down by Jubilee Villas to wait. I smoked the cigar I had been carefully preserving for this very occasion. After a while, I got the feeling that the numbers in the Company had diminished somewhat. People were drifting off. 'Sergeant Major, what's going on? Where is everybody?'

'Come with me, Boss.'

He gently led me round the corner and a short way along the street. The marines had found an open pub. And as if in answer to a Royal Marine's prayer, recalling our Globe and Laurel cap badge, it was called the Globe Hotel. By now the entire Company was crammed inside, every man with a can in his hand. Someone gave me a can of beer. My God, it was good. I don't know who was paying. It certainly wasn't me. There were some civilians in there. They were friendly and highly appreciative, although clearly they had no sense of smell. One of them asked if I wouldn't mind just taking my men down to the airport and machine-gunning all the Argentine prisoners. 'Give us another couple of beers, and we'll think about it,' said the Sergeant Major.

Out came my mouth organ for the last time, and the singing began. There may have been happier moments in my life, but just at that moment, I was damned hard pressed to think what they could be: standing there in this smoky, homely shack (apart from the occasional sheep shed, the first time I had been under a roof for a month), surrounded by 150 tired, singing, stinking, unshaven, filthy, lightly boozed, beautiful, glorious Royal Marines – my Royal Marines – this was a magical moment to be treasured for the rest of my life. It had been a long way to go for a drink.

Chapter 8

Returning

She had a million dollars' worth of nickels and dimes,
She sat around and counted them all a billion times.

We remained on board *Sir Percivale* for three days, washing, drinking, eating and sleeping. The atmosphere in the ship was not a happy one, with an officious Army ship's sergeant major doing everything he could to be unhelpful and obstructive. The men were supplied with an improvised communal bath which very quickly became revolting and unsanitary and probably contributed to the outbreak of tummy trouble that afflicted us. The food was barely adequate and the beer strictly limited. Many would rather have stayed ashore and dirty, foraging for ourselves. The probable truth is that *Percivale* did not have the ability to provide enough water and other services to meet our aspirations, and she was almost certainly short on many necessaries. But at least she was warm.

In the mess on the first night, someone played the sound track to the film *Chariots of Fire* on the mess stereo. When it reached the song *Jerusalem* everyone sang along, most with tears streaming down their cheeks in the realisation that they had survived. The sound of the song today still brings lumps to the throats of many who were there. I slept for ten hours the first night, but there were others who slept only fitfully and intermittently until their bodies had relearned how to relax for more than an hour at a time. We ate and drank the ship out of food and beer. The poor purser had never seen anything like it. Eventually we were sent ashore again, billeted in houses in Stanley, to do our part looking after prisoners and tidying up. Many men's bowels, having performed beautifully throughout the war, now inflicted them with vomiting and diarrhoea. Known as 'Galtieri's revenge' by the marines, it was more

175

likely to have been a result of the overworked Stanley water purification plant than the spite of the Argentine dictator: or perhaps we were just not ready for so much good living.

Those few days in Stanley were an interesting, agreeable time. All the mail we had not received in the previous weeks caught us up. We enjoyed examining the enemy's weapons and ruminating over his positions. We found the flatbed trailer on the airport road from which the Exocet had been launched that had hit *Glamorgan*. I met two Royal Air Force officers inspecting a mobile air-defence radar. They said it was rather good, and better than anything we had. The Argentines had deployed it very cleverly and had used its mobility to make it difficult for us to destroy.

Stanley was a mess. We did our bit at cleaning up but we felt sorry for those who would have to continue the work. Argentine ideas of sanitation were elementary. They had crapped anywhere and everywhere. One felt we would have found shit on the roofs if we had taken the trouble to look there. With so many British troops in such a small area, all on the look out for 'souvenirs', there was a whiff of anarchy which needed firm control. Helmets, pistols, and bayonets were all in high demand. Most sensible men ditched the more lethal souvenirs over the side somewhere between the Falklands and home, but one or two remained to haunt those who hung on to them in an increasingly firearms-sensitive society. Marine Gillon, having survived the battle and the Argentine rifle going off in his hands, was hit by a British soldier reversing carelessly in a 'liberated' military vehicle. He was taken to hospital but we were able to spring him in time to bring him home with us.

We 'spliced the mainbrace' at Her Majesty The Queen's command. We were not too sure whether this was to celebrate our victory, or the birth of Prince William. We weren't fussed which it was and celebrated both just to make sure we got the right one.

Many of us attended the thanksgiving service in the cathedral. The building was quite small and was packed with many familiar faces. While at home in Angus that spring, before the crisis developed, I had heard a wireless programme in which the congregation of that cathedral had sung the national anthem at the end of the service. Of course it never occurred to me at the time that, a few weeks later, I would be singing the national anthem myself in that same church. In his sermon, the local vicar, the Reverend Harry Bagnall, described what it was like to be invaded by a foreign power that knew nothing of democracy; how they had taken no account of the Falkland Islanders' personal possessions; how complaints to even the highest authority had met with empty promises. Their property had no longer been their own, their rights and liberties vanishing with the raising of the Argentine flag. His simple, dignified description of what it had been like for the Islanders was all the more powerful for being understated. He then described what it was like to be liberated from this, thanking us all for the part we had played. The humility, the sincerity and gratitude was palpable, and many a hardened soldier's face melted.

We in X Ray Company found ourselves guarding a warehouse full of prisoners. It was curious and illuminating to meet our erstwhile adversaries. They looked well fed and moderately cheerful. Presumably the prospect of going home was not entirely displeasing to them. I spoke to a number of officers, mainly about routine administrative matters but also about the war. They appeared to be agreeable, civilised men whom, under other circumstances, one might be happy to have as friends. But there were tell-tale signs that their army operated on different lines to ours. In particular, the relationships between officers and other ranks threw much light on their performance in battle. The notion of 'serving to lead'; the concept that the officer or NCO is first and foremost the servant of his men was not one that was in evidence. They showed astonishment, even distaste, that a marine could speak to an officer uninvited. That an officer and a marine could enjoy a natural, straight-forward, friendly conversation was a point of surprised remark. That orders and instructions might be given by British officers and NCOs courteously, without shouting, maybe even using the occasional 'please', or 'thank you' was observed with arched eyebrows. That those orders were actually obeyed immediately and to the letter was met with disbelief.

Argentine officers seemed to scorn their NCOs, and the soldiers were in the main treated like dirt. There was little evidence of the trust that is so necessary for a military organisation to withstand the audit of war. Fear seemed to be the means whereby discipline was enforced in the Argentine army and fear is a brittle glue. When fear of the enemy overwhelms the fear of one's NCOs and officers, unpredictable and unpleasant things can happen. We heard many and persistent rumours about the mistreatment of Argentine soldiers by their officers and NCOs, including the allegation that they wounded their soldiers to keep them from running away. These were unconfirmed, but generally the officers treated their soldiers as cannon fodder, and physical violence seems to have been routinely used as a means of control. We found bodies of men on Sapper Hill who appeared to have died of exposure and who looked poorly fed. It seemed that food was being eaten by those who had access to it, not necessarily those who needed it.

What we did see first-hand was a willingness to use the protection of the Red Cross, without scruple or regard to the rules. Many houses and vehicles in Stanley which had no connection with medical facilities as laid down in the Geneva Convention were marked with red crosses. I spoke to the manager of a warehouse in Stanley who told me that at least one of the 'hospital ships' that had arrived during the war had unloaded substantial quantities of weapons and ammunition. I myself supervised the clearing out of a garage with a large red cross on the roof. There were indeed some medical stores in there. There were also several tons of 30mm anti-aircraft ammunition – all conveniently adjacent to the anti-aircraft guns nearby. I thought of our unmarked bombed hospital in Ajax Bay.

Captain Mike Irwin, our adjutant, met an officer who was an enthusiastic polo player like himself. He asked him if he knew a certain Argentine officer who had been at the British Army Staff College at Camberley with him the year before. It transpired that not only did he know him, but the officer was here in Stanley as part of the Argentine commander's staff. Mike asked why then, with a Camberley graduate on his staff, was the Argentine general's defence so unprofessional? 'He was probably asleep in the lectures,' was the answer. Mike tried to find his erstwhile fellow student but was unable to do so in the time available.

It became apparent that there was more than one Argentine army in the Falklands. There were those who had endured the weather in the hills and fought us. Many, but not all, of the soldiers were conscripts. The officers were mostly inexperienced and not very competent, but among them were some who really cared for their men, and more than a few who were willing to fight to the death, as we had seen at first-hand. Then there were those who had stayed in Stanley. More of them were non-conscript, full-time officers, NCOs and older soldiers. One hesitates to call them professional for fear of being misinterpreted. They had not endured any great discomfort and had not been exposed to any great danger to speak of. I spoke to one clean, smartly dressed officer – a base wallah – who was contemptuous of the way the war had been fought by his own side in the hills. The incongruity of someone who had sat on his fat arse in Stanley throughout the war, complaining about the failure of those who had endured the conditions in the hills and had risked everything, seemed to pass him by.

What seems clear is that the divisions in Argentine society were reflected in their army and among the officer class the concept of service was immature and poorly developed. With these attitudes, it is hardly surprising that many of their soldiers felt disinclined to fight when it came to the rub. Their officer corps was shot through with incompetent, corrupt, self-interested, vicious, unscrupulous men whose hands were bloody from the 'dirty war' in which 30,000 of their own people had been murdered by the armed forces. In short, their soldiers had been betrayed by their officers and their politicians. It was lousy leadership that lost the war for them.

Unsurprisingly, we were now keen to set off for home. We hoped earnestly that we would not be consigned to a ship like the *Percivale*. Our prayers were answered and when we finally said farewell to the Islands and sailed north, we were once again in the bosom of our great grey mother, the *Stromness*, having climbed up the same homemade scrambling net that we had climbed down a month before. With mixed feelings, we discarded the clothes we had worn continuously for over a month. Heaving and filthy they may have been, but they were rather like faithful old friends who had come through everything with us. The fresh set that we were given were newcomers: strangers to whom we would need time to adjust. There were no mixed feelings about the long hot showers, which were unambiguously relished.

To begin with, we saw icebergs and 'Mother Carey's Chickens' or storm petrels, apparently running across the surface of the water. We also watched with awe the albatross; supreme master of the glide. With fascination we observed them use the waves to help them take off. The bird would slide down the side of a large wave, gathering speed and then, as the wave rose underneath it, it would use the uplift action to give it a leg-up into the air, rather as a Sea Harrier uses a ramp. And off it would go: the very manifestation of grace, beauty and aerodynamic perfection. These creatures gave way to porpoises and flying fish as we advanced into the tropics. It was a good party, that journey home. Since it was now mid-winter in those latitudes, 25 June was declared to be Christmas Day and we celebrated accordingly. Having rather got into the hang of this southern hemisphere thing, we celebrated New Year on 1 July for good measure. We played deck sports together. We performed 'sods' operas', those peculiarly naval, hilarious reviews where no holds are barred; and above all, we started talking. We talked and talked all the way to Ascension Island. We talked to each other about what we had done. Sections, troops or whole companies convened together over a beer or three, spinning yarns, sharing and comparing experiences, airing grievances and generally relieving stresses and mental strains. All this contributed to our readjustment from the feral beings we had become, in time for our return to the normal human world.

Battle isolates. It is such an extraordinary, unnatural experience that it is impossible to describe to one's own satisfaction. A man's memory remains the most private recess in his body. However well-meaning, however kindly and intelligent the inquirer, it is impossible to describe in words such profound memories to those who weren't there. In this regard, you share more with your enemy than you do with your own family. Many men, faced with trying to describe the indescribable, resort to silence and this is why our fathers and grandfathers, and their fore-fathers, may not have been overly forthcoming about their war experiences. We understand so much more now about post-traumatic stress disorder than we did then. There are many factors which contribute to any given person's mental resilience, but if men can talk to others who understand what they are talking about, it is a wonderful safety valve. Unconsciously we used that safety valve to good effect. As far as I am aware, only one man in X Ray Company showed signs of suffering mentally from our experiences. There may well have been others and perhaps more to come even now, especially when one considers that the injury can present itself many years after the event. More vulnerable than most must be those who were wounded, and who were brought home outside the community of their mates, who then watched us come home after them to the adulation of the country.

The damaged hearing and the cranky feet are permanent reminders for many men, but for most time is a great healer. Still, there are some tormented by their dreams and pursued by their anxieties, which get worse and worse until their personality changes, and only by talking it all through with someone who *really* understands, will they find a prospect of salvation. Therefore, the fact that we had the opportunity to stay together afterwards for three weeks and talk to each other worked hugely in our favour. By the time we were delivered back to our families, we were much healthier than if we had been whisked straight home. This process has now been formally recognised and modern warriors are usually given a similar recreational opportunity to decompress, before they return to their families. But on the other hand, given that so many Royal Marines took part in the Falklands War, there could even be more psychiatric damage among those who did not deploy, than among those who did ...

We flew courtesy of the Royal Air Force from Ascension Island. We were bound for RAF Leuchars in Fife. For those returning in the *Canberra* and other ships, an extraordinary outpouring of national euphoria awaited them. Many of us who flew home earlier wondered if it might have been good to be part of it. Others felt that on balance, being home and able to watch it on the TV with one's family would do well enough. It was somehow in concert with the spirit of 45 Commando that we should deploy to the Falklands without fuss, out of the glare of publicity, and that we should return in the dead of night to an RAF airfield in Scotland, back whence we came.

As we approached, we were told that we might have to divert to Glasgow. Leuchars was enveloped in the famous east coast fog – the haar. We weren't expecting a great welcome party, but any arrangements that might have been made would now go by the board: all a bit of an anti-climax, even for us. The pilot had one attempt at bringing us in to Leuchars. No go: full power went on just before touchdown. He promised us one more attempt, but if that failed, it was Glasgow. This time we hit the runway with a convincing thump, to a loud cheer from the passengers.

We were genuinely surprised and touched by the welcome party. The RAF Leuchars Volunteer Pipe Band, the Commanding Officer of Leuchars and many others were there to greet us. General Pringle, supported by sticks, newly out of hospital after being blown up by the IRA, gamely stood and shook hands with every man. HM Customs and Excise, not normally given to jocularity at the best of times, let alone at one o'clock in the morning, managed a smile as they waved us perfunctorily through.

We boarded the waiting coaches. As we drove through the Fife and Angus countryside, and Dundee, it was evident that pubs had stayed open or parties had been gathered for the purpose of welcoming us home. People appeared from pub gardens, behind hedges, on driveways and at roundabouts to wave at us. Someone asked the coach driver to turn the bus video on to see what was showing. It was the *Blues Brothers*.

Chapter 9

Reflecting

Hi-de-hi-de-hi-de-hi!
Ho-de-ho-de-ho-de-ho!

On 9 April 1982, Admiral Fieldhouse, the Commander-in-Chief of the Fleet at Northwood, had made it clear that Rear Admiral Sandy Woodward, the carrier group commander, Commodore Michael Clapp, the amphibious task group commander, and Brigadier Julian Thompson, the landing force commander, were all to answer directly and equally to him at Northwood. This, incidentally, was contrary to standard amphibious doctrine according to which the commander landing force should have been under command of the commander amphibious task group until completion of the landing, at which time the landing force commander would then answer directly to Northwood. However, such subtleties were lost in the noise.

Rear Admiral Sandy Woodward was therefore not the operational in-theatre commander, but being the senior officer present it was – and still is – widely assumed that he was. Confusion over who was in charge persisted throughout the operation in many quarters, including Northwood, where Woodward was seen as a *primus inter pares*. Judging from his own memoirs, that confusion was shared by the Prime Minister Margaret Thatcher and by Woodward himself.

By treating Woodward, a submariner with no experience in joint, amphibious or air warfare, as a first among equals, Northwood did nothing to ameliorate the difficulties arising from the absence of an in-theatre commander. There are parallels between joint warfare and living in a bivvie. Cooperation, collaboration, understanding and communication are much in demand in both activities, but judging from accounts of those who had to deal with him, Woodward's style and personality made him something of a 'tent rhino'. If he had been a Royal Marine in a bivvie, so to speak, he would have been a ripe candidate for an early punch on the nose.

However, he carried a huge burden and had to wrestle with many uncertainties in those early weeks of the war. It is often the first steps in any great endeavour which are the most daunting and it was Woodward's force that first engaged the Argentine navy and air force, before the rest of us left Ascension Island. Like his First World War predecessor, Admiral Jellicoe, Rear Admiral Woodward could have lost the war in an afternoon – long before we even attempted to land and recover the Islands. His job was firstly to try to establish a sea blockade to isolate the Argentine forces on the Islands, and then to reduce the effectiveness of the Argentine air force. Later he would provide the airpower and the escorts supporting the amphibious and logistic ships, as well as the naval gunfire in support of the amphibious and land battles. This necessarily meant putting his ships where they could be attacked, yet he was fighting with one hand behind his back because he had no airborne early warning. As ship after ship was damaged or sunk, and weather and time exerted their inexorable attrition on the mechanical efficiency of his fleet, Woodward knew that his war might perforce be over by the end of June, whether we had won or not. By then, a large proportion of his surviving ships would be in need of significant repairs; repairs that could not be made on the high seas in winter, thousands of miles from a dockyard. Central to his task was the imperative not to lose either of the mission-essential ships in his group, the aircraft carriers *Invincible* and *Hermes*. In the event he didn't lose either of them and the land war finished in victory before his sea war petered out for lack of serviceable ships. Rear Admiral Woodward received his just reward in the shape of a knighthood.

Major General Jeremy Moore, who commanded the land forces in name from 12 May and in reality from 30 May, also received a knighthood. To him fell the task of propitiating Northwood; a headquarters divorced by distance and culture from the brutal complexities of an inshore naval battle and a land war on a blasted heath, and yet with a tendency to drive from its 8,000-mile-away back seat. Others could have lost the war in an instant, but only Moore could win it. His knighthood was an appropriate punctuation mark at the end of a career already studded with remarkable achievements. His understated, collegiate, but effective style chimed with the moment and it gave much pleasure to all who knew him to call him 'Sir Jeremy'. When he died in 2007, Margaret Thatcher attended his funeral.

Commodore Michael Clapp, who commanded the amphibious task group, and Brigadier Julian Thompson, who in reality commanded the land forces from the beginning of the war until Jeremy Moore arrived, were both made Commanders of the Order of the Bath. They deserved more. This was an award which had the reputation of being given to two-star officers, who were not going to be promoted to three stars. It had thus acquired the nickname 'the kiss of death'. Given the normal progression of events, both men might have expected to receive it in due course. But like Sandy Woodward, they could have lost the war in a moment, and rarely in our history has the fate of two governments – in this case the British and Argentine – not to mention the lives of several thousand people, rested so starkly in the hands of such relatively junior officers. However, their relationship with Northwood had not been an easy one, they performing mere miracles when their masters were expecting the impossible. Moreover, they had been the keepers of the flame of amphibious warfare and one can imagine how the establishment did not much enjoy being reminded how heavily it had depended upon the guardians and the practitioners of a capability about which it knew so little, which it had neglected for so long, and which, had events not intervened, it would have consigned to the scrapyard. Michael Clapp retired after the war. Turning down the offer of promotion to rear admiral for personal reasons, he reverted to his substantive rank of captain Royal Navy and became a stockbroker. Julian Thompson became a major general and, after retirement, a distinguished academic, writing many acclaimed books on military history.

Lieutenant Colonel Andrew Whitehead was made a member of the Distinguished Service Order for his command of 45 Commando Group during the war. We, his centurions and his legionnaires, were very proud of this. His service had indeed been distinguished. It had been highly professional, he had been rock-steady, and he had been parsimonious with the lives of his men. We had indeed been in good hands and we were delighted it was thus recognised. He went on to command 3 Commando Brigade and eventually retired as a major general.

Captain Mike Barrow commanding HMS *Glamorgan* was also made a member of the Distinguished Service Order for the outstanding handling of his ship throughout the war, including the contribution his ship made to the battle for Two Sisters. Captain Barrie Dickinson who commanded the *Stromness* with such style and resolution was made an Officer of the Order of the British Empire. Commander John McGregor was similarly decorated for outstanding performance of his engineering duties, including the planning of the removal routes of the bombs from *Sirs Galahad* and *Lancelot*. He of the acetylene torch, Mechanician Gordon Siddle, was Mentioned in Dispatches. Of the professional bomb disposal men, Staff Sergeant James Prescott, who defused one of *Argonaut*'s bombs and was killed while trying to defuse another in *Antelope*, was posthumously awarded the Conspicuous Gallantry Medal. His team mate and boss, Warrant Officer John Phillips, who lost an arm in *Antelope,* received the Distinguished Service Cross. Lieutenant Bernie Bruen received the Distinguished Service Cross and Flight Lieutenant Alan Swan the Queen's Gallantry Medal. Chief Petty Officer Graham 'Piggy' Trotter won the Distinguished Service Medal, and Fleet Chief Petty Officer Mick Fellows clearing *Antrim* won the Distinguished Service Cross. Lieutenant Commander Brian Dutton, who worked away for a week removing *Argonaut*'s bomb, won the Distinguished Service Order, an especially high accolade for a relatively junior officer. Fellows also enjoyed the distinction of being invited to Downing Street by the Prime Minister who kissed him full on the lips saying she 'always wanted to kiss a sailor'.

Lieutenants David Stewart and Chris Fox both won the Military Cross for leadership on their respective patrols into the Two Sisters. David became a colonel and Chris left the Royal Marines soon after the war, becoming the first Royal Marine to transfer to the Special Air Service Regiment. Marine Gary Marshall was decorated with the Military Medal for covering the withdrawal of his troop with his machine gun and giving fire control orders to others, while himself under fire. He later became a colour sergeant and a physical training instructor. Corporal Harry Siddall also won a Military Medal for his part in clearing Yankee Company's objective; he subsequently joined the Scottish Prison Service. Lieutenant Clive Dytor won a Military Cross for his battle-winning charge, and Corporal George Hunt, who supported him so resolutely and who led his men with him, and was wounded, won the Military Medal. Clive took Holy Orders, became a priest and later the headmaster of the Oratory School in Berkshire. George Hunt became a major and a helicopter pilot and was subsequently Mentioned in Dispatches for his performance in Northern Ireland. Lance Corporal Andrew Bishop was decorated with the Military Medal for taking over command of his section when his section commander was hit, rallying it and leading it into battle most effectively. Corporal Julian Burdett, was awarded the Distinguished Conduct Medal for directing artillery fire and assisting other wounded, while himself seriously wounded. Bombardier 'Nozzer' Holt won the Military Medal for his performance with Harry Siddall. He retired as a warrant officer and became a traffic warden in Inverness. Lieutenant Chris Caröe was Mentioned in Dispatches for his leadership in the fight for X Ray Company's Sister. Chris was badly injured in an accident a few years later and left the Royal Marines. Captain Jeff Niblett won the Distinguished Flying Cross for many gallant acts in his helicopter, including the evacuation of British and Argentine casualties from Two Sisters. Major Sam Drennan, who flew the wounded Paul Denning out in his Army Air Corps helicopter, was similarly decorated for his gallantry, repeatedly evacuating casualties from exposed positions in appalling weather conditions on Tumbledown Mountain. Colour Sergeant Brian Johnston, whom we watched rescue sailors from the stricken *Antelope* and who was later killed with five of his landing craft crew, was awarded a posthumous Queen's Gallantry Medal. Captain Mike Cole was Mentioned in Dispatches for his command of Zulu Company on Two Sisters, and Major Rupert van der Horst was similarly decorated for his stalwart supervision of the unsung, resolute back-up we all received from the Commando logistics and administrative organisation. And Marine Keith Brown, who left his safety catch on while trying to shoot Mirages, became a politician and the Minister for Housing and Transport in the Scottish Government.

Marines Dave O'Connor and Howie Watson did not go to jail. Instead, their careers flourished. O'Connor was awarded a Mention in Dispatches for his part in the battle. Ten years later, he and the Royal Navy officer he was escorting at the time were taken hostage by the Khmer Rouge in Cambodia. After their release, he was made a Member of the Order of the British Empire for his coolness and professionalism in this dangerous situation. He became a British National Shooting Champion, and retired as a widely respected warrant officer. Watson was accepted into the Special Boat Service and rose to colour sergeant. Marine Keith Simpson, who celebrated his 18th birthday in Port Stanley, also entered the Special Boat Service and became the Regimental Sergeant Major. Marine George Wiseman, another 17-year-old, and Marine Graham Adcock, both became majors, and Sergeant George Matthews retired as a lieutenant colonel. The ever-faithful Marine Dickie Birch became a sergeant, but died of a brain tumour aged 51. Captain Derek Dalrymple, Yankee Company's widely liked and respected artillery observation officer who sent the Iron Lady her artillery fire plan, also died of cancer much too early, as did the gentle, rock-steady Corporal Mick Tagg.

Our much-loved ship, the *Stromness*, eventually joined the United States Navy where she served for 28 years as the USS *Saturn*. In October 2010, she finally met the fate that she had avoided in the South Atlantic. Off the coast of North Carolina she was sunk by gunfire and missiles by the USN who used her as a target.

There is a tendency now to look back at the comparative quality of the opposing forces in the Falklands War and assume that a British victory was a foregone conclusion. This is to ignore a number of important realities that were certainly apparent to us at the time. It is hardly surprising that, on 20 May 1982, a commentator such as Tam Dalyell MP warned of a 'military defeat of the first magnitude', and the Official Historian says in his introduction to the second volume, 'This was a war fought with a small margin of error ... final success could by no means be taken for granted.'

It may be convenient to group warfare into three components of fighting power: physical, conceptual, and moral. On the physical side, the British were attacking a numerically superior enemy 8,000 miles from base, having given him time to consolidate on ground of his own choosing. Argentine equipment was the match of ours in quality and quantity in almost every area, in some cases better. We lacked airborne early warning which gave them a significant advantage in the air, although we had other factors which counted in our favour, nuclear powered submarines and Sea Harriers being chief among them. Nevertheless, physically, the Argentines had much going for them and they were certainly not seriously mismatched with their adversaries.

The Argentines lost the war on the conceptual and moral fronts. Conceptually their plans were flawed and took no account of the worst case from their point of view: namely, that we could land intact, ready and willing to fight. Their leaders made the same mistake that politicians of every stripe have made many times in many countries: they forgot that virtually every war in history has lasted longer than the people who started it expected. They seemed ignorant of the eternal truth that when you start a war, you unleash forces that are beyond your control and the war always takes a course that you did not anticipate. The Argentines thought the war had ended on 2 April 1982. Instead, they got themselves into a war for which they were neither equipped nor prepared.

The root Argentine mistake was inextricably linked with an original British failure, which it is possible to see as the greatest single cause of the war. The source of all Argentine difficulties was that they underestimated their enemy. Everything they did, including the invasion itself, was based on the assumption that the British would cave in as they had done before. Had they believed that the British were able and willing to come and fight them, they would not have invaded. All wars are started and finished by politicians. This one was no different, and it was started by gross British political failure: a failure of deterrence. The British had placed a military garrison on the Falklands as a tripwire. They had thus implicitly declared that they were ready to use military force to defend the Islands. But no one had been convinced. A tripwire with no bang to follow is an empty, useless gesture. If you do not appear to be willing to fight for what you hold dear, paradoxically, you increase the chances that you will in the end have to fight for it. Because the British had forfeited their credibility, they had to fight to win it back. How fortunate they were that the Argentines invaded just before they had got round to getting rid of their only means of doing so.

All organisations seem to have a corporate memory which tends to fade unless events force them to remember hard-won lessons. Military organisations striving to deter war are especially vulnerable to the sclerosis of success. The Royal Air Force started bombing Germany in 1939, ignoring many of the priceless lessons it had learned about bombing in the First World War. The Royal Navy went into the Falklands War with ships and attitudes which ignored many of the key lessons of the Second World War. In the Falklands, British Army battle doctrine and its kit reflected an army which had not been tested seriously since the Korean War. British politicians allowed deterrence to fail in the years preceding 1982, a lesson which they should not have had to learn again.

The Argentine air force was very successful initially: as well as sinking six British ships and damaging others, it forced them to take protective measures which brought serious penalties to the flexibility of their logistics. The Argentines tried to sink the British carriers, which was logical enough. If they had succeeded, it is difficult to see how the British would have been able to carry on. However, the carriers were relatively well protected and were, as much as possible, kept out of harm's way. British logistic ships – all manned by civilians – were every bit as mission essential as their carriers, but they had to be exposed again and again to enemy attack to do their jobs. Had the Argentines thought their objectives through, they would have made every effort to hit these vital ships. It is true that once in San Carlos Water, the British made it as difficult as possible for the Argentines to hit the logistic ships. But they couldn't protect them entirely. The *Canberra* sat like a great white whale for 18 hours in San Carlos Water while bombs rained down on the ships around her, but had she herself been sunk or badly damaged, the headquarters and two companies of 42 Commando, who were sitting on board her as the Brigade reserve, could have been rendered non-operational. The loss of the one major cargo ship that was sunk, *Atlantic Conveyor*, had serious repercussions on the tempo of the British campaign, but it had been hit by mistake. In short, if they had sunk as many logistic ships as they sank warships, the Argentines could have stopped the British in their tracks.

Moreover, if the Argentines had made any serious attempt to counter-attack the landing force at its more precarious moments, they could have given the British serious cause for concern, at the very least. For instance, at dawn on the second day during the battle for Darwin, with their commanding officer dead, low on ammunition and the battle stalled, 2 Para was in a highly vulnerable condition. The appearance of a spirited counter-attack brought in by the helicopters which they certainly had, could have produced a very different outcome. Similarly, no significant attempt was made to counter-attack any of the hills around Stanley.

The Argentines were within range of their own artillery, they had the transport and the troops, but they did not have the will – or the moral strength.

The moral aspect of warfare is arguably the most important of all. Napoleon certainly thought so. He said; 'In war, three-quarters turns on personal character and relations: the balance of manpower and materials counts only for the remaining quarter.' Montgomery thought so, too: 'The morale of the soldier is the most important single factor in war.' It is also the most difficult area to quantify. Leadership, fighting quality, training, battle discipline, judgement, and morale all come under this heading. All can only be measured subjectively and you will only ever know how wrong or right you have got it *after* the event. Excellent equipment can be bought off the shelf at very short notice; a half decent plan can be worked up by most staff trained officers. But the resilience of your soldiers to every physical and mental assault that the violence of the enemy and the dice of Mars can pitch at them; the ability to withstand the shock of battle and the vagaries of climate and geography, and still be willing to expose themselves to danger and fight to the death: these are only achieved by assiduous attention applied over many years, by successive commanders with a profound, instinctive understanding of the nuances that motivate men to die for a cause and for each other. You don't need Napoleon or Montgomery to tell you that if your men won't fight, you will lose. The British had the stomach for a fight because they were well trained and well led. The Argentines didn't, because they weren't. This is in many ways the most interesting of all aspects of warfare and the area where the relative capabilities were most divergent. People talk about excellence, but do they understand where it comes from? It doesn't come because you recruit only excellent people. It only comes when you consistently get the best out of ordinary people. We are all of us, after all, ordinary people.

Who were the young men whom Britain sent to the South Atlantic in 1982? Then, as now – and now they include young women – they were ordinary people from every sort of background in the country, who joined the Armed Forces for a variety of mostly superficial reasons. The attraction of a secure job, the prospect of adventure, an escape from boredom or unemployment, the love of sport, and so on: these were, and are, more influential than the love of country. However, the reasons for staying in the Services are never the same as the reasons for joining; once one is in, very quickly another more profound set of motivators becomes engaged. A sense of duty, a wish not to let oneself, or friends or family – or country – down, a feeling of belonging and contributing to a very worthwhile team, starts to become prevalent. And if the training goes well and the leaders are of the kind who serve their people, this in turn develops into a selflessness, an absence of cynicism and a willingness to put the needs of others before one's own in the interests of the whole – even to the point of death. But they are still ordinary people and they themselves would be the first to say so. The magic is to get ordinary people to do extraordinary things.

Except there is no magic. The infantry foot soldier in war has the most difficult job in the world. The truth is if you haven't invested in time, care and equipment for your people; if you haven't treated them with respect and given them information, inspiration, enthusiasm, training and yet more training, especially the people in the front line, then you deserve only failure. If you haven't built up all of your people so that they can take decisions on behalf of their bosses, you and they will be overtaken and overwhelmed by the fast moving, unforeseeable, uncontrollable caprice of war. Sufficient of the British establishment understood this well enough to give them a war-winning edge. In a word, it was leadership which beat the Argentines: leadership in all its manifold complexities and facets at every level. There is a direct relationship between performance and leadership. It is leadership which makes people fill that gap between what their natural instinct tells them they want to do and what their duty tells them they should do. It is leadership which makes ordinary people excel. This is perhaps one of the most important and least widely understood realities of war, business, and everything else.

What about the financial cost? In the House of Lords Debate of 21 February 1985, Lord Trefgarne, the Parliamentary Under-Secretary of State for the Armed Forces, in answer to a question on the cost of the Falklands War said that, in 1982–83 we spent £780 million on the war. Over the following two years, provision of £550 million was made for residual campaign costs and the replacement of lost equipment. A great deal of money, perhaps, and much more was subsequently spent in building a new airfield and securing the Islands in the long term. However, to put it in perspective, those with long memories will recall that the civil servants in the Inland Revenue went on strike in 1981. As reported in the Lords on 11 February 1982, the cost to public funds, in terms of interest on the additional borrowing resulting from delays to the collection of revenue, amounted to £450 million to £500 million. So, relatively speaking, the cost of replacing the lost ships and equipment was hardly more burdensome than a civil service strike.

Was it worth it? The burden of war is always unevenly borne. You cannot expect the family of a killed or maimed soldier, sailor, marine or airman to give the same answer as a Falkland Islander or a politician. However, few of those who listened to the Reverend Harry Bagnall's sermon in Stanley Cathedral, after the war, would be in any doubt that it was indeed worth it. Moreover, much that was positive came out of the war. The Falkland Islanders were a declining, dwindling community in 1982. They have now doubled in numbers. They are not without their problems, but financially they are thriving and their prospects are brighter than anyone might reasonably have imagined before 1982. Most importantly, they are free and living under the government of their own choosing; and although one needn't expect any thanks from the Argentines, the country got shot of a very nasty government and is now also a democracy of sorts. Overall, they are in better shape now than they were then, even if they still want to colonise the Malvinas. And if you look at the wider view, because British credibility had been maintained, all the other small places that we were responsible for, like North Norway, Belize, Berlin, Gibraltar, Hong Kong, the Balkans: all were that much safer afterwards. The Cold War was pretty chilly in 1982. It is too easy now to remember only the dysfunctional, morally and physically bankrupt giant that was revealed by the removal of the Berlin Wall. In 1979, American impotence had been demonstrated by the overthrow of the Shah of Iran and the imprisonment of American hostages in the US embassy in Tehran. The Soviet invasion of Afghanistan the following year sent further shivers down the Western corporate spine. Imposition of military law in Poland had a similar effect. Although in fact the reverse was true, it appeared then as if the Soviet star was in the ascendant, and any sign of weakness in the Atlantic Alliance would be noted and fed into Soviet calculations. So the Russians, too, were deeply interested in what we were doing. They wanted to know if we would fight. What might our reaction be to a similar piece of adventurism on their part to test us? The fact that we were willing and able to sail 8,000 miles and fight for a piece of barren rock, upon which only 1,800 of our people lived, was as much a dislocation to their expectations as it was to the Argentines and it played a part in hastening the end of the Cold War. Naked aggression had been beaten in its own coin. By any reasonable standard, the results justified the effort and the sacrifice.

We are all of us changed men. For many, it was the pivotal event in their lives. The time 'before' was innocence, while 'afterwards' was a particular form of adulthood that not many ever see. At least one Falklands officer veteran, formerly an enthusiastic hunting, shooting and fishing man, now kills nothing. Certain things bring back memories involuntarily and instantly. The sudden sound of low flying aircraft still triggers an instinctive 'duck' and takes me straight back to Ajax Bay. Music from the *Blues Brothers* whisks me to the *Stromness* and the smell of peat fires, wet clothes, and boggy mud still elicit visions of the yomp. For others, it will be individual, very personal, random sights, sounds and smells that impressed themselves on the mind at a moment when all their senses were charged to the point of torment, when they thought they might not live out the hour.

It must also be acknowledged that more than just a few men, although they might not have said so at the time, positively enjoyed the war. We should not be surprised or shocked by this. They were doing the job they had joined and trained for. They were with their friends, they were at the top of their game and they were on the winning side. For them, combat was the most fulfilling, satisfying, exhilarating thing they could ever have experienced. The fact that others depended upon them for their lives and that they had risked their own lives to live up to that promise, meant that whatever may have happened to them before or after that event, they had at least once in their lifetime achieved a supreme utility that could never be taken away.

We were under no illusions about the relative scale of our achievements. Even the hardest fought battle in the Falklands was a mere skirmish compared to many Second World War fights and comparison with what happened in the First World War might invite ridicule. Notwithstanding notable exceptions, generally, our enemy had no real stomach for a fight and we had it relatively easy. We in 45 Commando only fought one major battle, although we did the intellectual and spiritual preparation for two. 2 Para fought two battles and there were others, like the naval gunfire support observation teams, who seemed to gatecrash everybody else's party. One doffs one's hat to them. One also respects deeply those of our forces in Afghanistan who are in the front line now in 2012, knowing that their percentage chance of not completing a six-month tour without injury or death is calculable. What it must have been like for those of our forefathers in the two World Wars who went into action time after time, beggars the imagination. I think particularly of those bomber squadrons that on average suffered 3 per cent casualties on every raid, accumulating a loss of 50 per cent over the war: a casualty rate exceeded only by the 75 per cent losses sustained by German U boat crews, in the Second World War.

It was a famous yomp, but in truth we didn't walk very far, or very fast. The historical achievement, if there was one, was to remain a cohesive, fighting-fit body of men in that difficult environment, carrying very heavy loads, and sometimes on short commons for nearly a month. We were also proud of the fact that we had delivered what we had been paid for. There was no build up. There was no carefully structured training and preparation period drawing on the lessons from previous deployments. We had been firmly at peace, yet when called to war from our beds, we were not found wanting. Our peacetime efforts had been audited by war and found to be good. Like those Roman legions described by Josephus, our war had been a bloody exercise. We had not let a long peace atrophy our war fighting qualities, and, in that regard at least, we might bear comparison with the British Expeditionary Force in 1914.

The other, less spectacular but no less extraordinary, achievement was the supply of logistics. From the assembly in the UK and delivery to the ships of war stores, right through to the distribution of food, fuel and ammunition to the front line 8,000 miles away, the provision of essentials was a masterpiece of organisation and improvisation right across the board. This is very clearly described in Julian Thompson's outstanding book *The Lifeblood of War*.

The normal procedure of reducing notice to move, thereby allowing preparatory work to be carried out, had necessarily been ignored by the higher level headquarters. From a standing start, at a weekend at the beginning of Easter leave, men and women in every organisation, civilian and military, swung into action with a will. Nothing was too much trouble. There was no mission, no contingency plan, no initiating directive and none of the other standard framework instructions for planners to refer to at the beginning of an operation. So there was no guidance about what should be loaded where, or in what order. The driving imperative was a political one: sail as soon as possible. Making intelligent assumptions, a workable loading plan had been devised by 3 Commando Brigade but it was soon overtaken by events, so if there was any logic to the loading sequence, it was either accidental or the result of local initiative. Thereafter, the discovery of the whereabouts and the tracking of items remained a constant headache for the staffs.

The Commando Logistic Regiment, the logistic unit of 3 Commando Brigade commanded by Lieutenant Colonel Ivar Hellberg, was configured to supply the three manoeuvre units of the brigade and their supporting units and sub units – about 3,500 men. This number rapidly grew to five units, and when the logistically skeletal Army brigade, 5 Infantry Brigade, entered theatre, another three manoeuvre units were added to the list of customers – a new total of more than 9,000 men. Ascension Island, being located halfway between home and theatre, allowed some of the activities normally conducted in a forward mounting base, but it was still 4,000 miles from the war. There was no port where ships could be conveniently reloaded, and such cross-loading as did take place was done with small craft in a heaving Atlantic swell. It is no surprise that the airfield on Ascension was the busiest in the world for a short while in April 1982. But the easy bit was getting the stuff down there.

The real logistic problems multiplied exponentially on arrival in theatre, the greatest challenge being one of distribution. The original logistic plan was based on the promise that the Navy would secure air control for the landings. It was therefore intended that the landing force would be supplied directly from ships as it advanced across the island. When the Argentine Air Force refused to be controlled, it became clear that ships could not move about inshore with impunity, so the supplies all had to come ashore straight away, or disappear off out to sea. The only place ashore with any hard standing was the derelict meat factory at Ajax Bay. This confined space became the overcrowded focal point for all logistic activity, including the hastily assembled field dressing station. In the unpromising, filthy wreckage of a building next to the slaughterhouse, this facility did the work of a full-blown field hospital. Out of the 880 British and Argentine casualties who passed through the 'Red and Green Life Machine', many of whom were most grievously wounded, only two died in their hands and a further three died after being transferred on to the hospital ship *Uganda*. This was truly a stellar achievement. And all this with two unexploded bombs lurking within a few feet of the operating table.

Getting at the stuff that went back out to sea was made more difficult by not having an overall commander in-theatre who could see and understand the difficulties, and who could lay down priorities between the carrier group, the amphibious group and the landing force, all of whom were answerable separately back to Northwood. The commander of any operation, just like the commanding officer of a commando or battalion, needs to be able to see what is going wrong and be in a position to do something about it. Admiral Fieldhouse, commanding from Northwood, could do neither. During the most critical phase, the amphibious landing, the commander of the land forces, Major General Moore, was at sea in the *QE 2* without effective communications and was thus a commander in name only. But enough supplies were got ashore to keep things going – just. In retrospect, the idea that a headquarters 100ft under Middlesex could command effectively an amphibious landing 8,000 miles away flew in the face of every lesson of history, but the Royal Navy, used to operating nuclear submarines in this fashion and substantially uninformed about the complexities involved in joint and amphibious warfare, did not see it that way.

Before the Falklands, all logistic planning had been based on the assumption that distribution would be done with wheeled transport. Helicopters would be secondary assets. But in the Falklands there were no roads. The only usable vehicles were the very limited number of small over-snow vehicles. The availability of helicopters was severely constrained and became even more so when three-quarters of the heavy lifting assets, the Chinooks, were lost together with many important stores in *Atlantic Conveyor*.

The enemy air force was a lethal threat. The weather conspired against movement and even the erection of tents was difficult in the wind.

And yet, enough fuel got through to keep the Rapier generators going, the over-snow vehicles moving, the radio batteries charged and the helicopters flying. Enough ammunition was brought forward for us to fight and for the artillery to support our battles; our casualties, and those of the enemy, were successfully evacuated and treated. Some of us went short of food from time to time, but we were able to resort to the time honoured stratagem of living off the enemy.

This describes only the logistics of the landing force. The conversion of merchant ships to amphibious support ships over what amounted to a long weekend, the supply of fuel, ammunition, food and all the hardware required to support, maintain and repair a fleet with over 100 ships at war, 8,000 miles from base, is yet another extraordinary story.

All this was achieved against a background of corporate amnesia and cultural snobbery. Many hard won lessons about the importance and complexities of land logistics from the Second World War had been forgotten, or put to one side for the sake of budgetary expediency in the name of 'cutting the tail'; forgetting that in war, your tail usually turns out to be your throat. The maxim that operations are the art of the logistically possible had not been given its full due. The Naval Headquarters at Northwood could barely appreciate the scale of the logistic problems faced by their amphibious subordinates in theatre, while deeply ingrained in the Army was a snootiness about logisticians, rather akin to the sniffiness of the Victorian aristocracy about 'trade'. And yet, like those Victorian aristocrats, they were looking down their noses at the very people who allowed them to be what they were.

Logisticians are not accustomed to receiving plaudits. Being taken for granted is their normal lot, except when their customers turn on them when the bacon fails to arrive. But for all those men and women in the factories, depots and dockyards in the UK, in the RAF air bridge to Ascension, through to the hard-pressed staffs in 3 Commando Brigade, the Commando Logistic Regiment, the amphibious staffs, and the logistic echelons in the commandos and battalions, let the trumpets sound long, loud and clear. There are not many medals to be won by humping ammunition in the dark in the freezing rain, or wracking one's brains through the night in a windblown tent over a helicopter flying schedule that has been wrecked for the umpteenth time by circumstances unforeseen and beyond control; but the war was won by those who did these things and their ilk, just as surely as by those whose names appeared in lights.

For those involved in the fighting – and for their families – the uncertainty matched that for our forebears. We were attacking a numerically superior enemy on ground of his choosing, a long way from home, and the action was intense enough for the brief period of hostilities. We knew that at least one government was going to fall. We had to get it right first time and, traditionally, the British have not always been good at this. We experienced additional doubt about how long the resolve of the Government, and the British public, would hold. That we had got off lightly only became apparent to us after we had won. During the fighting, the prospect of having one's block knocked off was real enough – and like the call for mobilisation, the memory of that sensation is not dimmed by time.

The respect and friendship that grows between men who fought together is well known and we certainly experienced that. The bond that exists between men who have endured and shared a war is not something readily described, but it is different to all other bonds. I watched 17-year-old marines bloom into mature men in 27 days. My three troop commanders, who had always shown potential, became in that short period experienced, balanced all-round personalities. I learnt yet again that every day one lives hereafter is a bonus to be cherished and I have tried not to waste a minute ever since.

And what is it like to have led men successfully in battle? Imagine you are the captain of a world-class sports team, representing your country in an international tournament. There were no cheering crowds on Two Sisters and in that misty, snowy, black night, there were certainly no cameras or lights, except the lights of machine-gun tracer, exploding shells and burning flares. But no winning captain of any Six Nations Grand Slam, or any Football World Cup; no winner of a Wimbledon Tennis Singles Championship or an Olympic Gold Medal, can ever have experienced the elation and satisfaction that comes with having fought a night battle in a snow storm, up a 1,000ft rocky mountain, and won. Churchill once said something to the effect that the most exhilarating feeling a man can experience is to be shot at and missed. In my experience, that is true, and moreover, all my marines had been missed as well. Not a single man had been lost. The exhilaration did not come immediately. After the adrenalin ceased pumping through every vein, we all seemed to have a bit of a downer, saddened by the loss of good men in the other companies. Moreover, we knew we would probably have to repeat the performance a couple of nights later. But once the fighting was over, the thrill of our achievement began to register. Buddhists have a story of a man being chased by a tiger. He falls over a cliff and hangs on to the root of a tree. He looks to one side and sees growing there some wild strawberries. With one hand, he reaches out, plucks one and eats it. It was the most delicious strawberry he had ever tasted. None of us had fallen over a cliff, or eaten a wild strawberry, but the gratitude for our survival was strong and in later life, when I have encountered the occasional piece of barbed wire or broken glass in my path, I have found it helpful to recall the surge of relief and gratitude we felt then.

Furthermore, many a commander who has had men killed under him is struck with a sense of guilt to a greater or lesser degree. He may often ask himself, 'Would I have lost those men if I had done it differently?' I had already survived desperate battles in the mountains of Dhofar in Oman, where I had suffered the sorrow of having good men killed under my command. I knew this feeling of guilt. I knew how precious and fragile life is, and how easily things can go wrong. But now, to have fought and won a battle without loss among my own men – to have brought home the same number of live marines that I had taken to war – this was a privilege and a joy which has abided with me all my life, and barely a day passes without a humble, grateful thought.

Poor Min, poor Min, poor Min.

_____

See all things,
Change some things,
Fear nought but God;
Honour the men.

St Bernard of Clairvaux
Author of the *Rules of the Order of the Knights Templar*

Glossary

AMFU	Adjustable Military Fuck-Up
bivvie	Shelter, improvised from a waterproof poncho supported by sticks and rubber bungies
Blowpipe	British man-portable anti-aircraft missile
Browning .5 inch HMG	Tripod mounted heavy machine gun of .5 inch calibre and an effective range of 2,000 metres
Carl Gustav 84mm	Man-portable, shoulder-fired recoilless anti-tank weapon with an effective range of 500 metres
cook-off	Term applied when ammunition explodes, when burned in a fire
CMFU	Complete Military Fuck-Up
Commando	Either a person who has passed the Commando Course, or a battalion-sized unit of Commando trained personnel about 700 strong, commanded by a lieutenant colonel. Normally comprises 3 rifle companies (see Rifle Company) plus supporting weapons
GPMG	General Purpose Machine Gun – a man-portable, 7.62mm belt-fed machine gun with an effective range of 800 metres. Normally scaled for one per section in infantry units (see Section)
Hexamine	Solid fuel block supplied to cook food in the field. Not unlike the standard fire lighter
LMG	Light Machine Gun – a portable 7.62mm magazine-fed machine gun. An adaptation of the Bren Gun of WW2 with an effective range of 600 metres
Milan	Man-portable, powerful wire-guided anti-tank missile with a range of 2,000 metres
NCO	Non-Commissioned Officer. All ranks from lance corporal up to warrant officer

pepperpotting	Low level infantry tactic whereby one group of men advances by zigzagging forward while another group provides covering fire
Pucara	Twin-engined, turbo-prop Argentine ground attack aircraft
Rapier	British anti-aircraft missile. Not man portable
Rifle Company	Group of 100–120 men commanded by captain or major, comprising 3 troops (see Troop). Normally 3 companies in a Commando or battalion (see Commando), of which they are the principal fighting elements
SAMFU	Semi-Adjustable Military Fuck-Up
sangar	Stone-built defensive position. Usually made when it is impractical to dig trenches.
Section	Group of 8 or 9 men commanded by a corporal comprising a rifle group of 6 men and a gun group of 3 men with a GPMG (see GPMG)
SLR	Self-loading Rifle – a 7.62mm rifle with a magazine of 20 rounds. Reloaded by the gases discharged when fired. The standard British rifle
Troop	A group of 30–34 marines, comprising headquarters and 3 sections. (see Section), commanded by a lieutenant, or second lieutenant – the Royal Marines equivalent of an Army platoon
66mm LAW	Once-only, lightweight disposable anti-tank shoulder-fired rocket with an effective range of 200 metres
81mm mortar	Mortar used by British with a range of 5,560 metres
105mm Light Gun	Artillery used by British with a range of 17,200 metres
120mm mortar	Heavy mortar used by Argentine Army with a range of 7,200 metres
155mm artillery	Heavy artillery used by Argentine Army with a range of 20,000 metres

Appendix 1

Equipment carried by X Ray Company Commander during the battle for Two Sisters

	lbs	oz	kgs
Fighting order webbing plus poncho	7	5	3.25
Two full water bottles	6	6	2.83
Pick head	2	8	1.11
Pick helve	1	12	0.77
Ration pack for 24 hours	3	8	1.55
Mess tins	1		0.44
Hexamine fuel for cooking		13	0.36
Torch		12	0.33
Binoculars	2	12	1.22
Schermully flares × 2	1	12	0.77
Packet of mini flares		8	0.22
7.62mm Self-loading rifle and bayonet	11		4.88
Image intensifier night viewing sight	6	8	2.88
Full magazines × 5 for rifle (20 rds each)	8	2	3.61
L2 hand grenades × 2	2	4	1.00
Phosphorus smoke grenades × 2	2		0.88
50 rds × 7.62mm in bandolier	2	4	1.00
Helmet	2	8	1.11
PRC 351 Clansman radio and battery	13		5.77
Frame for carrying radio	3		1.33
Service knife		8	0.22
Hip flask		14	0.38
Mouthorgan		4	0.1
Plus clothes, boots, cigarettes, maps etc.			
Total	**81**	**4**	**37.01**

Index